All that day we ploughed into the lonely green waves that rolled out of the west beneath a heavy layer of grey cloud . . . This was the Western Approaches, and it was here that the U-Boat battle was being fought and won . . . It was a long, cold, hard death-grapple, fought against the most cunning of all enemies, under an almost continuous waterfall of salt spray . . . in those vast wastes of the sea.

'The writing is simple, often trenchant in criticism, and the sense of humour never far below the surface of the narrative gives an added edge to this story of one man's war—a brave man's war—in the Western Approaches.'

Manchester Guardian

Commander D. A. Rayner
D.S.C. and Bar, V.R.D., R.N.V.R.

Escort

The Battle of the Atlantic

Edited by Captain S. W. Roskill, D.S.C., R.N.

Futura Publications Limited

A Futura Book

First published in Great Britain in 1955
by William Kimber and Company Limited

First Futura Publications edition 1974
Reprinted 1975

ISBN 0 8600 7016 6
Printed in Great Britain by
Hazell Watson & Viney Ltd
Aylesbury, Bucks

EDITOR'S FOREWORD

By Captain S. W. Roskill, D.S.C., R.N.
Author of the Official History of the War at Sea

Commander Rayner's story came to me in snatches at various times when we met after the end of the war. Not until quite recently did it occur to either of us that in it lay the material for a book. When men have lived through periods of great strain there often is, I fancy, a strong reluctance to commit their experiences to paper, at any rate until the passage of time has assimilated them into the whole pattern of their lives. The scars then still remain, but the wounds themselves are no longer raw, and by a process of healing relaxation the mind no longer shrinks from memories that for long could only hurt. It was at my suggestion that Commander Rayner began to write about the war at sea as he saw it, and it may have been mere chance that I made the proposal at the time when, at last, he felt able and prepared to record his experiences.

I do not for one moment suggest that this true story of one man's part in the Atlantic battle is unique in all, or even in many respects; for there were Escort Commanders who brought in more convoys than Rayner, and who also sank more U-Boats. Some men also certainly fought for as long as he did, or even longer, in that protracted struggle. But I do believe that in one respect this story, if not unique, is very nearly so. I know of no other officer, let alone one of the Royal Naval Volunteer Reserve, who served continuously for more than five years in command of escort vessels; nor of any other who graduated from a trawler at the very beginning to a corvette, then to a small destroyer, to several larger destroyers or groups of destroyers, and finally to command of a group of new and greatly improved war-built escort vessels. This astonishing continuity of experience and, if I may say so, of endurance gives to Commander Rayner an authority to speak on his subject which can hardly be questioned. Furthermore, the discerning reader will, for all the modesty with which the story is told, have no difficulty in detecting the deep confidence which Rayner inspired in the minds of the senior officers under whom he served. He was for a long time in Commander Howard-Johnston's redoubtable 12th Escort Group; his ships came through the severe tests imposed by Commodore (Vice-Admiral, Retired) G. O. Stephenson at Tobermory with flying colours; and he won the high regard, even affection, of that great leader and shrewd judge of character, Admiral Sir Max Horton.

But I have other reasons for feeling glad that the public will be able to read this story. We British do not like to be reminded of how narrowly, through our own negligences and follies, we have escaped disaster; nor of how in our thoughtless selfishness we have often left our safety in the hands of very small bands of men who had the vision to see what was needed, and the devotion to fulfil the needs themselves. It cannot be doubted that the pre-war R.N.V.R. officers, of whom Rayner was one, come within the latter category. They were prominent among the first properly trained reserves available to man the small ships; and to a considerable extent it was that tiny nucleus which made possible the enormous expansion of the R.N.V.R. as the war progressed. If it serves no other purpose than to remind us of these simple facts, this book will have been well worth writing.

I have neither added anything significant to, nor subtracted anything from, Commander Rayner's account. I have verified matters of time and place, and such suggestions as I have made have mostly been concerned with the manner of presenting the story. In its details as well as in its broad relation to the war at sea as a whole, I believe this story to be accurate; but it does, of course, view tremendous events through the comparatively narrow lens of one man's vision. I would emphasise that where matters of opinion are expressed they are Commander Rayner's and not necessarily mine. I have not thought it a proper part of an editor's functions to modify or alter sincerely held opinions on such matters as anti-submarine tactics and weapon development, on pre-war naval policy, or on the design of some of our ships. Though I would not always accept Rayner's views, I feel that his long experience at sea fully justifies his expressing them; and that they will therefore command respect, if they are unlikely to receive universal agreement.

Where I believe the book may have lasting value is that, at least to my mind, it rings absolutely true in its picture of the men who manned the little ships. Their endurance under conditions of appalling discomfort, their unflagging persistence in carrying out the tasks allotted to them, their ribald humour and unfailing good nature, and, above all, their great-hearted humanity, are all recorded here. Of course they grumbled. British sailors always have done so. But they rarely complained, and never whined. Perhaps it was these qualities of which Commander Rayner's narrative will vividly remind all who took part in the Atlantic struggle, which contributed most to bringing the nation through to victory.

It has been a privilege to be asked to edit this contribution to the story of the Royal Navy from 1939 to 1945.

S. W. ROSKILL

PREFACE

I have long wished to write a book on the Western Approaches, but the subject is so vast, and the people who served there were so many that it has been very difficult to see how this could be done.

As I saw it there were three possible alternatives – a fictional tale, a story of the war in those seas embracing everybody, and lastly an autobiography. Fiction I think always reads as fiction; it can never quite be believed, and one never knows where truth ends and imagination begins. To write the story of the Western Approaches as a serious war book would be to invade the preserves of the official historian to the Admiralty : and even so there would be many people left out who should have been mentioned. I have therefore very reluctantly chosen the third alternative. I say very reluctantly because I would rather have written about anybody other than myself; yet to attribute my experiences to another person would at once produce the illusion that I was writing fiction.

Here it is then – the story of the war at sea *as it affected me.* I emphasise this most particularly because I have been throughout most careful to include no single incident that did not actually happen to me. If I had included all the events that to my knowledge happened to other people I could fill twenty books. If I were to include just one thing which did not happen I should be untrue to myself, and untrue to all those less fortunate than I who perished by wind, by wave, and by enemy action.

Throughout I have used the names and ranks of people as I would have used them had I been speaking of them at the time. I have nearly always refrained from interrupting the narrative by inserting after the name of Commander Blank, for instance, the words 'now Admiral Sir John Blank, K.C.V.O., D.S.O.' It can be assumed that age and experience have added to the rank and honours of all the officers of Her Majesty's Navy who figure in these pages.

It is also, in more official writings, the custom to place after the name of every ship when first mentioned the name of her captain. Once again, and for the same reason, I have refrained from doing so, unless the name was necessary to my story.

I write only of ships and of men, both of whom have character, and change from one generation to another. These I would try to fix in a moment of time as I knew them. I do not write of the sea, which has no personality of its own and does not change. The sea is neither cruel nor kind. It is supremely indifferent, and wholly lacks sensibility. Confined by the great land masses its surface is moved by the wind. The greatest ship ever built by man is no more than a fly on the wall of its immutability. Although its face may appear different in the Atlantic to that which it presents in the Indian Ocean, it is the same element. Any apparent virtues it may have, and all its vices, are seen only in relation to the spirit of man who pits himself, in ships of his own building, against its insensate power. To conclude otherwise is to diminish its majesty.

This book is dedicated to the memory of all those who lost their lives or their health in the Western Approaches, and in particular to the officers and men who were lost in H.M.S. *Warwick*, 20th February 1944.

D. A. RAYNER

Burghclere,
 June 1955

ACKNOWLEDGMENTS

I acknowledge with a deep sense of gratitude the help that I have received from Captain S. W. Roskill, D.S.C., R.N., without whose encouragement this book would surely never have been printed. To him, too, I am greatly indebted for much valuable advice and for a great many suggestions.

I would also express my gratitude for the help that my wife has given me; and to Miss Joan Waldron, who has had the thankless task of turning my handwriting into typescript.

AUTHOR'S NOTE

It is the fashion to place a glossary at the end of a book, with the result that many people do not discover what they have been reading about until it's all over.

In writing this book I have found cases where abbreviations entirely intelligible to the specialist would yet mean nothing at all to the layman. To describe each one as they occur would unduly interrupt the narrative, and as the abbreviations are really very few I have placed this 'glossary' in the front of the book in the hope that the reader will see it before he embarks on the story itself.

C.-in-C.	Commander-in-Chief. Followed by the Sea Area or Fleet commanded.
F.O.I.C.	Flag Officer in Charge. Followed by the port which he commanded.
N.O.I.C.	Naval Officer in Charge. Followed by the port which he administered.
Captain (D.)	Captain administering one or more flotillas of destroyers. In wartime in the Western Approaches he also had the administration of frigates, corvettes, and trawlers. In the case of Londonderry after Commodore G. W. G. Simpson had been appointed for this purpose he was known as Commodore (D.)
First Lieutenant Number One Jimmy Jimmy-the-One	The officer next in seniority to the Captain in any warship up to the size of and including a destroyer. This officer is responsible to the Captain for the appearance, and day-to-day organization, of the ship.
Coxswain.	The Senior Chief Petty Officer who

takes the wheel in action and when entering and leaving harbour. He also is the ship's 'policeman', and is responsible for the victualling in a small ship. He is very much a confidential servant to both the Captain and First Lieutenant.

Yeoman of Signals. The Senior Signalman. Again very much in the confidence of the Captain, particularly in wartime, when a number of signals are received and sent whose contents should not be divulged to all and sundry.

Quartermaster. A rating who steers the ship at sea and who keeps watch at the gangway in harbour. There will always be one for each watch.

Bosun's Mate Bridge messenger at sea and companion of the quartermaster at the gangway in harbour.

H.A. Gun. High Angle Gun (capable of firing at aircraft).

L.A. Gun. Low Angle Gun (for use against surface targets or for bombardment of shore objectives).

CONTENTS

PLANS

Map to show limits of escort at various dates and the air gap

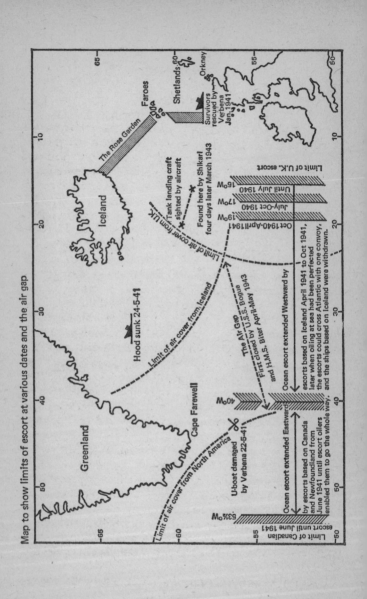

The Rose Garden

Faroes

Shetlands

Orkney

Survivors rescued by Verbena Jan. 1941

Iceland

Limit of air cover from U.K.

Tank landing craft sighted by aircraft

Found here by Shikari four days later March 1943

Limit of U.K. escort

Until July 1940 16°W

July-Oct 1940 17°W

Oct 1940-April 1941 19°W

Hood sunk 24-5-41

Limit of air cover from Iceland

The Air Gap

First closed by U.S.S. Bogue and H.M.S. Biter April-May 1943

Ocean escort extended Westward by escorts based on Iceland April 1941 to Oct 1941, later when oiling at sea had been perfected the escorts could cross Atlantic with one convoy, and the ships based on Iceland were withdrawn.

Greenland

Cape Farewell

Limit of air cover from North America

U-boat damaged by Verbena 22-5-41

40°W

Ocean escort extended Eastward by escorts based on Canada and Newfoundland from June 1941 until escort oilers enabled them to go the whole way.

53¾°W

Limit of Canadian escort until June 1941

CHAPTER I

PREPARATION

How very difficult it is to see where any particular matter starts, especially when the subject is one which has filled so great a part of your life. Delving into the depths of memory, you may follow the roots of a particular experience while they change from strong growth to the minutest tendrils of memory no thicker than a hair. When I do this to myself I find I lose the thread where, as an inky schoolboy eight years of age, I first seriously considered sinking U-Boats. This was in the First World War, and my drawing of the machine by which the enemy was to be destroyed earned me a beating for defiling the pages of the geometry book which I had misused, presumably because it was the largest sheet of comparatively white paper on which I could lay my hands at the time. The infernal machine which brought me such uncomfortable consequences was nothing more than a bottle of petrol inserted, by a gentleman suitably clad in a cloak and provided with a dagger, into the pocket of the U-Boat Commander. When a lighted pipe was placed in the pocket the U-Boat blew up. Diagrammatically portrayed, this spoilt the page – I can see that now. At the time I was bitterly disappointed that what I considered an excellent idea should earn such payment.

Next I remember that an uncle by marriage, who was a real First Lieutenant of a real destroyer, was the cause of an almost continuous border of destroyers appearing round the pages of my school books. This was followed in later years by an endless stream of model destroyers, some so small that a flotilla of eight could be carried in a matchbox and others of grander proportions which really floated, and were fitted with systems of propulsion varying from elastic to electric motors.

Leaving preparatory school for public school did not reduce the destroyer output, although I had suffered a severe set-back when I was rejected for the Navy on the score of flat feet. However, unkind fate did offer a loophole. At the Wembley Exhibition there was a most realistic reproduction of the attack on Zeebrugge, and afterwards an officer climbed on the stage and gave a lecture about the work of the Royal Naval Volunteer Reserve. I decided at once that as soon as I left school I would join – flat feet or no. On return to school I refused to take the Certificate A examination in the Officers' Training Corps; told the Corps Commander that I was going to join the R.N.V.R. as soon as I left school, and firmly declared that I was not going to have any army label on me whatever.

Within a month of leaving school I was knocking at the door of the Captain's cabin in H.M.S. *Eaglet*, the drill ship of the Mersey Division R.N.V.R. The establishment of officers was full and there were no vacancies. I went back the next month, and I called during the first week of every month from March to June 1925. By the end of that time Captain Maples was getting to know me quite well.

In those days it was extremely difficult to enter the R.N.V.R. as an officer. The applications far outnumbered the vacancies and it had become the practice, at any rate in the Mersey Division, that when a vacancy did occur the Captain would ask the gunroom officers to nominate two or three of their friends, and. from these he would make the final choice. Unfortunately my family had only recently moved to the district, and I had no friends amongst the junior officers who might have helped me. However, my pertinacity was finally rewarded, and when I called in July it was to be told that there was a vacancy, and that, provided I passed the doctor, I could consider myself a Probationary Midshipman.

Such was the start of my twenty-four years' service with the R.N.V.R. By 1939 length of service and the passing of a few examinations had brought me to the rank of Lieutenant-Commander. Throughout those pre-war years I had to attend drill on at least one night every week, and preferably on both the drill nights. I had to give up first one month and then fourteen days of my yearly holiday to service with the Navy. But it did not seem very much to pay for the good fellowship and all the social functions we enjoyed in return; nor was it very onerous while we remained unmarried. After marriage it became for many a burden too great to be borne. Those of us who carried on after we had found ourselves a wife did so only by the grace of our ladies. To the R.N.V.R. wives who found themselves grass widows on one or two evenings a week, and who had their holidays with their husbands cut short, should go much of the credit for the efficiency of the force at the outbreak of the war.

In every generation there are ships which by some happy choice of name, by particular beauty of appearance or by some individual action, have won popular regard above that of their less fortunate sisters. Once this has been achieved they seem to gather further fame unasked. They become the crack or 'tiddly' ships of the Navy. The appointments office of the Second Sea Lord sends to these lucky ships the best officers at its disposal. The drafting depots of Portsmouth, Plymouth, or Chatham send them picked ratings. They become at once the testing ground to promotion for both officers and men. A young officer appointed to one of them would already feel a tenuous halo forming round his head. A halo which might with the passage of years become changed into a 'brass hat' and commander's rank.

I call to mind five such ships, *Queen Elizabeth*, *Warspite*, *Tiger*, *Ark Royal*, and the mightiest of all – that ship which to my eyes was the most beautiful steamship that ever man devised – the incomparable *Hood*.

I was fortunate enough to serve in two of these five. For one month as a midshipman in the *Tiger* in 1926, and for three months in the *Hood* in 1932. In those ships I saw the Navy at its very best. It was efficient yet gay, strictly bound with the panoply of age-old custom, but warm with the benevolence which only perfect discipline can afford to bestow. One day in 1945 I picked up a Navy list. Nearly all the surviving midshipmen of the *Tiger's* gunroom and all the lieutenants of *Hood's* 1932 commission were then commanders. Even allowing for the expansion of war this was a remarkable verdict on the efficiency of those two ships.

Throughout the R.N.V.R. it had been generally supposed that Gunnery was the branch in which it was most worthwhile to specialise. This had come about not only because the gun was so obviously the weapon of the Navy, but because it was the easiest weapon in which to train in a drill ship. In the *Eaglet* we had an excellent gun battery fitted with all the manually operated guns from the big 6-inch to the 4-inch breech-loading and quick-firing guns. These were controlled by a director tower which was coupled to an ingenious device for teaching officers the principles of gunnery control. Gunnery was a branch in which both officers and men could reach a high state of proficiency, in spite of the inevitable limitations of a drill ship.

To be confirmed in the rank of Lieutenant it was necessary not only to pass an examination but also to undergo a qualifying course in some specialist branch, such as Gunnery, Navigation, Signals, or Torpedo. I dare say that at the outbreak of war 97 per cent of the officers on the active list of the R.N.V.R. had qualified in Gunnery. I was one of the few exceptions.

Early in 1932 I had asked the Captain of the Mersey Division (then Captain E. Elgood, as Captain Maples had retired some years previously) for permission to take a specialist Navigator's course. He explained to me, at first kindly, and then more emphatically as he saw my obstinacy growing, that I had much better devote my time to gunnery; that the Navy would never allow a ship to be navigated by an R.N.V.R. officer; that I should end up as nothing better than a 'tanky' (navigator's assistant); that in any case I was a bloody fool; and finally that if I wanted to spend the whole of the next war correcting charts I was going the right way to do so.

However, it was rather like asking the Captain's permission to grow a beard. The request to grow 'a set' is a formality laid down to prevent the lazily unshaven from claiming that their condition is only the start of a bigger operation. The commanding officer could only note the fact, he could not really prevent its happening. I took my navigator's exam.

I have never worked so hard before or since. To everyone's surprise, no less than to my own, I passed with the percentages of 94 and 98 in the two papers. The Admiral Commanding Reserves wrote a complimentary letter to Captain Elgood and thus spiked the Captain's guns. He now had to accept that he possessed an embryo navigator in his Mersey Division. Later, as war came nearer, the Admiralty began to offer more and more exciting courses. The new twin 4 in. high angle gun was mounted in the *Eaglet*, and training was begun to ensure that R.N.V.R. gunnery officers would be mobilised with the guns' crews whom they had trained in peace time, and that they would all be sent to the same ship to take over a complete 4 in. A/A turret.

Out of the hundreds of R.N.V.R. officers only a handful had specialised in navigation, but even these were not forgotten. In 1936 the anti-submarine school at Portland required officers to act as Unit Commanders in the fleet of trawlers which would be formed from the big Iclandic and White Sea trawlers in the event of war. For each group of five trawlers one trained Group Commander and two Unit Commanders were to be provided. The Group Commanders were to be retired Navy officers, while the Unit Commanders would come from the Royal Naval Reserve and, if any chose to volunteer, from those few Volunteer Reserve officers who had specialized in navigation.

This seemed to me to be too good an opportunity to miss. Once again I went to see Elgood. Again he told me I was crazy. War would – so he said – almost certainly come, and even at this late hour I could still qualify in gunnery, and would then almost certainly become gunnery officer of a destroyer, perhaps even of a cruiser. To this I replied that I wanted to get command of an anti-submarine vessel, for I had heard that when the war construction programme got under way they would have to use the Group and Unit Commanders to provide commanding officers for the new ships.

'You'll never get command, Rayner – the Navy won't give R.N.V.R.s command of a ship, no matter how long the war lasts.'

He tried hard, but could not shake my resolution. In 1937 I took the first part of the course. I was to have completed this in the autumn of 1938, but the Munich Crisis intervened.

I received a telegram ordering me to report to Naval Officer in Charge, Kirkwall. All the other officers of the Mersey Division were going off to join the fleet, or to man ships of the Reserve Fleet. The only difference between their telegrams and mine was that mine instructed me to join 'with all despatch' whereas their only carried the words 'forthwith'. Now there is a subtle difference between the two. 'Forthwith' in naval language means without wasting time. The meaning of 'with all despatch' is peculiar. It is stronger than 'forthwith'. It tells you that you must get there whatever happens. If you are in a ship and are told to 'proceed with all despatch', it allows you to take risks beyond what normal prudence might dictate. It indicates that you are expected to arrive as fast as you can; and in some measure the officer who gives such an order accepts responsibility for what follows. I explain all this because it was to have unexpected results.

On the way north I fell in with another R.N.V.R. officer, Lieutenant J. Black, also a navigator, and also bound for the same destination with a telegram worded the same as mine. We travelled together from Glasgow to Perth and on to Inverness, where we hoped to get a train northward to Thurso, in which port a fleet minesweeper was said to be lying to ferry us across to Scapa.

Arrived at Inverness we heard that Chamberlain had flown to Munich, that the last train to Thurso had already left, and that there would be no further train that night. Inverness station was a seething mass of officers and men. There was no chance of getting a bed, and very little chance of food.

Black then displayed a most competent knowledge of the railway system. He found a man who answered to the title of Controller, and having showed him our telegrams we asked him if it was quite impossible to go on northwards. He assured us that if we really wanted to go north we could do so if we took a local train to Helmsdale where a trainload of A/A ammunition was waiting. He would arrange for a carriage to be hitched to the back of the goods train, but of course it would be unheated. Even this appeared to be a better fate than Inverness at that moment and we were at least complying with instructions. Collecting a warrant officer whom we had met and who seemed likely to prove a good travelling companion, the three of us set off in the local train. In due course we steamed into the little wayside station of Helmsdale, only to find that the ammunition train had already gone on. We seemed to be in a worse mess than ever. I went to talk to the engine driver. He telephoned to some authority, and was told to take us on himself. On we went – three officers in a three-carriage train. Two of us, Black and myself, were becoming a little apprehensive, but the warrant officer was still full of cheer. However there was nothing we could do, so we waved to the children gathered at the little stations to see the 'special' go by, and bided our time. Soon it was dark, but the train rumbled on. At last it stopped. I got out and went to see the engine driver again, since wherever we were, it obviously was not Thurso. A bitter wind whipped across the open moors, and there was no shelter at all in all that waste of heather except a small brick station hut.

'I'm sorry, Sir, this is as far as I can take you. My ticket only covers the line to Wick.'

No argument, no expostulation, would make him change his mind. Here the line divided. To Wick he would take us. Nearer than this to Thurso he could not go.

We unpacked ourselves and stood shivering in the wind. A human form appeared out of the shadows of the hut.

'Somebody on the phone to speak to the senior officer of the special.'

I looked at the others.

'That's me,' I said, 'I'll answer it, and if there's trouble you two can take to the heather for the night.'

I went to the telephone.

'Hallo.'

'This is Movements Officer Thurso speaking. Is that the Senior Officer of the special?'

'Yes, sir.'

'You've two hundred men there haven't you?'

'No, Sir.'

'What have you got?'

'One Lieutenant R.N.V.R. and one Warrant Officer.' It sounded a very inadequate cargo for a whole train.

'Good heavens, is that all?'

'Yes, Sir.'

'What's your name?'

'Rayner, Sir.'

'What, the one from Mersey Division?'

'Yes, Sir.' There was heartfelt relief in that answer. The owner of the voice obviously knew me, and had become much more friendly.

'What the hell are you doing in the middle of the night with a special train and one Lieutenant and one Warrant Officer?'

'It's a long story, Sir. . . . Who are you, Sir?'

'Crick of the *Hussar*.' I knew him of course. Only a few months before the First Minesweeping Flotilla had visited Liverpool. Lieutenant-Commander T. G. P. Crick had then been in command of H.M.S. *Hussar*.

'What are you doing as Movements Officer Thurso?' It was my turn to ask a question.

'I'm running the ferry over to Scapa – you'd better spend the night aboard, there's a bunk or two free.'

'Thank you very much, but how do I get on from here?'

'There's a little branch-line train I've got working for me. I'd already sent it down the line before I got through to you. Bring it straight back, won't you?'

He sounded apprehensive.

Shortly it hove in sight, we bundled ourselves in and set off for Thurso.

'Well,' I said as we stretched ourselves out in the warm

24

carriage, 'we may be the subject of the first court martial of the war, but at least we travel in style.'

We spent the night in warmth and peace, and decided the next morning to go by civil aircraft from Thurso to Kirkwall. We felt that it might be healthier to by-pass Scapa. It was as well that we did so, for we heard afterwards that enquiries were being made. Crick did not give us away, and no one thought of bothering about making enquiries in Kirkwall. Very soon Chamberlain flew back from Munich, and we all went home. But Crick remembered me, and when the real war had come and in 1941 he had to choose a number of corvettes for a special purpose, he chose mine.

The reason for our appointment to Kirkwall was, we discovered, concerned with establishing a contraband control base. Being navigators we were to be used as boarding officers, a prospect which filled me with gloom. I determined that as soon as possible I would complete my anti-submarine course.

As I was one of the first two officers to arrive I was given the job of billeting the men on a population willing enough to receive them, but justifiably indignant at being offered only three shillings and sixpence a day to do so. In vain I pointed out that this was a sum fixed by Government in about the year 1870 and that nobody, least of all the base Paymaster, could do anything about it. They were only silenced when I told them that by law this sum was supposed to pay for an armed man and his horse, and added that they were very lucky not to be asked to keep the horse as well.

When I got back to the *Eaglet*, Captain Elgood proceeded to point out just what a fool I was. I was the only officer who had not had an interesting appointment. He begged me to change before it was too late; but I still remained firm to my convictions, and rushed down to complete my anti-submarine training at Portland.

It was a busy winter for us in the R.N.V.R. The Admiralty had given approval to increase the strength of the division above the eleven hundred men we were allowed.

Our numbers rose steadily until we had sixteen hundred men, and sometimes as many as four hundred men in uniform drilling on a single night.

The R.N.V.R. had, between the wars, and contrary to the generally accepted opinion of the public, made remarkably little impression on the yachtsmen of the nation. To join the R.N.V.R. meant giving up so much leisure that it was almost impossible to combine the two. I did so myself, but only with the greatest difficulty. Now in a last minute attempt to sweep the yachtsmen into the fold, the Admiralty created the Supplementary Reserve, R.N.V.S.R. Many of them took a fortnight's holiday with the fleet and an attempt was made to teach them navigation and gunnery in the drill ship on nights when the R.N.V.R. was not using her. But it was not much more than a list of names. Elgood seized on me and placed me in charge of their navigational instruction, so that often I went down to the ship three nights in a week. I had already been teaching our own junior officers for the last three or four years, and therefore found this new job easy enough; but nothing short of the imminent prospect of war would have made me give up so much of my time. Now there was an urgency about our preparations that had been lacking before. Training went on apace, and when mobilization came Captain Elgood had the satisfaction of sending off more than forty officers and sixteen hundred trained men from Merseyside.

CHAPTER 2

SO THIS IS IT

Four days before the outbreak of war I received my telegram ordering me to report to the Sparrows' Nest Trawler Base at Lowestoft, to which I was sent, in the Admiralty's polite phrase, 'for disposal' as Unit Commander of anti-submarine trawlers.

I had already packed my bags, set my affairs in order

and seen to the laying up of my yacht. As I was one of the last to be mobilized I had time to get myself ready. In that I was luckier than many others.

When I joined the Sparrows' Nest there was no cause to wonder why my mobilization had been delayed. As a base it simply did not exist. Even the taxi driver at Lowestoft station did not know of it, except in its pre-war guise as a park with a pierrot show. He told me that he thought he knew of a house which the Navy had taken over and I agreed that we might as well go there to see if they knew anything about a base for His Majesty's Trawlers.

When I arrived at the house, which was in fact to be the base, I met Commander Gardiner on the doorstep. He and I were, as yet, the only staff. The Captain was due to arrive at four o'clock that afternoon, and we would receive the first draft of men on the following day. We had twenty-four hours to get the base working. I dumped my bags in the house and we walked together down the road to the tree-lined park. Passing inside the gates we came to a large concert hall. Sounds of music and singing could be heard. We went round to the stage end of the building, and came upon some of the artists sunning themselves in deck chairs and drinking coffee. Others were on the stage rehearsing. Gently but firmly we told them that there would be no show that night. We had come to take over the building.

By lunch time two more unit commanders had joined, as had the base Paymaster and his staff. Early in the afternoon lorries arrived from Chatham bringing stationery, mess tables, forms, a small working party and a few writers, stewards and cooks.

We might be getting off to a late start, but the organization behind the Paymaster's side of the base was obviously superb, and the cases had been packed with great intelligence. The first to be unpacked contained twelve waste-paper baskets. The whole operation had been planned in that sort of detail. All we lacked in that first twenty-four hours was man power, and executive officers. Obviously someone had said, 'Oh, the trawlers will not be ready for a week or two. Those unit commanders we are sending there can turn to and run the base until their ships are ready.'

During that night and the next day a dozen or so officers and a like number of ratings working with their coats off, man for man and without distinction of rank, had created a working base out of absolutely nothing. We were dog tired, but we were ready for the first incoming draft on the evening of the second day. To my lot had fallen the key position of Drafting Officer, and I sent off the first crew to join their ship at eight o'clock on the second morning. As assistant I had Lieutenant Lord Churston, R.N.V.R. For a week we drafted crews to the minesweeping trawlers. At the end of that time the base was a flourishing concern. We had accommodated over six hundred Patrol Service ratings, had manned over eighty minesweeping trawlers, and had built enough air raid shelters from sand-filled fish boxes, commandeered from Lowestoft fishing harbour, to house our men while they were awaiting draft. They were more than usually odiferous shelters, and their architecture was unique. It was perhaps fortunate that they were never tested.

Soon we began to hear rumours that the first anti-submarine trawlers would be ready. It took considerably longer to fit a trawler for A/S work than for minesweeping. The vessels chosen for the former purpose were the big modern 900 ton Arctic trawlers sailing mainly out of Hull, whereas the minesweeping trawlers had been drawn from the smaller Fleetwood and Grimsby boats and were 600 ton vessels. Even so there was a great difference between individual ships – an individuality that was well known to the men, a great number of whom had actually sailed in or knew intimately the ships whose names were now beginning to appear on the list of A/S trawlers which had completion dates beside them.

Lord Churston and I would have shown the character and self-denial of saints had we not taken advantage of our peculiar position. We set about collecting five good ships' companies for our own group intending, when the time was ripe, to choose our ships in the light of the knowledge we had gained from the men, and then to draft ourselves and them together. After all we had come to fight a war, not to be Drafting Officer and Assistant Drafting Officer of the Royal Naval Patrol Service Base Lowestoft. There were, we felt, plenty of officers who, for one reason or another, would be more suited to carry out those duties.

We each chose the skippers for our own ships. Fate led me to make a supremely good choice. Skipper Lang was a perfect example of the Devon trawler skipper. Although he had not often handled ships as big as the 900 ton *Loch Tulla* to which we eventually drafted ourselves, he had risen from boy to become master of a sailing trawler out of Brixham; and then, after a period in steam trawlers, he had been appointed harbour master of that port at a remarkably early age. A harbour master must have a great deal of tact; and a tactful man Lang certainly was. He could get men to work because he knew just how far they could be driven, and everyone in the ship knew that he could do any job better than they could do it themselves.

He was a first rate seaman and knew things about the way of a ship at sea which no one not trained in sail could have understood. He would have made a great sailing master in any earlier age. His tall figure, topped by a head of short and crisp grey hair, for he rarely wore a cap, could easily be visualized in trunk hose on the decks of one of the English ships which chased the Armada up-Channel, or in white breeches and blue coat on the deck of a privateer running down upon one of Napoleon's fat supply craft. He gave me an enormous store of weather lore, whose accuracy astonished me. Later it was put to very good use, when I had to decide such questions as whether to let the escorts of a convoy go on oiling or wait for better weather.

'Wind'll freshen from the south'ard before midnight, Sir.'

'How so, Skipper?'

'See those gulls, Sir, throwing water over their backs – sure sign of a southerly wind that, Sir.'

'Thick weather or clear, Skipper?' I'd ask.

'Oh thick, Sir, with a mizzel of rain. Did you not notice how red was the rust on that buoy we passed a while back – blood red it was. 'Twill be thick as the Earl o' Hell's riding boots tonight.'

Probably this conversation would take place at noon in bright, clear weather with no sign of the approaching 'warm front' beloved of the meteorogical men. Later as I peered with strained eyes into a driving mist that formed into drops on my eyelashes, I would remember the conversation only too plainly, as I strove to make out the dark and unlighted headland which was the northerly limit of our night patrol line.

He had a hundred more such sayings, and all equally true. They were important enough to me then with a thousand horse power in a steam kettle below me, but how much more valuable they would have been a hundred and forty years earlier!

Lang had a great mistrust of all aids to navigation, and to him even the compass was more of a convenience than a necessity. In all the twelve months we served together I never remember seeing him fix the ship's position by navigational methods. He found his way about the sea as much by instinct as by knowledge. I well remember once, when I was teasing him about this while I was fixing the ship, he said, 'But you don't really need that, Sir! We are here,' and he pointed with a large and slightly spatulate finger to a particular spot on the chart. My 'fix' proved him to be as correct as made no matter. He must have had a three-legged station pointer built into his brain.

On another occasion I was a good deal worried because our compass had developed quite extraordinary errors after a depth charge attack in narrow waters. I thought this would mean having the compass re-corrected and re-swung, but Lang remarked: 'But why bother about correcting it so long as we know the error? Lor' bless you, Sir, in my old trawler we used to go down-Channel nor'-nor'-west and come home nor'-nor-'est. It's just a question of knowing how wrong it is.'

We got to know each other very well indeed, for of course we had our meals together in my cabin. I thus came to know his wife as well, although I never actually met her. He was very much a family man, and all his comments on the food, which was not always as well cooked as it might have been, were delivered as from her tongue. From this I gathered an impression of a very kindly house-proud woman, and an excellent cook. How we longed for her pasties!

So Churston and I let two or three groups of trawlers go by, until at last our men gave us the green light.

'That *Loch Tulla*, Sir – that's a fine ship for us, Sir. Built special she was, Sir, for an Icelander – a very big man he was – and everything about her of the best – and the *Regal*, *Brontes* and *Istria*, Sir – there's three good sound ships – not as you might say extra modern, Sir, but real good sea-boats that any man would go fishing in. The *Davy*, Sir? Never heard tell of her – reckon she's a new boat.'

Churston and I drafted ourselves. There was no lack of unit commanders waiting to step into our shoes. We fixed our own reliefs, and went to say good-bye to Commander Gardiner and the Captain. 'But you can't do that – not yet.' Apparently it had occurred to no one that two young men in our position would help themselves. But it was too late, the signal had already been made. We handed over to our grinning reliefs and left. We heard later that Lieutenant-Commander Bruford, R.N.V.R., who had taken over from me, had found a ship to his own liking within twenty-four hours. After that they got a proper Drafting Commander, and the racket closed down.

The fine weather which had set in with the start of the war still held – and mercifully so; for the conditions aboard the ships when we arrived in Birkenhead were indescribable. There were ninety-two men working on *Loch Tulla's* upper deck, and more than half of them had in their hands some tool to which either an electric cable or a high-pressure air pipe was attached. The upper deck looked as if an enormous spider, possessed of a sense of humour and slightly inebriated, had attempted to spin a gigantic camouflage net. The remaining forty-five men, carrying brushes and pots of grey paint, went solemnly round the ship, repainting wherever the tool men had blistered the previous application with their oxy-acetylene welders, or had riveted on some new fitting since last the painter had passed that way.

There had been no one to meet us; nor was there any

organization to cater for our wants, which were many. If a ship had been declared ready to receive her crew on a certain day – well, she was ready and the crew must live in her. Luckily the firm of Cammell Laird came to our rescue. They threw open their canteen to us and fed us for three days; then they put a large moulding loft at our disposal, and we used that as a mess deck. There were a hundred and one things to see to. Watch and quarter bills had to be drawn up so that every man would know what watch he was in, what was his action station, and in which mess he would eat and sleep. There were standing orders to write and get typed, ammunition and naval and victualling stores had to be embarked. And all the time these duties were interrupted by tests on gun mountings and depth charge throwers; tests on the water tightness of the asdic fittings; on the magazine flooding arrangements, and on many other of the new machines that were being put aboard. Each one of these tests must be attended by a ship's officer; and there were only two of us, Lang and myself. It is true we had a petty officer, called a 'mate', who was supposed to be a watch-keeper and more of an officer than a rating. This rank was never a success, and as soon as the Patrol Service got properly under way it was dropped and the mates were replaced by young Sub-Lieutenants. Very few of the mates had actually served as such in fishing trawlers; for the only qualification needed was the possession of a Board of Trade fishing mate's ticket. The mate of an Arctic trawler would almost certainly have had his Skipper's ticket, and could then have been a Skipper in the Patrol Service, receiving quite a useful yearly retainer through the R.N.R. grant. Ours, who looked better than most, was a sorry sight when the first days of seasickness had taken the curl out of his hair. Both Lang and I considered him quite unsuitable as a watch-keeper, and thus began our long months of 'watch and watch.'

Lying astern of us in the fitting-out dock was a big Cunard liner being converted to an Armed Merchant Cruiser. Beside her the piles of first class mattresses grew, as her passenger accommodation was ripped out and made into mess decks.

Returning one night to the ship I paused to talk to our quartermaster.

'It do seem a shame to see all they mattresses going into store where the rats will nest in 'em, Sir.'

'It does that, Quartermaster.'

'How would it be, Sir – ?'

'I'll have nothing to do with your sinful thoughts, Quartermaster.' I made my way to the companion hatch that led down to my own accommodation. As I was half way down I paused :

'Quartermaster.'

'Sir?'

'You realize I shall not inspect the mess decks until after we have left Liverpool. Goodnight.'

My cabin was in the after end of the old fish hold, separated from the new mess decks by a bulkhead. For the next half hour sounds of men handling bulky and awkward bundles reached me through the thin partition, and there was a constant shuffle of feet on the deck above my head.

In the morning one corner of the pile appeared to be lower, and some of the mattresses looked very rough to have come from the staterooms of a liner. I could only imagine that the local rats had been quick to seize the opportunity to provide for their own nests.

As soon as the ships were ready we went down the Mersey River for compass swinging and gun trials. We returned to a berth in Birkenhead docks. For one night we lay in the dock which was just inside the main lock. We then received orders to go alongside a shed in another dock to embark our naval stores. As this was some distance away I telephoned to Flag Officer Liverpool's staff, and asked for a dock pilot. I was told that all were too busy, and that anyway trawlers were expected to find their way about without recourse to dock pilots.

We started. I thought I knew Birkenhead docks fairly well, as they were so near my own home. 'It doesn't really matter,' I had said to Lang, 'I know it well. I'll act as pilot if they won't give us one.' All we had by way of a plan of the docks was the rather small one on the chart of the

Mersey. This showed a certain opening between two docks, and feeling proud of ourselves we took her towards this place with reasonable speed on her. We came round the corner of the dock to find a brick wall barring our path. The Harbour Board had decided to close this particular passage between one dock and the next. We came to a grinding stop, and *Loch Tulla* was ten feet shorter than she had been a moment before.

Fortunately she was what is known in trawler phraseology as 'a soft-nosed ship'; that is to say the real stem of the ship was the forward watertight bulkhead. The idea was that if, when fishing in the White Sea or off Bear Island she should run into pack ice, the bows would crumple rather than split. So, although we had spoilt her looks and her immediate readiness for war, we had not done any great structural damage.

We were dry-docked the next day for repairs. They took only four days to fit us with a new stem and bow plates. I had feared that the shock might have cracked the engine bearers, and such damage would have taken a long time to repair. Fortunately our soft bow had taken the jolt out of the crash, so that the only damage was to the bow itself.

During those four days I was summoned to a Board of Enquiry at the office of the Flag Officer in Charge in the Liver Building.

Addressing me the President of the Board asked:

'You are in command of H.M. Trawler *Loch Tulla*?'

'No, Sir.'

He looked over his spectacles at me.

'What do you mean, "No Sir"? – of course you are.'

'No, Sir. I am in charge, not in command – Skipper Lang is the commanding officer.'

'How can he be? So long as you're there, you're the senior.'

'I'm the Unit Commander, Sir – in charge of the operational conduct of one unit of anti-submarine trawlers. I live in *Loch Tulla* because she is fitted as a unit commander's ship, the other trawler of my unit is not so fitted; but I can, if occasion demands, equally well go to sea in her.'

34

'Well, how did it happen?'

'We'd asked for a dock pilot and been refused one. We are a 900 ton ship, Sir – I don't think the staff realize just how big these Arctic trawlers are; people think we are no bigger than a drifter of 120 tons. With that gun up forward and all the fishing gear out of her she is riding two foot above her normal trim forward. You've got to handle her fairly fast or her bows will blow off down-wind. As unit commander I'm entirely satisfied with Skipper Lang's conduct. It was in my opinion an accident that could hardly have been avoided once we had taken the wrong turning.' I felt that I was now no longer the prisoner in the dock, but counsel arguing a defence.

However the Paymaster Commander, who was acting as Secretary, intervened. Speaking to the President he said :

'You know I think we'll have to adjourn until we've seen the Admiral on this, the board was to be held on Lieutenant-Commander Rayner, I don't think we can switch it to Skipper Lang just like that, Sir.'

'When does the Admiral get back?'

'Tomorrow night.'

'We're sailing for Portland tomorrow morning, Sir,' I informed him.

The President looked up at me and smiled. 'Aren't you lucky!' he said.

We sailed, and we never heard anything more about that episode; but for weeks I scanned the mail anxiously and looked at every buff envelope to see if it had come from the Flag Officer Liverpool.

On the afternoon after the enquiry I had been down to the *Eaglet* to see Captain Elgood. He was still in command of her although she was now flying the flag of F.O.I.C. Liverpool, and was being used as a training ship for the Defensively Equipped Merchant Ships (D.E.M.S.). When a gun had been fitted to a merchantman, crews would be sent to the *Eaglet* for training in its use. The gun deck was loud with the slamming of breech mechanisms and the sharp orders of the gunnery drill, as three or more crews were put through their paces. It was all much the same as when she had been our own drill ship, less than one month ago, and yet it seemed that an age had passed during the thirteen days we had been at war.

Elgood's command was titular more than executive. His war work had been completed when the division had been mobilized; but he was a man of action, and hated the backwater into which he had fallen. But I think that illness had already laid cold fingers upon him. He was pleased to see me, and pleased that I had called, and when I bemoaned my invidious position as 'in charge but not in command' he answered me :

'Rayner, I have always told you so, but you'd never listen. The Navy cannot give command to an R.N.V.R. officer. Your experience today proves what I've always said. The discipline of the Court Martial means nothing to us. If you were dismissed the service tomorrow Elizabeth and your kids would not starve, you'd just go back to your shoreside job. Now with the R.N. it's entirely different. A severe reprimand will lose them the chance of promotion, and an R.N.R. could lose his Board of Trade certificate.'

'Oh well, it's too late to change now, and you know, Sir, I wouldn't anyway.'

'You always were a bloody fool,' he said as he shook my hand.

Words which were so typical of the man's sincerity. Although he always succeeded in conveying just what he meant, his thoughts were never as fierce as the words that clothed them. He had been a good master to serve, so long as one stood up to meet him sure of one's own ground. The training he gave me in dealing with senior officers was to prove most useful to me when, in later days, I was serving under Admiral Sir Max Horton in the Western Approaches; for the two men were singularly alike. Alas they were the last words I ever heard Elgood speak.

CHAPTER 3

LOCH TULLA AND SENIOR OFFICER
14TH ANTI-SUBMARINE GROUP

As the rest of the group had gone ahead while we were having the new stem fitted, we sailed alone from Liverpool to Portland. The plan had been that we should go there for a week or so to 'work up' and receive a final training before going on to our war stations. However, after the *Athenia* sinking, Mr. Churchill, speaking as First Lord, had promised the country that eighty anti-submarine vessels would be on their stations within a fortnight. The rush that followed killed the 'work up' plan. We arrived at Portland at 5 p.m. one night and sailed at noon the next day – a certified operational anti-submarine vessel.

Because his ship had developed some defect and remained behind, our own senior officer was not present. It therefore fell to *Loch Tulla* to lead the 14th Anti-Submarine Group through the breakwaters of Portland harbour. From the yardarm fluttered a string of flags, new and brilliant in the bright sun. 'Order One, George ten', form line ahead, speed ten knots. It was the first order I had ever made to a group of ships, and I was proud of myself and my command. As the three ships took up their stations astern of me, perhaps a little uncertainly, I leant over the after end of the bridge and watched. Astern of me *Istria* was shuffling into station, her high bow slicing the short channel seas, astern of her was *Regal* with Churston as unit commander leading the second division of the group. The last ship in the line was the unknown quantity *Davy*.

Loch Tulla was unique amongst trawlers. If I was to say that she was the most handsome trawler ever built the commanding officers of all the other trawlers would rise up and tear me limb from limb. Let us leave it that she was different. She had been specially built for an unusual man.

37

Regal, Istria and *Brontes* were as much alike as three pins. It was not until they developed little idiosyncrasies of their own under their new commanding officers that you could tell them apart at a distance of a mile. The *Davy* again was different. As we had guessed she was a new ship taken fresh from the builders. Looking at her one had the impression that her designer had tried to do something special, but the arrow of his thought seemed to have missed the target. To a seaman it did not appear that the bow matched the stern. Somehow or other the lines of her hull did not flow evenly along the length of her. As a ship she had a lean and hungry look; and she was to prove light-headed and irresponsible. This is not to belittle the officers and men who manned her. Her commanding officer, Skipper Mackintosh, was as good in his way as my own Skipper Lang. Mackintosh came from the Moray Firth. His men were always both smart and happy, and he ran an excellent ship. But I know the *Davy* nearly drove him to despair. She was a nightmare to take alongside. Without warning her high thin bow would suddenly blow down-wind, and there was nothing for it but to go astern and try again. Although she had two foot more freeboard forward than any other ship in the group, she was the wettest sea boat of the five; and in a steep head sea such as often fell to her lot on patrol in the Pentland Firth with wind against tide, she would take fantastic quantities of water over her bow. As befitted one who came from the north-east coast Mackintosh was a good Presbyterian. He was never heard to swear aloud, but the *Davy* must have tried his patience hard.

The 14th Anti-Submarine Group was bound for Rosyth, where we would be used to patrol the entrance to the Firth of Forth. Our one evening at Portland had been a hectic one. The camber where the anti-submarine trawlers lay was crowded with ships, moored four and five deep. Most of the group and unit commanders knew each other, and we were all eager to find out where our friends were going. The groups were bound to so many ports; patrol groups to Alexandria, Malta, Gibraltar, Rosyth, Portsmouth, Plymouth, Liverpool, Belfast and the Clyde; groups specially selected for coastal convoy work to Harwich, Rosyth and Plymouth. We might have picked anything out of the hat.

We rounded the North Foreland as it was getting dark, threaded our way through the maze of swept channels and sandbanks which marks the entrance to the great port of London, and hurried on northward. The fine weather which had lasted since the day war was declared had gone with the sun, and a stiff easterly gale was rising. About ten o'clock that night one of the pins holding the compass bowl in the wheelhouse worked itself loose, and could not be found. Without a steering compass I could not lead the group up the narrow war channel, so I sent Churston on ahead, but it proved impossible to follow the last ship in the line with no compass for the quartermaster to steer by, so I hove to until dawn.

When dawn came we found the missing pin on the wheel-house floor, and I was able to refit it to the compass. The steering compass was the original one which had been in the ship before conversion. It was a merchant service pattern, and not a proper Admiralty fitting like the new binnacle on the upper bridge, which had been built above the wheel-house when she was converted to a warship.

When we had mended ourselves we hurried on northward alone, passing the Humber as night fell. The previous night's wind had eased considerably. The sea was littered with the lights of fishing vessels, and this gave us an idea. Why be a darkened shape, and so an obvious war vessel when if we had lights and looked like a fisherman we would actually be less conspicuous? There was always the possibility of a U-Boat. We switched on our navigation lights. An hour later the asdic operator reported a strong echo bearing north seventy degrees west, at a range of one thousand yards.

Looking along the bearing I could see no surface vessel. I rang down for dead slow on the engines and went into the asdic hut. It was true enough – it was just such an echo as a U-Boat might be expected to give. While I was considering the matter, I wearing one pair of headphones and the opera-tor the other, we both heard a very definite clanging noise followed by the steady beat of engines. The propeller noise stopped, and shortly afterwards there came another distinct clap. I went to action stations, and *Loch Tulla* ran in at full speed to fire her first pattern of depth charges.

We circled round afterwards. There was a strong smell of oil, a piece of grey painted wood floated in the water disturbed by the explosion of our charges. With the knowledge we then had it looked pretty conclusive. Later in the war we would have known better. It could have been a minelaying U-Boat and we could have killed it, but in those early days we did not realize just how close a depth charge must be to a U-Boat to cause lethal damage. We heard later that when two mine-sweeping trawlers were sent to investigate the area one was herself mined, which was an indication but not a proof that we had attacked our first enemy.

The next morning we arrived at Rosyth. I had to go ashore and report. The rest of the group were already on patrol, and before nightfall – so were we. There was, we soon found, to be absolutely no rest, no let-up at all, for the next six months.

Long lines of ships in convoy wound their way up the east coast. Destroyers of the east coast escort force fussed round them. One or two anti-submarine trawlers would be there, and we cast envious glances at them. At least they went from one port to another, whereas we flogged the same bit of sea, day in and day out. We began to feel the boredom of war. So it was not going to be all fun, and action was going to be a rarity. Were we not the Patrol Service? Patrol, patrol, and more patrol. Up and down the line, Ping, ping, ping on the asdic for days without number, until you knew every aspect of the coast bordering your beat. In fog it had peered at you dimly, and sometimes unexpectedly close. At night it would recede until you longed to catch a glimpse of landmarks which by day you hated because of their familiarity.

We were not left long at Rosyth, which had appeared to be a friendly base with the enchantment of the city of Edinburgh within reach – if ever we should be so lucky as to have a night ashore. Urgent orders sent us hurrying northwards. Captain Prien had taken his U-Boat into Scapa

Flow, and had there torpedoed the battleship *Royal Oak*. There was then no anti-submarine group defending Scapa. It is not for me to question the decisions of authority. It is always unwise for junior officers to do so, because they cannot know all the facts on which decisions are made. Perhaps there were not enough groups to go round, possibly the protection of a hundred merchantmen in the Firth of Forth was considered more important than that of Scapa Flow. Such a one as I should make no comment.

I was on patrol when our sailing signal came. *Loch Tulla*, *Istria*, *Regal* and *Davy* met and formed up. For the first time for a week we had all been in sight of one another. Already we were becoming a team, and we felt a warmer glow when a dark blur answered our signal lamp and we knew that it was one of our own group. We arrived off the eastern entrance to the Pentland Firth about four in the morning, and settled down to patrol until we could enter by daylight. As dawn came we sighted another anti-submarine trawler coming up from the south. It was our group commander in *Brontes*. He led the group into Scapa, and at once developed another defect.

The truth had best be told. Our group commander was a man who I am sure was as brave as a lion, but his health was simply not strong enough for war in a trawler. He would spend long hours brewing and drinking some herbal tea in his cabin, and it seemed almost impossible to winkle H.M.T. *Brontes* from her anchorage. It was hardly a week before he was invalided south, and the mantle of senior officer 14th Anti-Submarine Group fell upon me.

To patrol the approaches to the windswept and tidebound fleet anchorage of Scapa Flow was one of the most difficult and arduous tasks that could have fallen to any group. On the few days when there was no gale there was fog; and always there was a sluicing tide running first one way and then the other through the rock-encumbered Pentland Firth at eight knots. When the wind was against the tide the sea was indescribable; and when the wind and the tide were going the same way together it was almost impossible to make headway against their combined onslaught. We were not encouraged to ask for the shore lights except in an emergency, and it became a point of honour not to do so. As a matter of fact I do not remember any of the group ever asking for the lights.

The conditions of work were arduous in the extreme. With five ships I had to keep three patrol lines manned; and the two ships off duty were expected to anchor in strategic places within the Flow as a further guard against any U-Boat which got through the outer patrols, evaded the booms across the entrances, or was not noticed by the 'loops'. These last were electric cables laid on the sea bed which, connected to a galvanometer ashore, would detect the passage of any large metal object. With all these defences it might seem a little unnecessary to anchor anti-submarine vessels inside, but the truth was that half were still only in an embryo state.

To anchor the trawlers inside at instant readiness for steam was just as arduous as being on patrol. With the high windage forward caused by their being out of trim, and the extra windage of the 4-inch gun and its platform, they would have ridden to anchor very badly indeed even if the bottom had been good holding ground – which it was not. They were only too liable to drag their anchors, and a constant watch both on deck and in the engine-room had to be maintained. All of us preferred the days of patrol to the days at anchor, probably because the ship herself seemed to feel happier steaming into the sea than when yawing and snubbing at her cable.

Fresh food was almost unobtainable. There was no leave for the ship's company, and nowhere to go if there had been. Later Lyness was to become a great base with canteens for the men, 'Ensa' parties and surfaced roads. When we arrived it comprised only a few first-war huts in a poor state of repair, an old seaplane hangar, and miles of unsurfaced road. My first call on Admiral French, Admiral Commanding Orkneys and Shetlands, was to find him in a hut which was strangely reminiscent of a potting shed, or even of one of those other sheds which used to stand in farmhouse gardens before interior sanitation became common. The Admiral and his staff were supposed to be accommodated in

H.M.S. *Iron Duke*; but a German aircraft had seriously damaged her, and she was now beached off Lyness and barely usable even as a home. Later she was raised and taken round to Long Hope where, beached again, she became a houseboat for the auxiliary patrol craft.

From October 1939 to January 1940 with five vessels I kept the same patrols for which in the following winter fifteen ships were used. Of the first hundred days at Scapa I spent ninety-six on patrol. Only on four occasions did we have a night lying at anchor doing nothing. When we were out, Lang and I were watch and watch. Four hours for me, four hours for him. He who was off watch in the morning must work the hands. When I was not on watch in the afternoon I must do the paper work for the group. When we were in harbour for an hour or two for coal or water I would have to go by boat to see the Admiral, the Chief of Staff, or Commander J. M. ('Lampy') Heath in the defence office. I slept either from eight at night until midnight and from four o'clock in the morning until seven, or from midnight to four in the morning and took my chance whether I could get some sleep in the forenoon or not. The group never missed a patrol. I don't know how the men stood it. The devotion to duty of the seaman can be quite incredible. On the whole, morale was excellent. I only saw it crack once, and then for so short a time, and the mend was so good, that I could hardly believe it had happened.

Because one of the ships had developed a defect and we were out of step with our routine, we had had a particularly vile patrol – four days at the western end of the Pentland Firth instead of our usual two days on that hated patrol line. We entered harbour just as it was getting dark, the ship short of coal and the men short of rest. One hundred days and only four nights' peace. We were just slipping into Long Hope to anchor when Flotta signal tower called us, 'Coal from *Hekla* in Gutta Sound and be prepared to escort S.S. ——— to Loch Ewe. Sailing orders will be sent.'

We turned round and went to Gutta Sound. Lang berthed her alongside the dusty collier. Even as we tied up I sensed the men were grumbling. It was not that anyone said anything. It was just the way they threw the heaving lines. I always think that you can tell the morale of a ship's company from the way heaving lines are thrown. Heaving lines smartly thrown, and another ready at once to back it up if the first one falls short, then all is well. Heaving lines slackly thrown, in a 'take it or leave it' fashion – there is something wrong. There was something wrong with us. Lang went down to his cabin below the bridge as the first grab-load of coal descended on our deck. I went to my cabin below the forward deck. The men were standing round looking at the coal – just looking. The coaling shovels were stacked along the ship's side. No one moved to take them up. I looked at the men, I knew I had trouble on my hands.

I had to think quickly. I felt no anger towards the men. They were all fishermen, born and bred under trade union rules and regulations. Any leader of the Seaman's Union would have had a fit if he had served a month in any ship of the group – let alone one hundred days.

We were in sight of Flotta signal station, in sight also of two or three fleet destroyers. I had only to send a signal asking for an armed guard, and arrest the whole ship's company. But what purpose would that serve? To put my ship out of action for want of a crew? Surely that was not the way. I went into Lang's cabin.

'Sorry, Skipper, to turn you out, but the men won't handle the coal. Will you come and give me a hand? We'll start in, and my bet is that they'll join in too. Don't say anything – just take a shovel and pretend nothing has happened.'

Tired as he was he rose at once, heaving his long legs from the bunk in which he had already fallen fast asleep; for in those days to lie down was to go out like a lamp.

We each took a shovel and started. The men watched us. We were not working alone for long. First to come was a foul-mouthed red-headed little stoker. His exact words cannot be written, but they were to the effect that something very unnatural could happen to himself before he would let a couple of brass-bound Don Juans do his work for him. Five minutes later the storm in the teacup was over, and coaling was going with its normal swing.

In that instant of time when I had decided to deal with the matter in my own way I had climbed a further step up the ladder towards maturity. Now I felt that if I had the chance I could command a ship, because I would never again have any fear of men.

Clothing too was a great trouble. The men had come to war with only their uniform. There were no 'comforts' yet for Scapa, or at least not on an adequate scale. My mother, in London, had tapped a source of stockings and sweaters; but when these arrived we found they were so badly knitted as to be almost unwearable. A tiny foot, into which no seaman could force more than his toes, would be topped by a long leg that could have reached to his armpits. Two men could insert themselves into one sweater, or alternatively the garment clung to one like a corset.

By comparison my wife's aunts, of which she seemed to have an inexhaustible supply, sent us some beautiful garments; but they could not get enough wool. One night when we were lying anchored inside the gate I took all our useless garments down to the messdeck and set the whole ship's company to unravelling wool. Twenty-eight men unravelling twenty-eight garments. Quickly the number of balls of wool mounted. 'The aunts' were set up in wool for months. Soon well shaped sweaters and stockings began to arrive in a steady stream from their active needles. The *Loch Tulla*'s men were at last warm, and we could spare some for the rest of the group.

Life in an anti-submarine trawler was not of course always one long fight with the weather and the patrol lines. There is always, in any ship's company, the man who can raise a laugh however bad the conditions; and we had a first class crowd. We laughed a lot, and on the messdecks they sang a lot. Someone had a banjo, and someone a mouth organ and everyone had a voice.

I was most sorry for the signalman. He was a nice lad from the London Division R.N.V.R., for they had no signalmen in the Patrol Service. In private life he was clerk in a London office. On each and every night of his working life he had taken the public transport to his home along brightly lit streets. His first view of Scapa depressed him enormously.

'Oh, Sir – no trams – not even a lamp-post,' he had said when I asked him what he thought of our new base.

He was quite a good signalman, but absolutely unable to recognize one ship from another even after some weeks at sea during which he had often seen units of the fleet coming and going on their way through the Pentland Firth. Anything that was grey and floated was a ship, and might be the one to which he was supposed to be sending a signal. All he wanted was the answering flash of light at the end of each word, and he was quite happy.

On one occasion when the group had been hurriedly assembled from their patrol lines in order to hunt the area where a U-Boat had been reported, I told him to make a signal to the *Brontes* : 'You really must keep better station.' I had my head in the chart table as I was plotting our search scheme, and realized suddenly that he was passing the signal to some ship on the starboard side whereas *Brontes*, however badly out of station, should have been somewhere on the port side. Hastily raising my head I saw with horror that my signal had been passed to a 'Town' class (10,000 ton) cruiser which was rapidly coming up over the horizon.

'And what sort of reply do you expect from that?' I asked.

It came : 'Your signal not understood.' In the circumstances I considered it remarkably lenient. I made back.

'Sorry. Case of mistaken identity. My signalman cannot distinguish an acorn from an oak tree.'

On another occasion when patrolling off Holy Sound in a dense fog, a fleet destroyer showed suddenly through the mist.

'Quick,' I said to the signalman, 'make to him – "can you tell me where I am?"'

He took up the lamp and passed the signal. Almost at once I could see the reply coming back from the destroyer which was already disappearing from view in the fog. I spelt it out for myself. 'Regret-have-not-known-you-long-enough-to-venture-an-opinion.'

'That's a very curious reply. What on earth did you make to him?'

It turned out that the signalman had made 'can you tell me *what* I am?' Their signal made sense even if it did not help me much.

In some measure we solved the food problem by indenting for a 'harness' cask. I cannot remember in what book I discovered that ships on certain stations where fresh meat was not available could demand such a thing from the Naval Stores. It is a large butt of teak or oak, in which meat can be salted down with common salt and saltpetre. This seemed to be an excellent idea for us so I went to the Paymaster Commander at Lyness Base.

'Please, Sir, I want a harness cask.'

'Good God, I don't suppose anyone's asked for a harness cask since the last sailing ship went out of commission.'

'Well there's no harm in just trying, Sir.'

What a wonderful organization the Navy is, and particularly the Naval Stores Department! Within a month *Loch Tulla*'s harness cask arrived, and enough saltpetre to last us for years. Thereafter we could salt down a week's supply of fresh meat, when we could get it. All it meant at that time was that we could take in all the meat we could get without fear of it going bad.

Christmas 1939 looked as if it was going to be a particularly lean time. We had our Christmas dinner at anchor inside Hoxa gate. Much to my surprise I heard that we had been successful in getting some liver, and when I went down to the decorated messdecks I was amazed to find heaped plates of liver and bacon. I was even more surprised when my steward brought down liver and bacon for breakfast the following morning, instead of the usual bacon and elongated tinned tomato which was our normal breakfast dish. When liver again appeared on the menu at lunch time I said to Lang that we really must investigate the origin of all this liver. It seemed unlikely that honest means had been used to acquire what must have amounted to a couple of hundredweight of a delicacy which our wives told us was no longer part of the body of any animal used for food.

As I feared we were receivers of stolen goods. It transpired that a working party from a battleship had been sent to Lyness base to collect three wicker 'skips' full of liver for the twelve hundred odd men of her company. The jetty at Lyness was made of large planks, with a good two inches between one plank and the next. The battleship's party had put down the skips just above the place where *Loch Tulla*'s boat lay waiting for her supply party, who had gone ashore to draw our usual bully beef. It was more than human nature could stand, particularly when it had sharp knives. Holes had been cut in the wickerwork placed so temptingly above the heads of the boat's crew, and the succulent meat was abstracted until only a thin layer covered the bottom of each skip.

Although we had many alarms no alleged sighting of a U-Boat was confirmed. Perhaps they considered the area too unhealthy, or perhaps some of our supposed contacts really were U-Boats and they escaped us, having at any rate learnt that we were on the lookout for them. It had always intrigued me to discover how Prien did get his U-Boat into Scapa to torpedo the *Royal Oak*. Although the booms at Hoxa and Hoy were not complete when he carried out his attack I was fairly sure that the loops would have detected him had he used either of those routes. If ever a patrolling anti-submarine trawler got anywhere near the loops a signal would come at once 'Investigate suspected crossing on loop Number so and so' and we would have to investigate ourselves, and spend some time assuring the loop officers that it was only we who had agitated their instruments.

I took, therefore, an early opportunity of inspecting the eastern approaches to the Flow, which had supposedly been closed by blockships. I had with me at that time an article written by a German Admiral which describes his passage through Holm Sound in a German yacht. This had been quite a big yacht drawing a lot of water, and he had remarked that the fierce tide had worn a deep water channel round one end of each blockship; and that if you went through, as he had done, against the tide you were going so slowly over the ground that you had plenty of time to go carefully with the lead. It so happened that on the morning of the day when I first had suitable weather to explore these

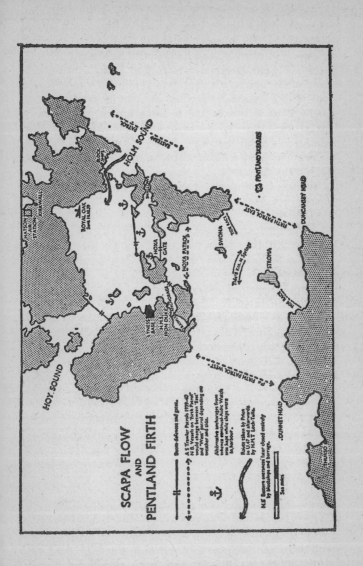

SCAPA FLOW
AND
PENTLAND FIRTH

HOY SOUND

HOY SOUND

HATSTON
R.N. AIR
STATION

KIRKWALL

ROYAL OAK
Sunk 14.10.39

HOLM SOUND

EASTERN PATROL

PENTLAND SKERRIES

HOXA
GATE

HOXA PATROL

SWITHA PATROL

DUNCANSBY HEAD

SWONA

TIDE RACE

TIDE RACE

THE KIRK of SWONA

STROMA

TIDE RACE

IRON DUKE 1914-39

U47

SWITHA PATROL WEST

DUNNET HEAD

THURSO

——— Boom defences and guns.

A S Trawler Patrols 1939–40
N.B. Vessels on 'firth Patrol'
and 'Wren' patrol depending on
weather and tide.

Alternative anchorages from
whence continual Arctic Winds
are kept while ships were
in harbour.

Route taken by Prien
in U47 and afterwards
by H.M.T. Loch-Ewe.

N.E. Eastern entrances later closed entirely
by blockships and barrage.

Sea miles

approaches, I had been involved in an acrimonious discussion with Hoxa gate. I forget now the rights and wrongs of the matter, but I was in the mood to damn the gate and its keepers to eternity. The flood would be running strongly out of the Flow in the afternoon, and I decided about an hour before high water to go into Holm Sound and take a look. With a leadsman sounding we went in steadily. It was so easy, that as it was time to leave this patrol, and as it was our turn to spend the night at anchor inside the Flow, I decided to go in that way instead of tackling Hoxa gate.

Dark had hardly fallen when we received a signal from Flotta signal tower.

'Admiral Commanding Orkneys and Shetlands to Senior Officer 14th Anti-Submarine Group. Report your position immediately.'

I replied, 'At anchor one mile north Hoxa gate.'

There must have been some telephoning between the staff office and the boom gate for it was an hour before the next signal came.

'By what route did you enter?'

'By Holm Sound.'

'My barge is being sent for you.'

It may have been a crazy thing to do, but I was convinced it was the way Prien took. We were just about the same length as a U-Boat and drew the same amount of water. *Loch Tulla* could be expected to steer more easily, and we had daylight. Prien of course did it all at night, and with enemy territory all round him.

Needless to say this escapade caused something of a sensation. It may have hastened the proper blocking of the eastern approach, because very shortly afterwards the channel was completely blocked. At any rate I did not receive quite the dressing-down I had expected.

Much to my surprise I found myself included in the first honours list of the war, but had no idea for what reason the D.S.C. had been given to me. I would like to have thought it was for our action south of Flamborough Head on our way north, and perhaps at the time I did think so. Later experience was to prove how very difficult it was to destroy a modern U-Boat. There can be no doubt that we in the anti-submarine branch had not made sufficient allowance for the advances in the technique of welded construction. The pressure hull of a U-Boat was believed to be far weaker than in fact it was. We had thought that a well carried out attack by an anti-submarine vessel in coastal waters would certainly effect a kill. At first it had been estimated that a depth charge exploding twenty yards from a submarine's hull would kill it. Later experience was to prove that this distance should be very much reduced.

But whatever may have been Their Lordships' reason for decorating me, nothing that I had done would have been possible without the willing co-operation of the men. The temperament of the men was peculiar. They were all volunteers and so showed to the full that typically British willingness to endure, no matter what hardships, so long as they felt they were doing so of their own free will. Once conscription is introduced much, if not all of this valuable quality is inevitably lost. The men were drawn entirely from the fishing fleets, and already their old comrades were earning very large sums of money for the food they gathered for the nation. By and large the fishermen who stayed at home were not working so hard as the men in H.M. Trawlers. Their innate morale could be placed on the credit side of the ledger, but on the debit side was a most curious refusal to service the ships properly. Until I realized the basic reason for this it caused me considerable worry. I discovered that apparent reluctance to take care of weapons and engines on which their lives might at any moment depend, was the result of the custom by which the crew of a fishing vessel left their ship the moment she docked, and only rejoined her when she was in the sea-lock ready to sail on her next fishing trip. During her time in harbour the ship would be taken over by a gang of men known by the delightful name of 'ships'-husbandmen', and they would go over her completely, refitting and renewing where necessary. The fishermen were, therefore, quite unused to servicing anything, and their natural inclination, when machinery became out of order, was to leave it to the shore staff to put right. Unfortunately for them there was practically no base staff available in those early months, and our only hope of repairing machinery lay in the workshops of Messrs. Cox and Danks, who had been salvaging the German warships scuttled after World War One. In keeping the patrols going my greatest difficulty had been to teach the ships to be self reliant. There were of course some technical matters which were beyond our own immediate control – in particular the asdic machines. But at Scapa we were blessed with a most hard-working anti-submarine officer, Lieutenant M. F. Isaac, R.N., who slaved without respite to keep our asdics going. It was nothing for him to arrive alongside in a motor boat at two o'clock in the morning, when we were at anchor six miles from the base. Such men have an influence far beyond the scope of their own work. If we were important enough for him to come out on a vile night across the Flow to service our asdic, then encouragement is given to the whole ship's company – for the men are no fools. The gunnery ratings will start to keep their guns just that much cleaner, and the engineers will see that their engines receive the little extra attention which prevents a breakdown. The efficiency of a ship, or of a group is extremely sensitive to the attention of the base staff. Throughout the war I was always to admire the unselfish, and so often unthanked, efforts of those who, living ashore and often in much worse conditions than ours, yet managed to keep our ships fit for sea. To us fell the thrill of action, and the feeling that what we did was of real use; to them the long hours struggling with defective electrical circuits while others slept.

By the middle of January 1940 we were getting some relief from the wretched watch at anchor within the gates. The *Iron Duke* had been converted into a base ship for the auxiliary patrol, which was composed of small drifters, officered often by the R.N.V.S.R., and manned by 'hostilities only' ratings. The drifters were equipped with an immature asdic, and were employed to steam back and forth within the booms. They intrepidly strapped a couple of depth charges to their sterns, and we often wondered what would happen if they ever had to fire one. Commander

C. A. R. Shillington of the Belfast Division R.N.V.R. was their Godmother, and he reigned benevolently over their comings and goings from the one-time Captain's cabin in the *Iron Duke*.

Their arrival released us to perform our proper duties and now, when off patrol, we could look forward to an escort job. Unbounded was our joy when we could actually steam for more than six miles in a straight line, after months of constantly retracing our steps. One of our favourite jobs was to escort the Trinity House ship round the outlying lighthouses, and it was on one of these trips that *Loch Tulla* came across and attacked what was almost certainly a U-Boat, although the staff ashore were inclined to suggest it was a whale. However, it had broken surface half way between ourselves and the Trinity House vessel, and was clearly seen by both ships to be on her side. Unfortunately an asdic defect prevented our continuing the attack, and by the time we had mended ourselves she could no longer be found.

To this period too belongs a hunt for a reported U-Boat when an extremely ill-matched pair of ships were ordered to investigate an aircraft sighting to the west of Hoy Sound. H.M.S. *Kelly* (Captain Lord Louis Mountbatten) and H.M. Trawler *Loch Tulla* were sent off together, presumably because we were the only two asdic-fitted ships available. Of course we found nothing, for the scent was more than a little cold when we got to the position. Then, as always until we learnt to develop proper air to surface vessel co-operation, the delay between an aircraft sighting and the arrival of the ships was so great that the chances of the latter obtaining contact were absolutely negligible. In this particular case no less than twenty-four hours had elapsed.

Let us consider the case of a U-Boat observed by aircraft to be in position X. We will, for the moment, overlook the fact that the aircraft, because of its relatively poor navigational facilities and its high speed, might have been anything up to ten miles wrong in its estimate of the geographical position. Even if it had reported the position correctly it is certain that the U-Boat, knowing himself observed, would move on at about four knots, so long as he was kept submerged by further aircraft patrols. Of course if the U-Boat was allowed to surface during darkness and get away using his diesel engines the position at once became hopeless. Assuming, however, that he could be kept down and that the hunting ships arrived one hour after the sighting report, then it was necessary to sweep fifty square miles of sea surrounding the sighting position. An hour later the area had increased to two hundred square miles; and two hours later the area was over eight hundred square miles. It will be seen therefore that theoretically it was almost useless to go to a sighting report unless you could arrive within an hour or two. In one hour a group of anti-submarine trawlers could sweep an area ten miles long and eight miles wide, but almost at once the zone to be investigated started to increase faster than they could search. Fortunately practice was rather more in favour of the hunting craft than theory. In coastal waters the land would often cut down the space to be searched, or there would be definite arcs of the circle which could be put outside the 'probability area'. After all the U-Boat was not merely engaged in avoiding the hunting craft. He was there for his own nefarious purposes, and could be expected to hang around convoy routes or, if sighted on passage to or from his operational area, it could be assumed that he would continue on his outward or homeward course. Even so, to go a-hunting twenty-four hours late was little more than a gesture of defiance. It was extremely unlikely to find the enemy. Successes were rare until later in the war when air and sea forces were put under joint operational control, and the aircraft which sighted the U-Boat had been provided with equipment to enable it to circle the position, and 'home' to it the ships of the escort group.

However, there was certainly a U-Boat nosing its way round Scapa Flow during the second week of January 1940, for the night before our search with the *Kelly* he had been over one of the outlying loops, and a day or two previously *Davy* had attacked a suspected contact to the eastward of the islands. By the time *Kelly* gave up our particular search and made the signal 'proceed independently', I had been without sleep for seventy hours. This experience interested me a good deal, because I found the period from twenty-four to thirty-six hours by far the worst. Thereafter I had felt peculiarly well, and quite recovered the competence which I had almost lost in the bad period.

Returning to Scapa we berthed alongside *Kelly* and I was invited by Lord Louis to dinner. Better even than that was the fact that Lang was also invited. For me it was a fairly common occurrence to be asked aboard a destroyer for a bath, dinner, or drinks, or for all three. *Kelly*'s captain was the first to ask my skipper as well. Lang made his excuses, but he was terribly pleased none the less.

In February, it was arranged that the group should go, one at a time, to Aberdeen to have 'de-gaussing' fitted as a protection against the magnetic mine. Fortunately when the first berth fell vacant, I took *Loch Tulla* down and went on to attend the first investiture of the war in Buckingham Palace. I was the only R.N.V.R. there, and so the last naval officer in the line. When it came to my turn His Majesty said conversationally, 'I'm so pleased to see one of you here today.' I was so surprised that I muffed my going astern and turn to starboard, so that the very senior Army officer who was behind me had to do a quick shuffle to avoid a collision.

In London I had two nights with my wife and then went back to Aberdeen to take *Loch Tulla* north once more.

One ship constantly away, meant more work for the remaining four, and by mid-March 1940 all the officers were in danger of going 'round the bend.' At the end of the month I went to see the doctor because I was having difficulty in seeing lights at night, and even such well-known objects as the buoys on the booms appeared to be double. I was given three weeks' sick leave, and a junior watchkeeper was provided to help Lang with *Loch Tulla.*

Arrived home, my own doctor took one look at me and put me to sleep with tablets for three consecutive days. Two days later my father-in-law returned from London with the news that there would almost certainly be trouble in Norway. I could not let my ships be taken into action by anyone else, so hurried back after only one week's leave. As I went north Hitler's legions went to Norway. I had sent a telegram to Lang telling him by hook or crook to get *Loch Tulla* on the western patrol, and to have a boat in Thurso harbour to meet me. I had no intention of going near Lyness base in case someone should prevent my going aboard. My plan worked smoothly. As the rest of the officers and ratings hurried aboard the Scapa ferry, I stepped into *Loch Tulla*'s seaboat and was rowed off to my ship. There I sent a signal to A.C.O.S., 'Have resumed command of my group.' I don't suppose anyone cared a tuppenny damn what I was up to. They were all far too busy.

Groups of anti-submarine trawlers were coming in every day, fuelling and going on to Norway. We were desperate with envy. We badgered all and sundry to be allowed to go too, but we were kept just where we were.

A month later they were coming back – what was left of them. By ones and twos they came through, paused to off-load the most curious assortment of army gear salvaged from the wreck, and went on southward. I spoke to many whom I knew. They all told the same tale. Airpower had defeated them – not the weather, not Hitler's surface forces – just airpower. They had learnt a thing or two about the German airmen. They were deadly – if you did nothing. They had no fear of the Lewis guns which were all the anti-aircraft defence we carried; but they would not stand a 4-inch gun. It did not matter that it was only a low-angle gun. The Hun could not know that for certain. So long as it was pointing in the right general direction and went off with a satisfactory puff of smoke, he would go away to bother some less excitable target. These officers also told me that in order to survive they had found it necessary to abrogate the age-old custom whereby fire was held until the Commanding Officer gave the order. They told me that things happened far too quickly, with German aircraft coming suddenly out of the clouds. Guns' crews must be allowed the initiative to open fire as soon as an aircraft was identified as hostile. What I learnt convinced me of the wisdom of their decisions. I at once issued orders that any aircraft that was obviously hostile could be engaged without waiting for an order from me. I continued this practice in every ship which I afterwards commanded. On three occasions in later years my ship was saved by this order. On no occasion was it abused.

Norway saw the end of the group commander and unit commander system. It had functioned well enough when we had more men than ships. It was wasteful of men capable of command. A group of five ships would have one group commander and two unit commanders in addition to the five Commanding Officers. Three officers capable of command were spare numbers. As soon as the new ships started to come along, the group and unit commanders R.N.R. were taken to command the new corvettes. Large numbers of war-trained officers were coming forward. A junior officer arrived for each of the trawlers. The old 'watch-and-watch' life was over. We should now be in three watches. The break-up of the old groups enabled reinforcements to be sent to those still functioning as groups. We received two ships, and were promised two more for July, and another group of five for the next winter. At the same time there was a definite shift of emphasis in anti-submarine tactics. So far we had patrolled the approaches to ports. Now the loops, booms, and auxiliary patrols had made the ports safe, and the emphasis slowly but surely shifted to escort work; for where would we be more likely to find a U-Boat than round a convoy? The convoy was at once our charge and our bait.

Now that the group consisted of seven ships, several of which were bound to be always at sea, I could not look after them all properly if I stayed in *Loch Tulla*. Gradually I was squeezed out of the ship. I had a small group office in the new depot ship *Dunluce Castle*. I was given a seat in the Extended Defence Office (X.D.O.) ashore at Lyness, and I had a staff title of Staff Officer Anti-U-Boats. It was arranged that in the event of a hunt developing I should go to sea in whichever of the group happened to be the emergency ship at the time. Dunkirk came and went without causing any difference to our routine. In July the other group arrived with Lieutenant-Commander I. J. Tyson,

57

R.N.R., in command. Although he was senior to me, by virtue of my staff title, I still continued to operate the patrols. There was now no need for me ever to go to sea. Tyson was more than capable of taking charge of the ships. Force of circumstances had driven me from my beloved ships into what was virtually an office job ashore. I began to plan moves to extricate myself from the position. I wrote a letter to the Admiral. Somehow it came back to me for my remarks. I minuted it 'I think he ought to go' and signed it; but it must have got lost.

As it was I was more than fully employed. I always had two ships in harbour and I persuaded the X.D.O., under whose authority we had been placed when our only job was the patrol lines, and who still retained a lien on us, to inspect each ship during her rest period. My own group had been at Scapa for ten months, and no staff officer had ever visited them. I felt that an official visit would help them to feel that they were part of the show. The inspections went very well indeed. The ships turned themselves out smartly, and Commander 'Lampy' Heath was an excellent inspecting officer. Inspecting officers vary a great deal. It is easy to be pernickety; to make caustic comment, and so do more harm than good. 'Lampy' was such a charming personality that he was a great success. We only had one disaster, perhaps because I only had one ship which, if not bad, was certainly always in trouble. It is a curious thing that in any group there is always one ship which is best in every way, a number which reach a high level of adequacy, and one bad boy. *Istria* was our bad boy and I had looked forward to her inspection with little expectation of a happy outcome. It started badly. As the inspecting officer's boat with Commander Heath and myself aboard, came alongside, there was nobody ready to receive us. They had somehow taken down the signal wrongly, and expected us an hour later. Worse was to follow, the ship was not over-clean, and a naked man was discovered shut in a cupboard where he had been bundled because they could not muster sufficient uniforms to clothe the whole crew. He was fast asleep and snoring when Commander Heath opened the cupboard door, and we peered with horrified faces into the dark interior. Slowly closing the door Heath turned to me. 'More ready for inspection by the Doctor than by me,' he said.

I wrote another letter to the Admiral asking to be recommended for command of a corvette. This time I was sent for and told quite plainly 'No.'

Lord Churston had left just before Dunkirk to take command of a trawler. I suppose I could have got out then, but I wanted a corvette and they were still too few and far between for an R.N.V.R. to hope to get one. I saw Churston occasionally as he was coming and going between the northeast ports and Iceland. After the fall of Norway it had been vitally necessary to secure the Faroes and Iceland for our use, and even more important to deny them to the enemy. It always seems to me that the German High Command made a fundamental error in not immediately following up their success in Norway by a determined raid on Iceland. A U-Boat base in Iceland would almost certainly have brought disaster on us in the Atlantic struggle. One can only assume that the German is mainly a land-based animal, and hesitates to leap into a boat to cross the water. The indecision which he displayed over those northern islands was to be repeated when he reached the Channel coast two months later. There he vacillated, demanded the impossible of his air force – and lost the initiative. The same was true of the northern islands. The German fights best with the odds heavily in his favour. It is fortunate that with us it is the other way round.

The supply of goods and services to the garrison in Iceland was intermittent, and consisted usually of one supply ship with one or more trawlers as ocean escort. I tried hard to get my trawlers a chance on this run, but already there was a notable tendency to use the trawlers commanded by patrol service skippers for the coastal work, and to employ those commanded by R.N.R. and the R.N.V.R.s for the ocean escort.

One of these trawlers, a member of the class named after famous football teams, and rejoicing in the peculiar name of H.M.T. *Preston North End* had a pet as strange as her name. There are few things more complimentary to the human than the unwavering devotion of a dumb animal. In this case the human concerned was the First Lieutenant of the *Preston North End*, and the dumb animal a young bullock which this officer had encountered on a walk over the hills behind Lyness. They must have enjoyed their walk together, for the bullock came down to the water's edge and mooed softly as its friend was rowed off to his ship. It continued to call in bovine language all night and was still there in the morning gazing, with longing eyes, at the trawler. The First Lieutenant, who had spent a night punctuated by the faint roarings of his walking companion, approached his Captain. What cajolery was used I do not know, but that afternoon the First Lieutenant bought his friend and this time they were rowed off together to the ship. The bullock was duly taken on the books as Able Seaman Bullock, and drew rations as fitted an able seaman – and what is more he waxed fat and sleek on a cannibalistic diet that consisted largely of bully beef. The animal developed a remarkable dexterity in getting about the deck even in a seaway, and appeared thoroughly to enjoy his new environment.

The expression 'I could hardly believe my eyes' was fully justified when, on my first visiting the ship, I saw a large bovine posterior, fitted with a tail and supported on cloven feet, disappear round the engine-room casing as I climbed aboard. This was some months after A.B. Bullock joined the Navy, and he was already causing concern because he was now far too heavy to be taken ashore easily in the ship's boat. In what way he met his end I never discovered, for I only made his acquaintance as *Preston North End* was going to Iceland. By the time she returned I had left Scapa.

In August and September the corvettes were coming forward in increasing numbers. I wrote to Lieutenant-Commander Manning, R.N.V.R., whom I knew to be in the Second Sea Lord's office and largely concerned with drafting officers to the new corvettes. I pointed out that I was one of the first unit commanders to get command of a group, that I was now fast becoming a staff officer, and that my job could be done by somebody who had less experience of anti-submarine vessels at sea.

There was no reply for a week, nor during the week following. I knew Manning was a very busy man, and that in any case he would probably send a query to the Admiral, and I would then get a 'rocket' for going behind the Admiral's back. I went to sea for a week's patrol in my old ship. On my return I found a buff envelope. Hastily I tore it open. 'Appointed *Violet* in command. Date to be reported.' I left that night for Middlesbrough after handing over the groups to Tyson.

I arrived the following night and having found from the office of the Naval Officer in Charge that the *Violet* was completing in Smiths' Docks, I took a room in an hotel for the night.

Early the next morning I called at the firm's office to make enquiries. I was taken down the yard. All around me corvette hulls reared their red painted skeletons to the sky. In the wet docks the launched hulls were tied up. *Violet* was one of these. She would be ready perhaps in six weeks, perhaps two months. Who could say? They advised me that I had better go back and ask for a month's leave, as I could do no good in Middlesbrough until then. I asked the manager to show me a corvette nearly completed. We went down to the river wall. There in the river lay a corvette almost ready. She was the first long fo'c's'le corvette, *Verbena*.

'Who's her Captain?' I asked.

'Well as a matter of fact it's a most extraordinary thing but they haven't sent anyone yet.'

'Get me a taxi – quick.'

He got me a taxi. I was back in N.O.I.C.'s office six miles away in Middlesbrough within half an hour.

I telephoned to Manning.

'Do you know *Verbena* hasn't got a captain and *Violet* won't be ready for months?'

'Are you asking me to change your appointment?'

'Yes of course.'

There was a pause while I could hear papers being flicked over.

'You're quite right. No one has been appointed to her. Thanks for letting me know, I'll make the signal right away.'

I took the taxi back again to Smiths' Docks. I was going to step aboard my first command. I would see the manager afterwards, just at the moment I wanted to be alone. I hurried down to her. She was lying alongside the fitting-out jetty. A shimmering haze above the funnel told me that at least one of her boilers was lit. There were wires and pipes all over the place. The smell of fresh paint mingled with the smell of fuel oil. The sharp rattle of riveting machines rose in a never ending cacophony. But I could only see her as she would be, slipping quietly out of the northern mists with only the hiss of her bow wave to disturb the sea birds, and the steady throb of her propeller beating like a heart. She was quite perfect.

CHAPTER 4

VERBENA IN THE WESTERN OCEAN

Few things could have been more exciting to watch than the metamorphosis of my command from a mass of metal into a warship. Gradually the grey paintwork of manhood crept over the red paint of adolescence. The long lines of electric cables and air pipes grew less as day followed day. Much as I would have liked to spend all the hours of each day aboard, it was out of the question to do so. There were too many other things to be done. But to go away from her even for an hour was to add zest to my return, for I always wondered what I would find completed when I came back. Things happened with remarkable suddenness, for corvettes enjoyed a very high priority. Naval uniforms other than my own began to be seen aboard. The Fitting Out Gunnery Officer might be found inspecting the gun mechanisms, or an officer of the torpedo branch checking the clearance of the depth-charge rails. One learnt to be careful how one addressed people. Strange figures in boiler suits emerged from unexpected places, and an engineer captain who has crawled on hands and knees through a shaft tunnel would look as much like a dockyard matey as he would dislike being addressed as one.

Already she smelt and felt like a ship. Commissioning day was advancing upon us at a gallop. There was not enough time for all I had to do, and never enough time to gloat over her as I would have liked. Standing on her deck in the gathering dusk it needed little imagination to see her as the finished ship, and I realized suddenly that as soon as she was commissioned I would be piped over the side whenever I went ashore on official business, and piped aboard again on my return. There is no sound that means more to a naval officer than the shrill fluttering notes of the bos'n's call. They link him for ever to all those captains of warships who have gone before, and to all who will follow after him. The tradition is not only stimulating – but just a little frightening. A new boy on his first day at his public school may wonder if he will make the grade or let his side down. There are few new captains who can feel such self confidence that, in their inmost thoughts, there does not lie a fear that they may prove unworthy of their charge. It is remarkable how the customs of the Navy aid one. When you come to think of it the surest way to help a man is to remind him continually of his position, and of what the men whom he has been called to join expect of him. The psychology of the Navy is excellent.

I had brought my wife and children from Liverpool to stay in an hotel at Redcar for the fourteen days before we actually commissioned. It was the first time I had really seen the children for a year, and except for one brief visit of *Verbena* to Liverpool I was not to see them for another year. At that time we thought that the ship would be based on Liverpool, and that I would see my family every time she was in harbour. As it turned out we were sent to work from Londonderry. My wife and I then had to decide whether she and the children should move over there, or whether it was not better to stay in our own home so that the children's schooling would not be disturbed. We chose the latter course, and I am sure it was the right one. Several captains did bring their wives to Londonderry, but I cannot think that at a time when ships never knew where they would be tomorrow, it was fair to place the wife in such a position of doubt and uncertainty. I well remember that when *Petunia* was detached from the group to act as a special escort and did not rejoin for some six weeks, her captain's wife suffered great anxiety, and that none of us could do anything to ease her mind because we had not the slightest idea where *Petunia* had gone.

On the morning of commissioning day the officers arrived. Two Sub-Lieutenants R.N.V.R. and a Midshipman R.N.V.R. They had come straight from H.M.S. *King Alfred*, the officers' training establishment, and not one of them had a watch-keeping certificate. They had all three been 'hostilities only' ratings, who had been selected from their fellows and made officers overnight. *Verbena* was the first ship in which they had served as officers. I had expected at least one Lieutenant R.N.R. or long-service R.N.V.R. who would have been my First Lieutenant. I went ashore and telephoned to Manning.

'Awfully sorry, but I've had to provide an extra officer for all the trawlers in the Western Approaches. The bag is quite empty. I'll send you a First Lieutenant as soon as I can. Possibly Liverpool base will find you one when you get there. If they do let me know.'

I went back to the ship. The Captain of *Verbena* and the Number One were evidently going to be the same person. At any rate they had known each other for thirty years, and were not likely to quarrel.

I cannot say that I viewed the immediate prospect with much pleasure. The Captain and the First Lieutenant are complementary to the other. However good the former may be, his ship cannot be a success unless the latter is efficient. If the Captain is responsible for the ship's body, to the First Lieutenant falls the charge of her soul. He is at once the translator of the Captain's authority to the men and their own ambassador at the court of that authority. In many ways it is more difficult to be a good First Lieutenant than a good Commanding Officer, for the Captain looks only one way, while Number One must look both fore and aft.

Fortunately the staff of the Second Sea Lord's office well knew from their own experience afloat the difficulty of finding good First Lieutenants. They were remarkably eager to help, and once assured that you would help them by recommending officers for promotion, they would replace those who proved unsatisfactory very promptly. There were two kinds of Captain whom they would not help – the man who selfishly kept back a promising officer because he did not wish to lose his services, and the man who recommended unsatisfactory officers just to get them removed from his own ship. Throughout the war I found that the more one tried to help the Admiralty Staff, the more they tried to help you.

There was little I could do about my present position. I only hoped that I should get *Verbena* safely through the training base at Tobermory. Terrible tales were already beginning to be passed round the anti-submarine world about the standards of efficiency demanded there. It was rumoured that Captains had been taken out of ships, junior officers relieved and ships almost recommissioned by the ruthless, eccentric, but essentially fair autocrat who ruled the training base – Commodore 'Puggy' (Vice-Admiral retired) G. O. Stephenson. Realizing that training and still more training was the basis of efficiency Admiral Dunbar-Nasmith the Commander-in-Chief Western Approaches had set up this base in the quiet waters of Tobermory. With its unerring gift for producing the right man for the job, the Navy had put in charge there a martinet of truly fierce aspect, who was a master of the small ship trade. Although he could be very frightening – and meant to be so – and many ships failed to reach the high standard he demanded, I do not believe that he ever rejected any officer who threw his heart and soul into the job; and it was not long before we found that the tyrant really had the kindest of hearts.

If we had commissioned when the bag of officers was

absolutely empty, the men at least were promising material. Unlike the trawlers, which were manned by the Patrol Service from their base at the Sparrows' Nest, the corvettes were major war vessels, and were manned by the Navy proper from the main depots of Devonport, Portsmouth or Chatham. *Verbena* was a west country ship manned from Devonport. The barracks had sent her a crew in which long-service ratings and 'hostilities only' men were mixed more or less evenly. At once it was obvious that they had sent me a first-rate coxswain, and for this I was truly grateful. In a small ship the coxswain is the third most important man, as far as the happiness of the ship is concerned; and without a First Lieutenant I was going to need him badly. Fortunately I had a nominal list of the crew, so that I was able to prepare a watch and quarter bill before their train arrived. At any rate the men would at once see that *Verbena* was going to be run properly. As a matter of fact the ship's company never gave me a moment's concern, from the minute they began to file aboard at five o'clock in the evening. All my officers were there with me, and the men were shown straight to their messes. We were able to pipe 'Liberty men' half an hour after the crew came aboard. Naturally not many men wished to go ashore the first night. It was just a gesture that the ship was a real ship. It was the 4th of December, 1940.

We began our acceptance trials the next day. She moved – she really moved! My own ship going down the river! A bitter wind blew from the north-east, but I was warm inside. I was desperate too to get my hands on her, to make her obey me; but the pilot had her all the time. She would not be mine to handle until she had proved herself, and I had signed the receipt. On three consecutive days we went to sea, for compass swinging, steaming trials, and gunnery trials. Owing to the danger from magnetic and acoustic mines we were not allowed to steam at more than eight knots, so the engines were never run at any speed. This caused some concern both to the Chief Engine Room Artificer and myself, because our engines had one peculiarity which I must explain.

In a reciprocating engine perhaps the most important gland is that through which the connecting rod rises and falls as it is carried up and down by the piston. In most 'push-and-pull' engines this gland is made up of pieces of special metal held in place by 'coil' springs. *Verbena* had been fitted experimentally with segmental pieces of metal held in place by a garter spring. It was supposed to be a more efficient gland packing, and so it was. But like so many small experimental alterations it was never properly followed up by those who thought of it. The result was that when running continuously at high speed we always suffered from the disease known as 'hot rods'. This can only be kept in check by the engine room artificer continually swabbing down the rods with an oily rag. Our work in the Western Approaches rarely called for long spells of high speed, but once we had gone to the Eastern Fleet we nearly always had to steam at our maximum speed. It was there that so much 'swabbing down the rods' had to be done that oil worked its way into the feed water and caused boiler trouble; and it was this that finally laid up the ship for nine months in Bombay dockyard.

The trouble with the engine, however, still lay in the future. In the present I had a much more pressing worry, for our charts had not arrived from the chart depot. Hectic signals back and forth had disclosed the fact that they had been destroyed in a bombed train. In desperation I took the chart folios which had been sent for *Violet*; but I had not got the up-to-date corrections which were so necessary in war time, and the best I could do was hastily to correct what charts I needed for the passage round to Tobermory from those kept in the Naval office.

We were ready to sail. I signed the receipt, and said 'good-bye' to the manager of the dockyard. *Verbena* was mine, and next morning I would take her to sea.

When I awoke I could hear the howl of the wind, and felt the short, fierce movements of the ship against the jetty. No need to go on deck to know that it was blowing a full gale from the north-east. I was faced with my first major decision – to sail, or not to sail. I had a ship whose engines were virtually untried, because of the restrictions imposed while she was in the builders' hands, and there would be a lee shore all the way up to Peterhead. Not for one moment in such weather could I stop the engines to make any adjustment.

I went ashore to the Naval officer in charge of the port. He was surprised to see me. I explained the position.

He was a busy man, anxious only to get rid of the ships that were building in the port. 'If you can't take your ship to sea I'll get someone who can,' he told me. I insisted on putting the matter up to Chief of Staff, Western Approaches. N.O.I.C. and I glowered at each other while we waited for the call to come through. Though I was sure that I was right, I felt distinctly uneasy about the outcome. There seemed to be no doubt in the Chief of Staff's mind. 'We want you badly, but we want you whole. Use your own judgment and get round to Tobermory as soon as you can.' I went back to the ship with a light heart.

The gale moderated with the turn of the tide in the afternoon, and we sailed at three. We put the pilot into his boat at the mouth of the river, and then she was entirely mine. As I turned her away northward into the war channel no man could have been happier.

She was obviously a first-class sea-boat. I had enough experience to recognize that as soon as she met the sea. She was the first long fo'c's'le corvette to be built. All the earlier corvettes, some fifty in number, had a break between the fo'c's'le and the bridge. This meant that a man going from the bridge to the mess decks must cross the low deck forward of the bridge before he gained the sanctuary of the mess decks. In *Verbena* the fo'c's'le had been carried right aft as far as the funnel, giving us a covered space in which the whole ship's company of seventy-odd men could easily be mustered. This arrangement allowed men to come on watch without being soaked through and, still more important, the cooks could carry the food down to the mess decks from the galley, which was between the bridge and the funnel, without the risk of losing it overboard. The earlier corvettes were very lively indeed in a seaway. In fact it was commonly said that it was impossible to get your legs into your trousers aboard one. The extra weight of the long fo'c's'le actually steadied them a great deal, and made them much better sea-boats. It improved their trim by putting them slightly down by the head, so that its weight detracted nothing from their speed – rather the reverse. *Verbena* actually exceeded her designed speed, and other corvettes, when altered, reported that they too had similarly benefited.

Originally the corvette had been designed as an off-shore anti-submarine vessel. It had never been thought that they would be used for long distance ocean convoy work. Now that we realized that the best way to sink U-Boats and to protect the convoys was to build up the escorts, they were being used for a purpose for which they were not designed. None the less after the long fo'c's'le had been added they were wonderful little ships. The hardly ever took green seas aboard, and although their movements were lively they suffered very little weather damage of any sort. Within the limits of the equipment that they could carry they were excellent warships, and their contribution to the battle of the Atlantic was a vital one.

I may have been a happy man, but I soon had my troubles.

Soon after settling to our course I fetched myself a cigar from my cabin and jamming myself in a corner of the bridge settled down to enjoy it. To my surprise I soon found everyone looking very glum. The asdic rating had turned a curious pea-green. The signalman was draped over the lee side of the bridge. The officer of the watch was gulping like a goldfish in a bowl. I took over the watch in all directions. Fixing the asdic headphones over my own head, I called the wheelhouse.

'Coxswain, are you all right?'

'Perfectly, Sir.'

'Thank God. They're all sick as dogs up here.'

His words came back to me disembodied by the voice-pipe between us, but still carrying the respectful tone of the trusted chief petty officer.

'Your cigar, Sir. Not used to it I expect.'

'Oh, thank you, Coxswain – you're probably right. How thoughtless of me.'

Later when the watchkeepers had recovered a little and Farne Island light was coming up, I told the officer of the watch to fix the ship's position. It was hopeless. Lessons learnt on the shore compasses in the *King Alfred* had not taught these officers how to take a bearing at sea. Obviously I must teach them everything. I started. I spent all the watch teaching. How lucky I had spent so much time teaching junior officers before this war started! Came the last dog watch, and another officer to teach. It was dark by then. Obviously I could never leave the bridge until they were proficient, so I had my first dinner in the asdic hut. I had no sleep that night. Not until the next afternoon, when we had rounded Cape Wrath and had the long run down the Minches ahead of us, was I able to sleep. Then I sent for my Lilo mattress and sleeping bag, and made up a bed in the asdic hut within reach of all the voice pipes, the alarm bell, and the officer of the watch. This was such a success that I used the asdic hut as my sea cabin all the time I commanded the ship. It gave my officers great confidence, because they felt that they could get instant help if they wanted it; and the men too seemed to prefer their Captain always to be at hand. Neither knew how totally inadequate he himself frequently felt.

In a glorious winter dawn five days before Christmas 1940 we slid gently into Tobermory harbour. Four corvettes were lying at anchor there. Two more and a submarine had been sighted going off to the exercise area before we entered. The old inter-island passenger ship *Western Isles*, now painted grey, swung at anchor in the centre of the harbour. We were told exactly where to anchor. As our anchor cable rattled out I took up the binoculars and looked at the *Western Isles*. From an upper deck scuttle peered an avuncular face, with tufts of grey hair sprouting below eyes which, so I learnt later, were of a brilliant blue and quite the most piercing I have ever encountered. So that was the 'Terror of Tobermory', the new Lord of the Western Isles. I felt sure that we had brought him something to chew on.

We had. We were beaten into bruised efficiency. At any time of the day or night the lash might fall. 'Send away a boat! Let go a second anchor! Rig sheer-legs, and hoist your boat clear of the water! Prepare to tow forward! Prepare to take a merchant ship in tow! Send a boarding part to *Western Isles*! Your ship is dragging her anchor, weigh and proceed!' Anything might happen – almost everything did. Crack went the whip and jump went the *Verbena*. At first we squealed as we leapt. Later we learned to achieve the leap without the squeal.

We were a very broken reed when we arrived. After a ten days' ordeal came our inspection, when the Commodore and all his staff came aboard. It was the final test. Afterwards in my cabin he said to me, 'Well, you'll do – but you must have a First Lieutenant. You can't carry the whole thing yourself. I've made a signal to C.-in-C., Western Approaches, and you'll get one in Liverpool when you arrive. You'll also get your evaporators put right. As far as I'm concerned you're an ocean escort now. Come and have dinner with me tonight.'

We sailed for Liverpool in the morning, still without our proper Notices to Mariners – those essential weekly publications by which charts are kept up to date. I had corrected such as I would need for the passage to Liverpool from the charts in the *Western Isles*. Perhaps I had not quite realized that we 'were an ocean escort now', certified as such by Tobermory, and that we might therefore be sent anywhere.

We left Tobermory full of confidence. We knew we were a long way from being perfect; but everything worked. Time would oil the wheels, and with luck we would be an efficient unit. We steamed on to the southward.

Passing the Mull of Kintyre we received a signal from Commander-in-Chief, Western Approaches. 'Fuel at Greenock and join outward-bound convoy estimated to pass Mull of Kintyre noon tomorrow as additional escort. Senior Officer in *Velox*.' So there would be no First Lieutenant this trip anyway; and no corrected charts either. I altered course for the Clyde. The morning's sun had now gone, and before we passed the boom gate at the entrance to the Clyde the night was dark and full of rain.

We asked the signal tower where the oiler was. They gave me a berth number, but it meant little to me. I had the tide under me, and the darkened shapes of anchored merchantmen were suddenly looming out of the murk. My only hope was to feel my way through the anchorage until I found the two bright lights that marked the oiler. To have lost my 'night sight' by looking into the lighted chart table would have been fatal. Oh why did I not take Elgood's advice and become a gunnery officer? At least it would not be my worry to look for one particular ship in a crowded anchorage, when I could not even see my own bows. When I did find the oiler – if I ever did – I would have to turn the ship and make my first 'alongside'. It was impossible. No one could find the oiler in that.

Was there a light? Yes I could see it – two little blue lights one above the other. I had to turn her.

'Coxswain.'

'Sir.'

'Have special sea dutymen piped. Lively there – we're very close. Port fifteen.'

'Port fifteen on, Sir.'

I see her bow start to swing – not fast enough.

'Increase to twenty.'

'Port twenty on, Sir.'

'Check revolutions.'

'Seventy revolutions, Sir.'

'One one O revolutions.'

'One one O revolutions on, Sir.'

'Ease to ten.'

'Port ten on, Sir.'

'Slow ahead.'

'Slow ahead on, Sir.'

'Midships.'

'Midships, Sir.'

'Coxswain.'

'Sir.'

'Can you see her now?'

'Plainly, Sir.'

'I'm going to put her bow on that second fender.'

'Second fender, Sir.'

The slap-slap of water between the two closing hulls – heaving lines snaking through the night——

'Port twenty. Half astern.'

'Port twenty, half astern on, Sir.'

'Stop engines.'

'Stop engines, Sir.'

The ship lurched slightly as her shoulder nudged the fender. Lines were passed rapidly. We were made fast.

'Finished with engines, Coxswain. Thank you.'

I breathed a sigh of relief, and patted the wet rail of the bridge with my hand. The ship had done me proud. She had spun round like a top when I asked her to.

Received signal, 'On completion of oiling anchor in position——'

Hell and damnation! I had hoped they would leave us alongside for the night.

I went down to my cabin to lie down. The extending of the fo'c's'le had only one disadvantage. It completely enclosed the captain's cabin below decks, and the only means of ventilation was through scuttles opening on to the covered flat outside the mess decks. I could not help hearing remarks by the men that were not intended for my ears. As I lay down that night I heard a rich west country voice saying: 'Cor – and don't e' ever tell me the wavy navy can't handle a ship. We wasn't more'n five minutes out in the bleeding rain.' It was balm to my spirit. As I drifted off to sleep I felt sure *Verbena* would be quite a ship.

We moved to our anchor berth at three in the morning, and sailed again to meet our first convoy at eight. We met them off the Mull of Kintyre. A long line of ships in two columns extending for nearly ten miles. Ahead of them was a 'V and W Class' destroyer – *Velox*. Signal lamps flashed from her. We were being given our stationing signal. A corvette bucketing cheerfully over the seas and looking, to our eyes, quite indecently efficient gave us a résumé of all the signals made since leaving Liverpool on the previous afternoon, and particulars of *Velox*'s own group orders for use in the event of an attack on the convoy. By the time she had passed all the signals it was getting dark. We were bound up the Minches, and until past the Butt of Lewis the convoy would stay in two columns. Once clear of the coast it would form up on a broad front. The two columns would then become eight, ten, or even more, with four or five merchant ships in each column. As this was a slow convoy, and probably made not much more than six knots, it took a long time to form up on the following morning. Some of the ships could not make more than seven knots, even if the leaders reduced to four, and it would be four hours before the rearmost ones had covered the twelve miles necessary to take up their stations. The morning was spent in getting the convoy into its ocean-going formation. *Velox* was zig-zagging across the front of the merchantmen; astern of the convoy was another destroyer, and there was a corvette at each corner. *Verbena* had been given the position on the starboard quarter.

Our first night was uneventful. We stopped zig-zagging at dusk and hung close to the nearest merchantman. No lights were of course shown; and in those days there was no radar. It was more important to remain with the convoy than to continue the zig-zag. In any case the U-Boats generally attacked on the surface, and in such conditions a visual look-out was a better protection to the convoy than the asdic. One senses that there had been a certain lack of realistic thinking about what would happen in war if the U-Boats should attempt to cut our sea communications in the Atlantic. Before the war we had beaten our chests with pride in our new asdic, and had confidently announced to all the services that we had the answer to the U-Boat peril. And so we had – so long as the U-Boat stayed submerged. But in the darkness of the winter nights he nearly always attacked on the surface, and until we could detect his presence with radar we fought him with our eyes, with seamanship, and with bluff. We had no other effective weapons against the surfaced raider.

On the second morning *Verbena* sighted a Focke-Wulf

long-range bomber, coming in low from the north-east. The Germans had stationed a number of these nuisances at Stavanger in Norway. Until our own Coastal Command got busy and chased them away for good they were a confounded pest. If they could get over the convoy they would bomb some luckless merchantman. In any case they reported our position so that the U-Boats should find us.

Hastily turning out the gun's crew of the watch *Verbena* fired a star shell. At night one was always kept loaded in the gun, and time was too precious to reload with high explosive. The burst of the star shell, bright even by day, hung in the sky in front of him. He banked steeply, probably wondering what it was, so we fired again. He went away into the mist that hid the northern horizon. *Verbena* had shown her teeth, even though they may have been false ones.

Although the officers on joining had been a disappointment to me because of their inexperience, I was already beginning to appreciate their qualities. They were terribly young and very earnest; and they tried so hard. Besides we had a reputation to keep up, or more correctly to make. We were the first corvette to be commanded by a Volunteer Reserve Officer, and it was many months before another corvette entirely officered by the R.N.V.R. was to join us. If we could make *Verbena* a success the way would be open for a flood of R.N.V.R.s to pour through on their way to command. It was a responsibility that I had pointed out to them. Before the war Sub-Lieutenants P. M. Whittaker and R. F. E. Pettifer had been clerks in an office, and Midshipman C. S. Edwards had been a schoolboy. They had each served nine months on the lower deck, and then three months at *King Alfred*; now they were keeping watch over twenty or thirty merchantmen. It was a transformation which the mind can hardly appreciate. On this our first trip, the midshipman was more sea-sick than anyone I have ever seen before or since. At last he collapsed entirely, and ate nothing solid for twelve whole days. We kept him alive on lime juice and sugar. On our return I offered to put him ashore, but he was determined to try again. Happily he was quite all right on our second trip.

The sea was too rough. We were not molested by the enemy. For eight days the convoy staggered on until it reached the longitude of 20° West, which was as far as we then could provide escorts. We would then leave it, and either go to meet an inward-bound convoy or return home to take out another outward one.

Our defective evaporator had allowed salt water to get into the fresh water tank, so tea, cocoa, and everything else tasted of salt. We sent all the available stock of wardroom drinks – beer, lime juice, and orangeade to the mess decks to try to help the men. There was nothing more we could do about it. As I had expected the coxswain proved a tower of strength. Tall, fair and good-looking he was a representative of the very best type of pre-war chief petty officer. He was always immaculately dressed, even in the middle of the Atlantic. This was a point of great importance in those days of hard work and little play, for it was very easy to let the men slide into slipshod ways; and once started on that road it was desperately difficult to stop. All through the war I insisted on certain standards of uniform and shaving for the bridge watchkeepers and as they included the look-outs, who changed round every two hours, it virtually meant that the whole ship's company kept themselves smart. I do not say that if a ship accepted a low standard in this respect she became inefficient in action. All that I do declare is that it was much easier to keep up efficiency if a high standard was rigorously maintained. In this the coxswain was an invaluable ally, for he was himself so smart a man. As a matter of fact he was one of the last men to carry the rank of Chief Coxswain. Most of those junior to him were Chief Gunner's Mates transferred to the new role. I was therefore all the more lucky to have him appointed to such a very small 'major war vessel' as my *Verbena*. Somehow or other he managed to keep the grumbles over the water situation within bounds at a time when they might have boiled up into serious trouble.

The escorts swept back to the Minches after we had left the convoy. With Cape Wrath just coming up over the horizon, and *Verbena* as usual the port wing corvette, we

76

sighted a merchantman to the northward obviously sinking.

We reported to *Velox*.

Signal from *Velox* to *Verbena*, 'Investigate.'

Report, 'Dutch merchantman sinking. Propose to pick up survivors.'

Reply, 'Proceed, but your attention is called to Notices to Mariners Number——'

We picked up one boatload of survivors. The rest of the group was still visible on the southern horizon, steaming back and forth waiting for us. *Velox* was signalling again, 'Your attention is called to Notices to Mariners——'

All right – our Notices to Mariners are lying blasted all over some midland railway station. We waited until the nearest corvette was out of line with *Velox*, so that the senior officer could not read our lamp and then made, 'What is Notice to Mariners – please'.

Back came the reply.

'Minefield – you are in it – we are not.'

'Newnes,' I said to the yeoman, 'don't you tell anyone about that – we can't steam away and leave the second boatload.'

'No, Sir – no – we couldn't do that.' He crumpled up the signal and tossed it over the side.

We got the second boatload and signalled to *Velox*, 'Have picked up master and all ship's company, including ship's dog.'

Reply, 'Well done – I'm glad it was not my decision.'

What could we say but, 'Thank you,' and make a resolution never to sail without our Notices to Mariners.

We went down to Liverpool. There we would get a First Lieutenant, our Notices to Mariners and our evaporators mended. We got our repairs and our Notices to Mariners; we did not get our First Lieutenant. Liverpool base was out to a clinch in every respect, and we were going to be based on Londonderry. Londonderry would fix us up with a Number One.

As we were the first of the new corvettes everyone wanted to see us. Admiral Dunbar-Nasmith was aboard almost before we had finished berthing, and as a constant stream of people came up our gangway, I could neither get home to my wife, nor could I see Elgood. I telephoned to the Admiral's office as soon as we arrived, only to be told that Captain Elgood was on sick leave. Alas he was very sick. How proud he would have been of *Verbena*, and how nothing on earth would have permitted him to show it!

We went to Londonderry. Leaving the dispassionate sea behind as you go up the River Foyle, the friendly, green land enfolds you. Further and further your ship noses her way up the tortuous channel, until an S-bend at Lisahally entirely shuts out all sign of the sea. Your ship steams on between the walls of woodland, so that her salt-encrusted sides are almost brushed by the overhanging branches; and your bow wave and wash, which for weeks have been lost in the immensity of the ocean, now slip-slop amongst tree roots, and stir the long tendrils of seaweed on half-tide ledges. Another S turn and there before you lies the enchanted city, silhouetted against the light of the noon-day sun. In the shadow of the wharf would be lying a long single line of escorts, mostly destroyers in those days – and many of them in need of repair. In later years the line became four or five deep, and ninety per cent of them were ready for sea. But the approach to 'Derry never lost its magic.

We tied up alongside an 'S Class' destroyer whose long lean lines captivated me. What covetous eyes I cast on her! But she was as far outside my reach as if she had been a battleship – or so I thought then. Perhaps there are still magicians in Ireland, for two years later I was to find myself appointed to *Shikari* and to have, as Senior Officer, 21st Escort Group, all the six surviving 'S Class' destroyers under my command.

Captain Ruck-Keene and his deputy Commander 'Jacky' Slaughter were creating a great Naval Base out of nothing. How they drove everybody, and themselves as well! Stores and services appeared from nowhere, and even jetties which had been falling to pieces, were repaired overnight. I had hoped to find 'B 12' Group which *Verbena* had been ordered to join, in harbour; but unfortunately they were at sea. In those days no escort capable of going to sea could be allowed to remain in harbour. I was told I would not immediately join the group, but must do one convoy trip to Gibraltar with another group. I was also told that there were no spare First Lieutenants in Londonderry. As Liverpool was only willing to look after its own chickens, that base took no interest in me once I had been sent to Londonderry; and the latter had no officers to spare, nor anywhere to accommodate them if they had appeared. I must sail without.

We joined an outward-bound convoy.

To be sent to another group was always difficult for the commanding officer. The Senior Officers of the groups were all busy inventing special tactics for their groups, and they gave these operations code words of their own. Later when Admiral Max Horton had become Commander-in-Chief, Western Approaches, with Captain Gilbert Roberts as his tactical adviser, all the various orders and manoeuvres were tried out on the floor of the tactical school. Those found to be most successful were then adopted and a general manual of operations was published. But in January 1941 to be attached to a strange group was to find oneself submerged by a flood of code words which meant just nothing to you. If you joined in the middle of the day perhaps you would get details of the more intricate manoeuvres passed to you by flash lamp. Sometimes, you would receive by rocket line a nice folder, parcelled in waterproof cloth, and containing all the group orders properly typed. But such an easy introduction was very rare, because you might be taken away as suddenly as you had joined, and then the Senior Officer would lose his orders as well as you. More often than not you would join at dusk, when all but 'Immediate' visual signals were forbidden. Then you would probably be awakened by the yeoman of signals in the middle of the night with some such ominous words as : –

'Krakatoa, Sir.'

'Krakatoa, Yeoman? What on earth's that?' you would say raising yourself from your couch.

'Seems to be a code word, Sir. Starshell on the other side of the convoy now, Sir – and rockets too. Funny group this, Sir. Wish we could get back to our own group – do at least speak English there, Sir. What the hell can you make of "Krakatoa," Sir?'

'Sorry, Yeoman, I just don't know. Better go to action stations and be on our toes. Press the alarm for me while I get this oilskin buttoned up.'

But what would you have? The attack by more than one U-Boat at the same time was then so novel. A number of intelligent men were independently striving to find some general tactics which, when carried out simultaneously by all ships of the group, would force the Hun to submerge. Once driven below the surface they would be targets for our only anti-submarine weapon – the asdic. Each group was working on different lines to achieve the same object. Each group developed remarkably similar manoeuvres, but they all differed in the code words which set them in motion. Each Senior Officer naturally thought his own solution the best, and it needed a very strong hand indeed to persuade 'Commander Blank' that his operation 'Krakatoa' was really just the same as the official operation 'Buttercup,' and that if he would only use 'Buttercup,' any additional escort sent to him from time to time would know exactly what was required of her.

We met the convoy off Inistrahull. This one was not going north through the Minches and then to Canada and America, as our previous convoy had done. It was bound to the southward. It would go out to the longitude of 208 West and then turn south to a position south and west of the Azores, where it would be dispersed. Some ships would then go on to Africa, some westward to Brazil and the Argentine, and some would stay with the escorts and steam eastward to Gibraltar.

The ships were already forming on to a broad front when we met the convoy. The Senior Officer was not like kindly *Velox*, who had shepherded the obvious new boy. The weather was vile, the convoy difficult, and whatever we did seemed to be wrong. It must be remembered that Senior Officers were often tired and exasperated. For them time in harbour was taken up by attending conferences, writing reports, and organizing the group. It could be just as tiring as a spell at sea, and in any case all men are not alike.

It blew almost a gale, with rain from the south-west. Now we were to discover the different character of each convoy. In the previous slow one all ships had been of approximately the same speed; but this convoy contained ships destined for many different ports, and their capabilities differed widely. Instead of a convoy speed of seven knots, we were trying to make nine. This was desperately slow for ships capable of sixteen knots or more, but was too fast for many of the others. They shuffled and jostled each other like strange horses in the same stall. Some carrying supplies for the Army in Egypt were deep laden, others were flying light. The beam sea and wind drove the lighter ships out of their columns. Striving to get back into position they called for so much effort from their own engines that they inevitably cast long wisps of black smoke into the wind – the chief bugbear of every escort commander. The convoy was more like a herd of cattle than an organized team. While the Senior Officer of the escort tore his hair and steamed back and forth across the front of the convoy, *Verbena* stationed astern, tried desperately to push the babies as they fell out of the bed. A continuous stream of signals flickered back to us from the Senior Officer. Signals which were difficult to read because his ship was always passing out of sight behind merchantmen, and his harassed signal staff would continue their signal whether we could read it or not.

'Number 14 is making smoke – stop her.'

'Number 23 is out of station.'

'Number 35 is out of station.'

'Why are you so slow in answering my signals?'

'Regain your correct station.'

So it went on for three days. I was up all day attending to the stream of signals; and at night when the Senior Officer was mercifully quiet (for it was before the days of the short-range radio telephones) I had to stay on watch for the safety of the ship. I had no experienced officers, and the weather was such that it needed experience to keep station on what was nothing more than an occasional dark grey flurry in the blackness, visible only when the last ship of the centre column lifted her propeller half out of the water in a burst of throbbing foam.

I had had three hours' sleep in three days when at last we turned south. I really did not know for how much longer I could keep it up. Then to complete the débâcle we ran into fog. Thick impenetrable fog. We settled down to the convoy course and speed. We could see little more than the bare outline of our own wash. We saw nothing all night, and when the dawn at last came, there was no sign of the convoy.

I had not attended the convoy conference in Liverpool, and no one had thought of telling me that this particular Commodore always signalled his convoy rendezvous (where ships would reassemble if they got scattered) no less than twenty-five miles astern of where he actually intended to be. I had received by light his convoy rendezvous for the next three days so naturally I went, as well as I was able, to each of them in turn. The weather was thick all the time and I had taken no sights. Indeed I had been running on dead reckoning ever since we left Inistrahull. Owing to the many jobs that had been given me it had been impossible to keep an exact track of my ship's comings and goings. In fact my dead reckoning was based on a guess at the convoy's speed. Before the days of radar, to keep in touch with the convoy in bad visibility was a nightmare for all commanding officers. Many escorts lost touch with their convoys, but given a chance of a sight, and if you knew the rendezvous, you could generally find them again. It thus happened that, in visibility which never exceeded a couple of miles we went to a position twenty-five miles astern of where the convoy actually was, and found it not.

At the end of three days I decided to go down the track of the convoy to Gibraltar, keeping more or less at convoy speed. I thought that once I got a sight I would report my position by wireless to the Senior Officer, and ask for a course that would enable me to rejoin. But for a week I had no sight. It was the season of the 'Portuguese Trades' – south westerly winds which carried with them low cloud shrouding both the horizon and the sun. We plugged on to the southward until we had been two weeks without a sight, and then, at six o'clock one evening we suddenly ran out of the murk into glorious sub-tropical sunlight.

Hastily I got the sight I had longed for, but at that late hour it gave me only one position line – the longitude. I was now about one hundred miles west of Gibraltar with my latitude very uncertain. I decided to steer in for the coast, and get a star sight at dusk. I had by then had plenty of sleep, and was feeling fine. The ship's company were really beginning to work together, and the officers to gain confidence. It had been a wonderful 'shake down' cruise, and we had exercised everything that we would ever be asked to do.

I prepared for my star sight, choosing stars to the north and east of us. I had the sextant in my hand when I noticed that the horizon appeared to be doing peculiar things. It was. All round us to north and east lay a thick blanket of fog. We plunged into it as if it had been cotton wool. The fog eddied round the bridge. It was something palpable and solid, catching at your throat. From the bridge the ship seemed to be cut off by the fog just abaft the funnel, and one could only dimly discern the look-out who had been sent to the eyes of the ship. It was even thicker above us, and the man in the crow's nest could be heard but not seen. Never before or since have I seen a fog as thick as that one. Fortunately the sea was dead calm, and in those perfect conditions our asdic would warn us of the approach of a surface vessel. So we steamed on.

At eight the next morning we should by my reckoning have been in sight of Gibraltar, or at any rate we should have seen one of the headlands north or south of the entrance to the straits. As we were still enveloped in fog I rang down for slow on the engines. Promptly we ran into a lane in the fog. Looking down this lane we could see land about six miles away. Obviously it was a headland – but which? The top of the headland I was seeking had a lighthouse on it, and I could have identified it from its shape – could I but see the lighthouse. But the top was hidden in the fog.

I could not go any closer until either I had recognized it,

or had rigged my sounding boom. While we rigged the sounding boom the fog closed in again. All we knew was that we were near the land. I assumed it was the south-west corner of the straits, and put her head to the northward, sounding all the time and going slowly. Another lane in the fog, and we glimpsed a low, red-cliffed coast. It seemed to be lying east and west, and across my path. I turned and retraced my steps. We saw nothing. We continuously found no bottom at thirty fathoms, which was as deep as my sounding machine would go. Two years later I would have had the whole position plain before me on my radar scan; but then I was completely lost. Just before noon the fog was thinning, and then sun came out. On our port hand as we steamed slowly south we could see the coast – high empty hills, a sandy beach on which the long Atlantic swell was breaking, and something was moving on the beach. It couldn't be, but it was – a camel! It must be the coast of Africa, but how far down it we did not know. We turned the ship and hurried north. There was the same headland we had first sighted but the fog still shrouded its summit. A destroyer suddenly came out of the fog ahead, and turned southward. I looked at her through the binoculars.

She was at sea with her quarter-deck awning spread. No British ship ever did that. She must be a Spaniard, and I was too proud to ask a Spaniard where I was. We waved to each other as we passed, and rather surprisingly she dipped her ensign to us as she swept by. With Spaniards to the north and camels to the south we could not be far away from our objective. In the log we entered the noon position, 'Fixed ship by camel and sombrero 260° Europa Point 20 miles.'

Gingerly we approached the fog bank from which the destroyer had come. The fog began to roll back and there, blessed sight, was an anti-submarine trawler on patrol. I called him up to ask where I was. He was just about to take the message when the fog rolled clean away, and there ahead of us was the Rock of Gibraltar. I changed the signal just in time to read 'Good afternoon.'

Gibraltar was very short of anti-submarine patrols, and

borrowed our services for a month. In exchange for this they did provide me with a First Lieutenant, but insisted in return on removing one of my subs. Which should it be? There seemed nothing to do but toss for it. Pettifer went, and I was sorry to see him go. I would have been just as sorry to lose Whittaker. The new Number One was an R.N.V.R. Lieutenant who had been in Mediterranean destroyers since the outbreak of war. He was an entirely competent officer, but as he knew he was only coming with us to make sure of a passage home he never threw himself fully into the ship's life, nor did she take him to her heart.

In Gibraltar our paragon of a coxswain suffered his one fall from grace. I was disturbed one night in harbour by the quartermaster who dived into my cabin and announced, 'Please, Sir, Coxswain's fallen down and hurt hisself.' He then rushed out again, I followed. There by the gangway lay the coxswain, stretching his long length upon the deck, his eyes closed and his face a deathly white.

'Quick – go and get the sick berth attendant,' I told the quartermaster. As he went forrard, I knelt beside the fallen man and gently raised his head to see if it was seriously damaged.

As I touched him his eyelids fluttered.

'Are you all right, Coxswain?' I asked.

His eyes opened. 'Yes, Sir. Just some "old ships" of mine I met ashore, and too much brandy, Sir. Thought this was the best way, Sir. Can you have me put in my bunk, Sir?'

'Certainly Coxswain, gently as a baby. Ssh – they're coming now with the stretcher.'

Solemnly he was rolled on to the canvas. The sick berth attendant having diagnosed the skull as still sound, the party bore the coxswain away to his bunk.

They gave us a boiler clean too at Gibraltar, and we persuaded the Naval Stores to give us enough paint to make the ship look really nice. When we had finished boiler cleaning we were going home, but first we must do one more patrol in the straits.

All night we beat back and forth and then, just as it was dawn, we sighted to the west of Tangier a Vichy French destroyer and two merchantmen. She was coming up inside territorial waters. A glance at the chart showed that she would certainly pass outside the three mile limit in the middle of the deep bay of Tangier if she held on her present course. The recognition manual showed her to be rather larger than a destroyer. The French had a class of super-destroyers called 'Contre-Torpilleurs' and this vessel was *Le Malin*, the name ship of the class.

She could see me as plainly as I could see her. She had five 5.5-inch guns. It infuriated me that she should sail by without altering course. I decided that if she came outside territorial waters I would stop her. Carefully timing our arrival to coincide with her coming outside the limit, *Verbena* ambled slowly across the straits with her men at action stations, but out of sight. Leaning over the bridge I called to Whittaker who was jammed tightly inside the shield of the 4-inch gun along with its crew :

'Mr. Whittaker, when you hear the signal lamp telling this Frenchman to stop I want you to bring your gun to the ready and keep it trained on his bridge all the time. If he tries any nonsense you may use your own judgment.'

The two ships were not two cables apart. I checked the position. We were outside territorial waters, and so was she. I turned on to a parallel course; the international code flag K for 'Stop instantly' broke from our signal halliards. Our ten-inch signal lamp repeated the order, and the guns swung round to cover her bridge.

The consternation on board was delightful. Her men were all closed up at the guns but they were trained fore and aft. Mine was pointing at his bridge at a distance of little more than fifty yards, and as the two ships rolled my gun rose and fell as it was kept laid on its target. The gun's crew, grinning like codfish, held fresh charges.

I leant over the bridge and opened up in my best French. For once the 'loud hailer' worked perfectly.

'Pardon messieurs. Je vous prie de ne pas toucher un de vos canons, et je désire que vous arrêtez votre vaisseau tout suite. Je vais vous rapporter a mon Amiral et peutêtre qu'il me demandera de vous prendre au contraband control.'

It was the longest and most singular remark I have ever made in the French language.

There was complete silence from his bridge, but there was obviously a very heated argument going on. The turbulence under her stern died away. She stopped. We flashed 'stop' at her convoy. They also stopped.

I made an immediate signal to Gibraltar 'Have intercepted contre-torpilleur *Le Malin* and two merchantmen outside territorial waters. Request immediate assistance to bring in to contraband control.'

The reply came.

'Emergency destroyer will join you. Await instructions.'

We waited. Half an hour later a destroyer could be seen leaving Gibraltar like a man getting out of bed in the morning. Puffs of black smoke rose first from one funnel then from the other. Soon she was racing towards us, the bow wave springing like wings from her stem.

Signals flashed.

'I will assume control of situation. You are not, repeat not, to hurt him.'

We returned to Gibraltar. That night someone somewhere woke up, and realized that those ships were carrying nine million pounds of Polish gold that had been left in Dakar when France fell; and the gold might be on its way to Germany. A general order to apprehend at all costs went forth; but it was too late. *Le Malin* and her charges had disappeared in the mist towards Oran, and could not be found. We were on our way back to England as additional escort to a fast convoy and could not take part in the chase. It was the nearest I've ever been to a gold mine.

The convoy home was uneventful, and we arrived back to find the group about to sail from Londonderry. We fuelled and joined them. From the mail I learnt that a First Lieutenant had been appointed to *Verbena*, and also another officer to replace Pettifer. When they arrived I should have a strong team.

It was a delight to join our own B.12 group at last, and to be able to speak the same language as the corvette ahead and astern – to be one of a team instead of the odd man out.

To have a senior officer whom you knew well, and who relied on you; who never, never fussed you with unnecessary signals, whom you regarded as the finest senior officer in the Western Approaches, and who so obviously had the best group. It is perhaps worth mentioning that probably all the western ocean escort groups felt the same about their own senior officers. The point I make is that these very mixed groups of ships were held together by a team spirit that neither wind, weather nor the enemy could break, and which more than cancelled out any disparity between the ships. I still consider Commander Howard-Johnston (now Rear-Admiral C. D. Howard-Johnston D.S.O., D.S.C.) senior officer of B.12 group, to have been a master of tactics. In all those terrible summer months of 1941 we escorted convoy after convoy without one single loss, once the protective screen of the group had been spread around the convoy.

It is true we sank only one U-Boat, but as our Escort Commander said, 'Our business is to bring home the merchantmen. The sinking of the enemy is only a secondary consideration at this stage of the war. Our turn will come later.'

I am sure that until we had perfected our radar, Commander Howard-Johnston was right. To other groups might go the glory of submarine kills – B.12 brought home the bacon.

Unfortunately *Verbena* was boiler cleaning when on the 29th June the group did slay U.651. This was a lucky meeting, as the U-Boat was found across the course of the convoy by daylight. She was not, I think, actually engaged in attacking the convoy rather was she, so to speak, overlaid in bed. *Malcolm* attacked as the convoy overran the U-Boat, but after firing once she had to break off the attack because the enemy was passing under the convoy. When the U-Boat came out at the back it was met by a hunting party comprising *Malcolm*, *Violet*, *Arabis*, *Speedwell* and *Scimitar*, and was blown to the surface. The next few minutes were hectic in the extreme, as every gun opened fire and shells went ricocheting all over the ocean. It was not without interest that the U-Boat's engineer officer, who was the last to leave, said that no damage had been done to the pressure hull by gunfire. As a means of damaging strongly constructed, circular sectioned hulls, 4-inch gunfire is indeed virtually useless. It may spoil their looks but can do no material harm.

What makes the achievement of Commander Howard-Johnston's group all the more remarkable is that throughout this period we were working from Hvalfiord in Iceland to escort outward and homeward-bound convoys between 20° and 40° West. This mid ocean stretch was the most dangerous to the convoys, and the most fruitful to the U-Boats; for we could expect no help from aircraft. There were I believe some Catalinas in Greenland, but owing to weather conditions we saw very little of them. For years those waters, where air cover was impracticable, were known as 'the gap'. It is no wonder that with such a successful record Commander Howard-Johnston was eventually taken from us to serve as Anti-U-Boat officer in the Admiralty.

In the middle of May the group was lying in Hvalfiord, when I saw a boat coming alongside, and a tall officer with a grin leapt aboard. There was something about the way he spoke to the quartermaster, something about the nonchalant way in which he left his luggage to find its own way aboard that appealed to me. I was standing inside the screen door and went out to meet him. The grin increased in dimensions. My memories of Jack Hunter are overlaid with memories of his wonderful grin. The worse the conditions the broader the grin. As he saluted me and said, 'Lieutenant Hunter. Come aboard to join, Sir', I knew that I had been lucky. Here was a trained officer sure of himself, and using the correct expression.

Hunter was a Scot from the East Scottish Division R.N.V.R. He had the physique of a Rugby forward, the modulated voice of a barrister (he was a Writer to the Signet in Edinburgh in private life), and a puckish sense of humour. He could always rely on his charm to get him out of the appalling scrapes into which the sense of humour would lead him. What could not be acquired by legal logic was secured by use of that formidable grin. The ship's company were enslaved from the first moment. Even now I am unable to think of him without beginning to smile. As one of my brother corvette captains remarked to me rather plaintively, 'It's all right for you and your bloody *Verbenas*. With a barrister for First Lieutenant any of you can get away with murder.'

The important words of course were 'any of you *Verbenas*'. We were no longer officers, petty officers, and men. This commanding officer of another ship had paid us the supreme compliment of classing us all together as '*Verbenas*'. This unity was Jack Hunter's contribution to my ship. He was the catalyst which changed the parts into one corporate whole, so that anything which affected anyone of us was felt by all. The sensation of being 'one' with the 'whole' gave me a feeling of deep satisfaction – a satisfaction which once I had left *Verbena*, I was not to recapture, until another First Lieutenant did exactly the same for me in the destroyer *Highlander*.

The commanding officer of even so small a war vessel as *Verbena* tended to be a very lonely man. Assumed by his officers and men to know far more than he usually did about future movements, he had at all times to keep a very close watch on his tongue. As the fountain head of the ship's discipline, and the ultimate arbiter of their fate at the 'defaulters'' or 'requestmen's' table the crew were only too ready to suspect the Captain of having tyrannical tendencies; while the officers, feeling that his exalted state might interfere with their more light-hearted moments, were inclined to indicate that it might be better if he kept away from some of their parties.

Hunter was able to charm away all these fears. Perhaps his experience as a barrister had given him a particular understanding of the frailty of human nature. The men would confide their troubles to him with absolute confidence, while if I should stay away from a wardroom party because I thought that the weight of my rank would damage the effervescence of their spirits, Hunter would be sure to follow me to my cabin and persuade me to return. I cannot recall that he ever had to use much persuasion.

He was equal to any occasion, even to extracting suspected malefactors from the clutches of the local police. Late one night in Londonderry we heard that one of our very ordinary seamen had been taken in charge for being in possession of articles for which he could not give a satisfactory explanation. The 'article' in this particular case was an immense marble clock of repellently ugly design. He had been taken up by the police as he staggered shipward very late at night, and the best tale that he could produce was that he had bought this incredible timepiece for the sum of five shillings from a civilian whom he had met in a public urinal.

The tale was so unlikely that no one could have believed it. Hunter, however, was for getting him out if humanly possible. The pair of us went ashore right away, but without the Inspector's permission the police would not release their captive. Next morning found us back again in the police station to meet the Inspector. I forget what legal quibble our counsel used to convince this officer that there was absolutely no case to answer, and that if he were not very careful he would find himself involved in a matter of wrongful arrest. Having thus carried the war well into the enemy camp, we departed with our retrieved seaman, who followed us back along the jetty to the ship, staggering under the sixty-pound weight of the ghastly clock.

It was May 1941 when Hunter joined. We went to sea almost at once to meet the homeward-bound convoy SC.31 in 42° west, which is about the longitude of Greenland. The convoy route crossed the fortieth meridian about one hundred and fifty miles south of Cape Farewell, the southeasterly point of the land. This time we were ordered to meet the convoy two degrees further west than usual, as U-Boats had been found to be working a patrol line as far west as the fortieth meridian. There is no doubt that had the ships been available the Admiralty would have provided anti-submarine escort for the whole passage of the Atlantic; but at this time we simply had not got the ships and even

escorting beyond twenty degrees west had only been introduced in the last three months. Generally speaking the Hun
liked his meat easy to kill. As soon as we had enough escorts
to give reasonable protection as far as twenty degrees he
withdrew further to the westward, and at once found more
easily-slaughtered targets. Early in 1941 the escorts had
received very important reinforcements from two sources.
Our own yards were turning out corvettes, of which nearly
eighty were in service, and the Prime Minister had obtained
fifty old destroyers from America. These latter were nothing
like ideal escort vessels; but they were ships manned by
British sailors, and that was what mattered most.

Each Atlantic convoy had with it an armed merchant
cruiser or an old 'R Class' battleship as protection against
surface raiders. SC.31 was to have been taken as far as the
meeting place with our group by the armed merchant cruiser
Salopian, but on the 22nd of May early in the afternoon
she was torpedoed in convoy.

Actually the group was early at the rendezvous, although
neither the Commodore of the convoy nor the Captain of
the *Salopian* were to know this; for we did not lightly break
wireless silence. The *Salopian* was sunk when the group
were only just below the horizon, and the Commodore gave
the order to scatter the convoy. Why this order was given
we could not tell. The Commodore may have been sent
warning that exceptional enemy surface ships' movements
were afoot. In which case he was justified.

The position of the Commodore of a convoy vis-á-vis the
Senior Officer of the escort should perhaps be explained.
The Commodore of the convoy was responsible for the safety
of the merchant ships against all enemies, and for their
control. The Senior Officer of the escort was responsible for
the safety of the convoy from U-Boat attack. It was a
divided command which worked well enough in practice
while there was only the U-Boat to be considered; for the
Commodore always, as far as I know, acceded to the requests of the Senior Officer of the escort, if he were asked
to alter the course of the convoy.

In this case the Commodore, having seen his ocean escort

sunk, and having no anti-submarine escort with him, may have expected more U-Boat attacks to follow quickly; he may therefore have decided to scatter the convoy so as to spread the target over the widest possible area. As soon as we in B.12 group heard the order given to scatter, Commander Howard-Johnston in *Malcolm* and the four other destroyers of the group went off at full speed to try to deal with the situation. Behind them the four corvettes plugged along as fast as they were able, and behind us again came the two anti-submarine trawlers.

The night was spent in a desperate effort to reassemble the scattered convoy. It was incredible how far away from each other the ships had got in the two hours before our arrival. When we did collect one or two together they had to be escorted back to the fold, where the *Malcolm* was dashing back and forth like a worried sheep dog. By midnight we had collected over half, and had driven them into some sort of order. Away to the northward Commander J. Boston R.N., in the ex-American destroyer *Churchill* had another ten merchantmen under his wing and, with the help of a trawler, was bringing them down to join the main body. Then, shortly after midnight, the *Elusa* a big Dutch tanker was torpedoed. At once she became a flaming pillar of fire as, with engines stopped, she lay beam on to the sea. Clouds of smoke and lurid bursts of flame drifted downwind. The burning oil spread from her torn side in a blazing arc.

Taking the *Churchill* up-wind of the burning vessel Commander Bostock brought his ship in with her bows at right angles to the tanker. Then, with as much coolness as if he had been exercising in harbour, and not in very close proximity to a vessel which might disintegrate at any moment in one huge explosion, he rigged a breeches buoy and took off every man of the crew and her master's wireless set as well. This last was given as a personal present to the rescuer of the *Elusa*'s crew.

In a British destroyer the feat would have called for superb seamanship, for there was quite a sea running. In an ex-American destroyer it was almost incredible, and this for

93

a purely technical reason. The Americans for some reason best known to themselves had built these destroyers with both propellers turning the same way. Although this peculiarity had little effect on the ships' speed, it did mean that they were just as difficult to handle as a single-screw ship. Having taken off the crew Commander Bostock returned to his charges.

Early on the morning of the following day the 23rd May, *Verbena* was ordered by *Malcolm* to return to the wreck of the *Elusa* and, if still afloat, to take her in tow until the arrival of the ocean tugs. At this period of the war we were salvaging anything which might again be made seaworthy.

As we approached the wreck we were astonished to see a surfaced U-Boat also going to inspect the result of the night's work. It was fully surfaced about four miles away, and coming directly towards us. We went into action stations and waited. He seemed to be taking no evasive action, and I could only assume that having found himself in that position her commanding officer preferred to fight it out with the gun, rather than submerge and face the inevitable depth charging. Alternatively if he chose to stay 'on top' and run away he could run much faster than *Verbena.* In his position I would have done the same. He was a very difficult target to damage, whereas *Verbena* was much larger and much more vulnerable to gunfire. I made a signal to *Malcolm*, 'Am engaging surfaced U-Boat with gunfire close to wreck,' and heard over the radio telephone *Malcolm* calling the *Churchill.* '*Verbena* is having a gun battle with a U-Boat. Go to her support with all despatch, and be prepared to pick up her survivors.'

I gave the order to fire when the range was about 2,000 yards. The spray from the shot must have wetted his conning tower. He turned swiftly into the sea and began to dive. Our second shot fell just astern of him. Closing watertight doors we went in to ram; but we had not the speed. As we passed ahead of his diving position depth charges flew from our stern. It was a gesture only, but we might have been lucky. He had dived at speed, and might then have been at any depth. He would have difficulty in getting his boat in trim, and because he must go fast to keep control, and use his pumps to adjust his ballast tanks, we would have a good chance with the asdic.

We gained asdic contact – loud and clear. He was making to pass under the *Elusa*. I tried to carry out an attack but had to break off to avoid hitting the wreck. I took *Verbena* round the stern of the *Elusa* and picked him up the other side. We attacked him, and opened him up. He was leaking oil now and steering up-wind. We went in for another attack, but he must have turned right round just as we lost contact ahead, because when we regained contact he was heading back for the wreck. Possibly he knew he was leaking, and wanted to get down-wind into the oil slick that covered the sea for miles down-wind of the wrecked tanker. We attacked him again. By certain signs I considered that he had gone very deep; and we had then not been issued with the special heavy depth charges for use against deep U-Boats. We were now short of depth charges, because at that time we had only stowage for fifty.

However, as *Churchill* was already in sight hurrying towards us, I decided to wait and put her in contact. Unfortunately the obsolete type of American asdic with which she was fitted was nothing like as efficient as our own British machines, particularly with deep U-Boats. By passing to her the range and bearing we were able to guide her over the target and she carried out one attack. This was a technique later to be developed to a fine art. If two ships could be used together, and all ships were fitted with radar, so that the constantly shifting range could be ascertained accurately, it was remarkably effective. At that time *Verbena* fired a 'pattern' of five depth charges. Later when converted for the use of heavy charges she fired a pattern of ten at a time – five light and five heavy, hoping that the U-Boat would be the jam in the sandwich between the heavy charges exploding below the light ones.

After this attack we lost contact, and hoped we had sunk our U-Boat. But as we could not be certain we stayed in the neighbourhood until dawn next day (24th May). Then, with our fuel reserves getting very low, we began, in company with the *Churchill*, the long trip of over 400 miles back to Reykjavik.

Shortly after ten we intercepted a report that the *Hood* had been sunk, but did not immediately know how or where. Soon any amount of signals were being received and we learned that she had fought and been blown up by the enemy battleship *Bismarck* in the Denmark strait between Iceland and Greenland, and no more than two hundred miles away. It was soon obvious from the reports of the shadowing cruisers, *Norfolk* and *Suffolk*, that the enemy were going to pass very close to us. I made a signal to *Churchill*, 'Any comments?' and received back the reply, 'Only watch and pray.'

Just before lunch we could see a big ship on the horizon hurrying to the southward; but she was hull down and difficult to identify. I made to *Churchill*, 'Are you reporting what I think I see?' and got back the reply, 'Better not – identification by no means certain. Might cause confusion. Gather *Suffolk* has the situation in hand.'

So the chase sped away to the south-east and we went on to our destination. There we rejoined Commander Howard-Johnston, who in the *Malcolm* had been sent to search for survivors in the area where the *Hood* had sunk. He later showed me an attaché case full of little strips of wood. They were all that he could find of the lovely *Hood*.

In the middle of June we went back to Londonderry for a boiler clean. We had been sending back one or two ships of the group with each homeward-bound convoy, for there were no facilities in Reykjavik. Thus we missed the group's U-Boat sunk on the 29th June.

At Londonderry we were told that when our next boiler clean was due we would be sent to refit. This meant that the very detailed 'refit list' must be prepared and typed in quintuplet. As corvettes did not carry a typewriter, and in any case we had no one aboard who was able to type, there was nothing ahead of us but a seemingly endless period of operating with one finger upon a typewriter borrowed from the base.

We were saved by Chief Wren Mackintosh. She really

was a wonderful girl. She was an invention of Jack Hunter's fertile brain, for he was an excellent mimic.

On the first occasion when she helped us, the refit papers were left at Captain D's office. Half an hour later Chief Wren Mackintosh rang up and said that *Verbena*'s defect list was to be typed at once. We collected it the next afternoon, making a passing reference to the kindness of the Chief Wren and how we really must buy her some chocolates.

The next day, emboldened by our success with the defect list, we took up a number of other letters and papers. The Chief Wren was just as efficient as before. We began to think that Aladdin's lamp was only a little better than our dear friend.

That night I was called to the telephone during dinner. It was a First Officer W.R.N.S. Very haughty she sounded at the other end of the line.

'Who is Chief Wren Mackintosh?' she asked me.

I replied that the poor girl had been drowned in a hole in the River Foyle – so sad.

There was an ominous silence and the line went dead. I returned to the wardroom.

'Number One, we must hold a "wake" for Chief Wren Mackintosh – she's been drowned.'

We held the wake. Considering we had no body we felt it was a very good wake.

The next morning I was sent for by Captain Ruck-Keene.

'About Chief Wren Mackintosh.'

'Yes, Sir, I am sorry, Sir.'

'Sorry she was drowned, or sorry she ever happened?'

'Both, Sir.'

'The base will be an easier place for me to run when you and your *Verbena* have gone to refit. Go away, and don't you or your First Lieutenant play these tricks on my staff.'

'Thank you, Sir.'

I was almost through the door.

'Rayner.'

'Yes, Sir.'

'I hate to tell you just at this moment, but I have to congratulate you.'

My head swam. Did this mean that the Admiralty had confirmed my claimed U-Boat by the wreck of the *Elusa*? Apparently not, that was still classed as 'doubtful'.

The news was something almost as good. I had been granted 'qualified status'. This unromantic promotion meant a lot to a Reserve Officer, for it made his position in the Navy's hierarchy of command the same as his seniority in his rank. Instead of my precious *Verbena* being the 'dog's body' of the Western Approaches corvettes she would be second senior corvette in her own group, and even ships commanded by Royal Navy officers who were junior to her captain would be junior to her. *Verbena* had grown up.

Captain Ruck-Keene recalled me to the present. 'You're getting on now, Rayner, and that's another reason why you should not indulge in these pranks.'

'Yes, Sir.'

Good advice, yes, but as his own Chief of Staff, 'Jacky' Slaughter, indulged in more pranks than anyone I have ever met before or since, I gathered that it somewhat depended on who had been 'pranked'.

We had one more sojourn in Iceland, and then in August returned to Londonderry with the whole group. We were going to refit in the middle of the month at Grangemouth near Edinburgh, but before we left we wanted to give a farewell party to the group. It was a little difficult to hold a party that would have just that touch of difference which we felt was *Verbena*'s due. Number One and I had a conference in my cabin. We emerged with smiles on our faces and went to see a stationer from whom we ordered invitation cards, printed in silver. We then went back to lunch in the wardroom.

A new officer, Lieutenant Cook, had just joined. He sat with his mouth open and a drink in his hand, while he heard our explanation. I am convinced he thought he had joined H.M.S. Madhouse.

'Edwards,' I said to the midshipman, 'prepare to assume the feminine gender.'

'Me, Sir?'

'Yes, you're going to be the blushing bride. Don't look so worried man, we've borrowed some feminine garments. Whittaker, on Saturday morning you are marrying Miss Joyce Edwards, and the reception will be held aboard this ship. The cards are being rushed through the printers, and will be distributed tonight. Number One is going to order the taxis. We'll invite all the group and Captain D's staff.'

As a matter of fact we nearly came unstuck over the taxis, because they had already been booked for a funeral. However, Hunter and his grin were able to persuade them that a wedding was much more important than a funeral, and succeeded in getting the interment put off until the Monday.

In clothes borrowed from a friend of mine in Londonderry, the midshipman made a wonderful girl. She had what I believe is called a boyish figure, and so the midshipman needed very little padding to fill the bill.

The ship's company of course got wind of our scheme, and were lining the ship's side, perched on every vantage point, when our guests started to arrive. Sharp on time the two white-ribboned taxis arrived, bearing Whittaker and 'Miss' Edwards in the first, and Hunter and Cook in the second. For myself I had decided to be the photographer, with a bootbox fixed to a theodolite that we had borrowed from a surveyor. The whole contraption was camouflaged with a large black flag.

Captain D and the party from the base arrived just at the right moment when the bride, desperately trying to manage high-heeled shoes, was almost carried aboard. Number One met Captain D and led him round the far side of the engine room screen while I, hastily getting rid of my photographic impedimenta, doubled round the other side to greet him officially.

Of course once in our wardroom the game was up – but not entirely, because we were determined to carry it through properly, and were going to see them to the train. When we came to leave after the reception, hundreds of ratings from the other ships had joined our own ship's company. A way was cleared with some difficulty, and down the lane ahead of the happy pair went the First Lieutenant handing out bags of confetti to the men. It was a wonderful send off.

There were quite a lot of people at the station too. And then, just as the train was starting Number One, who had secured from somewhere a train key, locked them in. As the train started to move the poor bride almost showed signs of hysteria and Jack Hunter, suddenly realising that they had no money, handed them a ten shilling note. Then they went off. We had expected them to get out at Lisahally, but the train did not stop there. It did not stop until it got to Coleraine.

There was still no news of them at dinner time.

Nor was there any news until ten o'clock when the dock-yard police rang up to say that an officer was trying to bring a girl aboard *Verbena*. We had to send the First Lieutenant down to the gate to recover the two of them.

It transpired that the money was just enough to pay for the fares and a beer each – and not a penny over. That was the trouble. 'Miss' Edwards discovered with horror just before the first return train that a penny was essential to her. As then dressed the 'Gentlemen's' was obviously out of bounds to her, and as she had no penny they must go outside the station to look for a bush. By the time the bush was found the train had come and gone; and there are not very many trains on the small branch lines.

It had been a wonderful party, but not all our time in harbour was spent in frivolities. There was training, and more training of asdic and depth-charge crews; and the continual chase round the base to repair defects, or to get little additions carried out for the efficiency of the ship or comfort of the men, was continual. Mostly it was the men themselves that provided the problems that kept the officers so busy.

The great majority of the defaulters who appear cap in hand before the Captain's table arrive in that situation from sheer carelessness – from the misfortune of a missed bus, or quite frequently from not having even bothered to look at the timetable at all. Just occasionally you meet a special brand of malefactor – the man who just does not care.

Something has turned him against the Service; perhaps some unfair punishment in his early years, or perhaps some matter which was not investigated thoroughly enough, has cast a blight upon him. These men are old by comparison with others of their own rating, and are often the best seamen in the ship. Sometimes they hold back from a definite desire to avoid promotion, because they feel themselves lacking in the ability to take command. At sea these men carry the whole weight of the ship. In harbour they are a confounded nuisance.

Verbena had two of these – an able seaman and a stoker. Regularly these two appeared at my defaulter's table, for they were 'chummy ships' and hung together. Each time the charge was the same. 'Absent over leave so many hours so many minutes; aggravated offence, ship under sailing orders.' It so happened that the seaman was a really first-class man, and the stoker more than pulled his weight in the boiler room. They knew that not to get back would let me down and let the ship down, for I had told them so often enough. They made great efforts to get back. The stoker was discovered one morning progressing on hands and knees along the dockside, with his finger in one railway line while the seaman used the other line as a guide. 'And keeping perfect station they was Sir, one singing out to the other every few minutes. Very keen to get back to the ship, Sir. So instead of taking them along to the station we brought 'em down here to see if you'd really be wanting them, Sir.'

Having signified our appreciation of the perspicacity of the local police, we duly accepted two human bundles and steamed off down the river.

But this was too much.

I gave them two days to recover and then, when we were comfortably at sea, I sent for the two of them to see me privately in my cabin. There, putting on what I hoped was a 'pained parent' expression, I addressed them. It was soon after our return from Gibraltar.

'First I suppose I must thank you for getting back to the ship. You know as well as I do the strength of the ship's company, and you both know you are carrying more than your fair share of work when we are at sea. But this last escapade of yours goes quite beyond reason. What can I do with you? What appeal can I make to you? I gather you want to stay in the ship or you'd have missed her long ago.'

'Oh we do, Sir. Never been so happy, Sir.'

They were like a chime going off together.

'What you mean is that you've never met such a bloody fool as I am who'll put up with you.'

'Not quite that, Sir,' from the seaman, 'you've treated us decent.'

'Now look, I want you to go for Leading Hand, and you for Leading Stoker. You can both pass easily.'

'No good, Sir. We'll only drop the "hook" next time in, Sir.'

'Oh no you wouldn't – not with extra pay; and besides haven't you got a girl? Surely you want to marry? Won't she be pleased to hear you've picked up a leading rate?'

'A girl, Sir !' The seaman answered me in much the same tone of voice he might have used if I'd suggested to him that he kept a tame elephant. As I knew he was no mean performer as a ladies' man I was a little surprised.

'Yes, a *Girl* – one of those pretty things on the beach. Haven't you one you want to marry?'

'Marry, Sir – not me, Sir. Why should I buy a book if I can go to the library?'

I gave it up as hopeless.

I was rather surprised therefore when, just before we returned to harbour, Jack Hunter came to me with a broad grin on his face.

'Something to please you, Sir. I've two requestmen. One to take the board for Leading Seaman and one for Leading Stoker.'

Their examinations took place on the same day, and of course they both passed.

Thereafter whatever they did ashore, they behaved perfectly within the ship, returning aboard with extreme regularity, and full of as much beer as they could conveniently carry – just one minute before leave expired.

A month or two later we returned to harbour to find

amongst the mail a draft chit for both. Devonport barracks, always short of leading rates, had seized them for another ship. However our own crew was stronger by then, and although I hated to see them go I had no real cause to try to alter things. On their last morning aboard two rather sheepish faces appeared at the door of my cabin.

'Just come to say "Goodbye," Sir.'

'Oh I hadn't forgotten. I was going to see you before you left.'

We said our goodbyes and then self-consciously they pressed three photographs upon me – one of each separately and one of the pair of them together.

'Taken special for you they was, Sir.'

I valued those photographs enormously.

In the second week of August we sailed from London-derry to Grangemouth to refit, and after the conference I rushed down to my home in Liverpool, for I had not seen my wife and family, except for one day, since the previous December. We took the children away for a fortnight's glorious holiday at Ambleside in the Lake District.

But fate intervened again. Four days before the end of my leave I was telephoned by Hunter from Edinburgh.

'Things are happening to her – strange things. I can't tell you over the telephone, but I think you'd like to know about them.'

'All right Number One, I'll be back.'

We packed up, took the children home, and my wife and I went up to Edinburgh together.

CHAPTER 5

VERBENA GOES EAST

Hunter met me at the station at Grangemouth, and we walked down to the ship together. I stood looking across the dock to where she lay, and could hardly recognize her. In ten days her appearance had been transformed. Now a huge structure resembling a gigantic pepper pot rose from the back of the bridge. It was higher than the funnel, and to my eyes, looked just about as unseamanlike a contraption as could be devised. To make matters worse it was not even on the centre-line of the ship, but was offset to port by at least ten feet.

No one knew what it was for. All we could learn was that Rosyth Dockyard was to fit whatever went inside it. But the pepper pot was not all. Awning stanchions were being fitted, and already the sailmaker who was to make the awnings had been aboard to measure the ship.

I went back to Liverpool to see the Chief of Staff to the C-in-C, Western Approaches. He told me that six of those corvettes which had been fitted for minesweeping were to be used for a very special purpose, and that we had been chosen by Commander Crick who was to be Senior Officer of the party; that for this operation we would need radar, and that as we were such very high priority the radar set would be supplied to us from the battle cruiser *Renown*. Naturally I begged for more information, but the Chief of Staff told me that the less I knew the better. I countered this by saying that the men would talk, and that we had best think up some tale. He suggested that I tell them that we were being lent to Freetown. The U-Boats were already working in the southern half of the Atlantic ocean, even down to Ascension Island and St. Paul's Rock off the Brazilian coast.

As that was all that he would tell me I went back to my ship.

As I journeyed northwards I cursed the luck that had put my ship into Commander Crick's mind. Had it not been for that madcap episode with the special trains he would probably have forgotten all about me. Now, told to pick out six corvettes, he must have run his eye down the list, and recognized my name. Thus I and my *Verbena* were taken. It was not that I objected to the chance of what promised to be an unusual operation. I had simply fallen in love with the job that we had been doing. It was so obviously one which was worth while; and there could be few sights more thrilling to see than an Atlantic convoy. The great concourse of ships, held together by the encircling fringe of escorts, would crawl home before the prevailing westerly winds. Rolling heavily, the deep-laden merchantmen, who held in their capacious bellies the food and armaments for a be-leaguered Britain, would spew white water from their scuppers. Poised on the Atlantic swell they would for a short moment be borne steadily forward on the crest, only to sink into the hollows with surprising grace as they waited for the next wave to overtake them. A few weeks later those same ships would be outward-bound again, butting bluff bows into the advancing waves. Still rolling, but more jerkily, and every now and then flinging a sheet of spray from their sterns as their propellers came half out of the water.

We had learned to think with genuine affection of our charges. We remembered them from one convoy to another, and sometimes formed real friendships with them. They too had characters as distinct as those of the individual escorts. Often they earned themselves nick-names. There was 'Smokey Joe', a great ugly surly brute of a ship, who was for ever making smoke. At the change of the watch the first thing the new officer would ask was, 'How's Smokey Joe behaving?' and receive the answer, 'Not so good. He was blowing tubes half an hour ago, and I had to tick him off again. But it's no use telling Smokey anything.' When you had steamed for a week within sight of him you had a special interest in him. When you found him in the next outward-bound convoy but one, you would feel a warm glow of friendship, you might even go alongside to greet him by loud hailer, knowing full well that within a few hours you would receive a signal telling you that Number 34 in the convoy was making smoke, and that the next time you addressed him your remarks would be far from polite.

Consider for a moment the men in those ships. In mid-1941 the U-Boats were sinking as many as sixty ships in a single month, as many as there were in one whole convoy – all lost. Yet there was no lack of men to man the ships. No British ship ever stayed in harbour because she could not find a crew. Was there ever a finer testimonial to our nation?

The bravest ship I ever met was one whom we christened 'Sinbad the Sailor'. We met him first on a homeward-bound convoy. He was immediately noticeable, and would have stood out in any company. From what junk heap of worn-out ships had he been rescued to fight in the most terrible of all wars? 'Sinbad' was a very, very old ship. Almost everything about him went straight up – straight bow, tall slender masts, a very tall and extremely thin funnel. Only his counter was as fine and delicate as that of a steam yacht. When we first met him smoke was pouring from his slim funnel. We had tried commands, arguments, cajolery – all to no purpose. Sinbad was smoking his pipe. That was only the start of it. Very soon he was falling out of bed repeatedly. We put him back time after time. He was so good-humoured about it all that we could not be really cross with him. His captain would come to the rail and wave to me as I called to him over the loud hailer. He was as old as the ship herself. He would stand, a short stocky figure wearing a bowler hat, swaying on the bridge of his ship. The wind fluttered his white mutton chop whiskers, and his red face was always split in a grin of welcome. One imagined that he was the owner as well as the Captain of his crazy charge.

But one day he could not get back to the convoy. Some defect in his aged machinery had reduced his speed to walking pace. I stayed with him as long as I could. At last as dark was coming I received a signal from *Malcolm*.

'Leave your straggler and resume your station.'

I knew why – there were six U-Boats shadowing the convoy.

I went very close alongside.

'Can you not get her going any faster?'

'Nay – Mister——' the words came slowly. I could just hear them above the whistle of the wind and the roar of waters between the ships. 'Nay – we – be – launched – over – fifty – years – ago. It's – an – engineer shop – I – be – needing.'

'I am sorry I must leave you – very sorry. We expect attack on the convoy. Goodnight and good luck.'

'Ay – you – get – off – to – the – convoy – Mister. We'll – be – all – right – you'll – see.'

If I ever prayed for anything it was that the U-Boats would not find our Sinbad that night. Next morning he was out of sight astern. There had been no S.O.S. in the night, and we had kept a special wireless watch for him.

Three weeks later we had taken some ships down to Liverpool. Coming out of the Mersey was a convoy and in the middle of it was Sinbad. Even as we watched a long trail of smoke spread from his high funnel. We could see a watchful corvette leap towards him. We laughed. We knew that one. She would have to do that many times. As we had left our own ships we went over to have a word with him.

He was delighted to see us. They'd almost rebuilt his engines for him. His ship was as good as new, so he said. As we left him we flung out from our yardarm in international code the signal 'Good luck'. In reply a puff of sooty smoke burst from his funnel, and a shower of ashes fell on our decks.

To go to sea in such a crate was to play with death. Yet he went – and had found a crew to go with him. No men could have been braver; and I was now to leave these men and this work which I knew and loved, to go elsewhere.

We took *Verbena* alongside the *Renown* in Rosyth Dockyard, and the complicated radar set was taken out of her and put into us. We felt very important that so vast a ship should be stripped of a new machine for our benefit, and I wondered more and more for what operation we were to be used. We were to sail to Londonderry to await instructions. Letters had told us that our own group would be in harbour, and that a group dance was to be held on the Friday night.

There were now many new faces in the ship's company. My years spent in training officers and men had given me a deep pleasure in seeing them advance. We had been six months at sea, and many men were now passing for leading seaman. Two of our leading seaman had passed for petty officer. The midshipmen, recommended for sub-lieutenant, had been taken away and Midshipman A. D. Townsend had his berth. Anyone in *Verbena* who wanted promotion was encouraged to try. This did not result in a lowering of efficiency. New people came up to take the place of old, and friendly relations having been established with the drafting officer at the Barracks, he sent us promising young ratings. Sub-Lieutenant Whittaker had been promoted to Lieutenant, but remained in the ship.

How greatly things had changed since I had taken her up the north-east coast ten months before! Then I was the only officer with any sea experience. Now I had three Lieutenants, all with watch-keeping certificates.

It was a Wednesday night when we left Rosyth, and by Thursday afternoon we were off Cape Wrath, the north-westerly corner of Scotland, and had every chance of making Londonderry in plenty of time for the dance. Rounding the headland we could see into the Minches, that stretch of tideswept water between the mainland of Scotland and the Outer Hebrides. At once we ran into a gale, with driving rain and fog. This was a special brand of Minch weather. It was surprising how often it could be clear outside and absolutely foul inside the Minches. There appeared to be nothing to do but 'heave to', or proceed very slowly. I thought then of our new radar. If it really did what it was supposed to do we might yet make Londonderry in time. I sent for its operator. Yes he could pick up the land. We tried it. It was wonderful. I asked the operator if he was game to work it for six hours at a stretch himself, because at that time he was the only rating in the ship trained in its use. We started off down the Minches at full speed, and I was amazed at the efficiency of the instrument. No more searching for a convoy in thick weather. Half the worry and strain of a commanding officer's life would be taken away by this wonderful invention. I even forgave it for its terrible outward appearance. In six hours we were through the narrows, and heading for Londonderry river.

It was a wonderful dance. Our friends had the same weather at Londonderry, and knowing when we had sailed they had never expected us to make the passage in time. We were kept very busy for the next few days, showing off our new toy.

And then suddenly, without warning, Hunter went sick. He must have an operation – and *Verbena* a new First Lieutenant. The good that Hunter had done was not easily undone. All that he had built stood firm, and showed no signs of cracking for many months.

A commanding officer is remarkably impotent to tackle many of the problems that arise. Service tradition assumes that both Captain and First Lieutenant are of the first class, as in peace time they usually are. In war this cannot always be so. A good commanding officer may have an efficient ship, but he cannot also have a happy one unless he has a good First Lieutenant. Looked at from below the Captain may appear as a deity, benevolent or otherwise according to his nature; but his powers are actually very restricted. He can function only through an efficient body of officers. It is the First Lieutenant in a small ship, the Commander in a big one, who brings to the Captain all the contentious matters, all the problems that arise. It is he who translates the Captain's decisions to the men. In this endless matter of go-between he must tread warily. His first loyalty is of course to his captain, but he must advise him tactfully. His second loyalty is to the men, whose viewpoint he must learn to understand, and often to represent. It is very much of a full time job, for he has his own duties as a ship's officer as well.

Very soon after Hunter had left it became plain that trouble was brewing amongst the crew. I went to see Captain (D) Londonderry, and he decided to replace the new First Lieutenant at once. Two days later we slipped down the river on a wonderful golden morning, bound for adventure we knew not where.

All we knew was that we were being sent as additional escort to join a convoy going to the southward, and that we and the five other specially fitted corvettes were to be detached with those ships of the convoy which were bound for Freetown, Sierra Leone. It was a forty ship convoy, which was small compared with those to which we were accustomed. The escort consisted of six corvettes and two ex-American coastguard cutters. These last were Lease-

Lend craft. They were big, unhandy brutes, and except for their long endurance they were not at all suitable for escort work. Even so we should have been able to give the convoy adequate protection. We steamed off westward at nine knots and turned to the south in 15° West. Nothing happened until we reached the latitude of Brest, when we were attacked by Focke-Wulfs. Although no damage was done they would obviously report our position, and I was not surprised when the following night a ship was torpedoed in the convoy. She was carrying ammunition and blew up with a terrific explosion. Oh for B.12 group! There had been no evening deployment to put down a shadowing U-Boat. We waited for orders that never came. The team had not played together before, and indeed we had no proper Senior Officer of Escorts with us. As the wind was moderate from the north, it was fairly obvious that the attack had come from astern. *Verbena* ran across the wake of the convoy dropping depth charges every five hundred yards. Whether this had any effect I do not know, but the U-Boat was content with his one victim.

The next morning found a large ship straggling. *Verbena* was told to guard her until she had mended herself. We steamed round her for twelve hours. The convoy was then one hundred and eight miles ahead of us. Although our straggler was a fast ship, and when mended could make thirteen knots we only had a speed of four knots in excess of the convoy. It would take us twenty-two hours to catch up. One day at full speed would reduce our oil reserves considerably. Already two corvettes had been sent to the Azores for fuel. By the time we caught up we also were running short of fuel, and had to go there too.

We arrived off Punta Delgada, only to find that the port was closed because of an onshore gale. The seas were enormous. We hove to and waited throughout the night. The next day was just as bad, and although the one after that was a little better, the port was still closed. The position was now desperate. Either we could try to make the harbour, or go and drift about in the Atlantic a prey to any U-Boat. I decided to take her into harbour. Going in was thrilling in

the extreme. A huge wave lifted us up and carried us towards the harbour mouth. It raced ahead of us, and we slid
down its back. Another came up astern. The entrance of the
harbour seemed to be rushing towards us with the speed of
an express train. We were surf riding in a vessel weighing
twelve hundred tons. The wave on which we travelled burst
on the harbour walls, and sent up a huge plume of spray to
a hundred feet. As soon as my bow was level with the tower
on the end of the breakwater I ordered the wheel hard-a-
port and the engines full ahead. She lay over as she spun
round on her heel and shot into the protected harbour. A
pilot boarded us. He was gesticulating madly and talking
nineteen to the dozen – a very excitable gentleman, and all
in Portuguese. At last he ran out of breath and said in
English, 'You very lucky man, Sah.'

'I'm much less trouble inside than being a wreck outside,'
I told him.

We took in fuel, water, sherry and a quantity of chickens,
and left at dawn the next day. They would not let us out
that night.

The convoy was now more than three hundred miles
ahead, and we received a signal 'Rejoin with all despatch'.
We knew why, for the Admiralty had signalled that U-Boats
were in the vicinity of the convoy. I had to comply, although
it meant using up fuel at a prodigious rate. Four days later
we had almost caught up the convoy. Then the escort signalled to us, 'Your friend straggling again. Please do the
necessary.'

By using our radar we found her in the night; but it was
morning before she got herself going again, and by that
time the convoy was one hundred miles ahead once more.
There seemed to be no end to it. During the day we heard
the escorts that were bound for Freetown being detached,
but we still had half a day's steaming to put our straggler
back to bed. Early the following morning we pushed him
in, said 'au revoir' to the senior of the ex-American cutters
and went off to find Freetown. At full speed we had each
day been using more than twice as much fuel as we would
have used at cruising speed. We had been at full speed for

a week, the equivalent of more than two week's steaming at ten knots, and we still had a long way to go. I wondered if we would make it. I had the fire drawn in the second boiler and continued on one. I did not know what there might be in Freetown, but had heard that there was practically nothing. It was unlikely that they would have an ocean tug. I had no fancy for spending any time drifting oil-less in the Atlantic, for when the engines stopped the electrics would stop also. There would then be no radar, and no asdic. I felt it would be better to be going somewhere, even if only very slowly. Besides to have to sail the ship would greatly encourage the men. There are few things so disheartening and so disruptive of morale as lying helpless at sea with the engine stopped. As soon as the steady beat of the propeller dies away and the ship, no longer answering her rudder, begins to drift aimlessly, a sensation of being utterly helpless and lost comes over all on board. It is as if the iron heart of the ship has been in some way connected with your own body. I can think of no punishment more vile for dishonest seamen than that they should be cast adrift in ships whose engines are destined to break down, so that they will drift aimlessly around the great oceans for all eternity.

We spent an amusing and quite profitable morning rigging the corvette for sailing.

The griping spars of the boats, each fourteen foot long, made two yards secured three-quarters of the way up the mast. These were fitted with slings, guys and lifts and stood out at right angles to the mast. They were capable of being trimmed to any required position. On the yard on the weather side we prepared to set the quarter-deck awning, and on the lee side yard to use the bridge awning. The fo'c's'le awning, which was triangular in shape, would serve as a jib. At midday the engineer officer reported that there was virtually no oil left. If we were to make harbour, we had to keep going for another four hours. On the wireless we could hear the other corvettes hunting a U-Boat to the southward, so we could not expect them to come to tow us in. We made a signal for a tug and, as we expected, the answer came back that no tug was available. A most curious smoke was now coming from the funnel, as the stokers burnt the sludge in the bottom of the tanks. The seamen were facetiously sending down to ask which of the stokers was being burnt!

At last the high land behind Freetown came in sight. Slowly our speed dropped. With the anchor ready for slipping we crept into harbour, and anchored as soon as we were inside the boom. After waiting there an hour or more a small tug appeared and towed us to the oiler.

Freetown anchorage was large. Except for the prominent hill behind the town it was curiously like the Solent. The red roofs peeping from the trees on the south side might well have been the village of Lee before it was quite so much built-up. The north shore was a long way across the mud flats, and showed only as a line of green trees on the horizon.

Lying in the anchorage was the most curious collection of shipping we had ever seen. There were landing craft with strange square bows and big ramps, and an assault ship hung round with dozens of motor launches.

The crews of the fleet oilers were the scandal-mongers of the Navy. Much of their life was spent in secluded anchorages, and the one break in the monotony of their lives was the arrival of ships wanting fuel. They acquired a nice taste in rumour and, subtle as a taster of wine, they could distinguish the genuine from the spurious. If they ran out of facts they were not too particular about spreading fiction. From the oiler we learnt that the strange shipping was an amphibious force intended for a landing on the French African coast. There could be only one objective – Dakar.

Naturally in such an operation they would want the minesweeping corvettes to sweep ahead of the landing ships. It was also now possible to hazard a guess regarding the purpose for which forty large and second-hand lorry tyres had been delivered to the ship before we left England. Up till now we had thought these rather a joke. But taken with an order we had received to practise getting out our minesweeping gear without stopping engines, they suggested that on our projected trip to the shore we should have barge loads of soldiers lashed alongside; and presuming that the 9.2 inch guns had not blown us out of the water first, our radar would enable us to arrive at the correct assault point.

The next day I discovered what I had suspected the evening before. I was one of those people who could not sweat enough to keep going in the tropics. I swelled. By noon my cap was two sizes too small for me, and my shoes were too tight. Men had been flown home who could not sweat. I sent for a carpenter's saw and a large block of wood, and started sawing after lunch. By four o'clock I had sawn that block all ways, and was sweating nicely and feeling a lot better. In the evening Commander Crick and the submarine hunting party returned, and I went with him to call on the Commander-in-Chief, Admiral Willis. Apparently the rumour we had heard from the oiler was right. It was to have been Dakar, but the operation had been postponed indefinitely. We were to be used for ocean escort work until a decision regarding our future was made. The assault craft hung about in Freetown until the following July, when they were used for the attack on Madagascar. *Verbena* unfortunately missed that action, because by then she had broken down and was in Bombay harbour.

It was in Freetown that I first ran up against serious trouble over my seniority. Commander Crick had picked a good team without realising the implications of 'qualified status'. When sweeping for moored mines the ships work in two sub-divisions; the second senior ship is the sub-divisional leader, and carries quite heavy responsibilities. Commander Crick had brought with him from the fleet minesweepers a Lieutenant-Commander, Royal Navy, whom he had expected to be his sub-divisional leader. However, all the other commanding officers of the corvettes were 'qualified officers'; and I was the senior of the four. To me therefore would fall the duties of sub-divisional leader. I was left in no doubt about the feelings of the R.N. Lieutenant-Commander. I could indeed sympathise with him, for although in the Western Approaches we were by then thoroughly used to commanding officers who were reservists, the main fleet had not yet met us in that capacity.

Commander Crick told me that before he left no one had warned him about 'qualified officer' status, but that he had no objection at all to *Verbena* leading the second subdivision. Even so I thought the whole position was more than awkward; for I was not only the second senior commanding officer, I was also the youngest. I went to Captain (D) Freetown, Captain Rupert Sherbrooke, now Vice-Admiral R. St. V. Sherbrooke, V.C., C.B., D.S.O. (he won his Victoria Cross in the Arctic on New Year's Eve 1942 when his flotilla fought off the *Lützow*, *Hipper*, and six German destroyers). After explaining the position to him I suggested that my qualified status should not be considered while I was working from Freetown. He replied that I was talking nonsense, and told me that he had just had my most difficult colleague calling on him to complain about the situation. He had told that officer that when his ship was as efficient as *Verbena* he would talk to him. Until that time he would not even meet him socially.

Partly to escape from so difficult a situation, and partly because we were not going to be used as minesweepers, I suggested that *Verbena* be detached to carry out a patrol off St. Paul's Rock on the other side of the Atlantic, where U-Boats were known to replenish from the special tanker submarines called 'milch cows'. We could have fuelled in Brazil, carried out another patrol and then returned to Freetown. Captain Sherbrooke promised to put the suggestion before the Commander-in-Chief; but before the reply was received a U-Boat was reported south of Freetown, and I was ordered to take the three corvettes commanded by the R.N.R. officers and search for it. We never found the enemy, but I did have a conversation with one of her officers over the radio telephone, and he very nearly tricked me into giving away the plan of my hunt. For a time the Germans did try the dodge of fitting their boats with a radio telephone on the same wave-length as our own, and supplying them with an English-speaking officer. They would break into our conversation in an attempt either to mislead the hunt, or to discover what we were up to. In this particular case I had sent two ships to one end of the 'probability area' while I, with the fourth, worked inwards towards the spot where the enemy had been reported. The U-Boat would therefore have ships to the north and south of him, the pairs of ships being out of sight of each other.

We were using as call signs the nicknames of the commanding officers, my own being 'Ben'. When 'Possum' was heard to call 'Ben' on the R/T and ask for my intentions, I might well have given him the plan of my hunt had the German not added, 'and what is your geographical position now?' As 'Possum' was the ship hunting with me it was a rather peculiar question, because he knew the whereabouts of the pair of us as well as I did. I called to him by light, 'Did you make that signal asking for my position?' and got back the reply, 'Not me.'

Had we been able to use visual signals to the other ships it might perhaps have been possible to double-bluff the Hun. With the ships out of sight I had to signal to the group. 'There is a Hun butting in on our conversation. All future signals to be coded.'

It was I think the first occasion that they tried to catch us in this way. An immediate signal was made to the Commander-in-Chief telling him of this new trick.

Only luck would have enabled us to catch that U-Boat, since it was one of those many hunts when the delay between the first sighting and the arrival of the hunters really made the position hopeless.

After this the four of us were ordered to take a fast convoy down to the Cape of Good Hope, refuel in Capetown and then bring another one north.

These ships were not like the merchantmen that we were used to escorting. They were big passenger liners, and they were full of soldiers going to join the armies in Egypt and the Far East. The speed of the convoy was fifteen knots, the same as our own best speed. It was a nerve-racking job because, if we lost station on the convoy it was impossible to regain it; and we could carry out no anti-U-Boat manoeuvres at all for the safety of our charges. An anti-submarine escort can only be fully effective when the escorting ships have a big excess of speed over that of the convoy.

On the way down to Capetown on the 7th December came news of the Japanese attack on Pearl Harbour, and on the 9th we heard of the German and Italian declarations of war on America. The United States were now in it up to the hilt. Not only was it nice to feel that we were no longer alone; but from our experience in the Western Approaches we well knew what a vast difference it would make to the convoy system in the Atlantic. Now perhaps we would really have a chance to take the offensive against the U-Boats. We longed to be back there to see that fight out rather than go eastward, for I had very little expectation of seeing Freetown again. Personally I had little to complain of. I found myself senior officer of four efficient corvettes, and so long as we were used for anti-submarine work I felt confident of our ability to do our job.

One by one the escorts were detached to refuel at Port au France in French Equatorial Africa. When our turn came I felt quite excited at the prospect of seeing a tropical port. In my imagination I had pictured a sheltered harbour, with great trees hanging over a land-locked bay; enormous creepers, draped like writhing snakes would be festooned from the heavy branches; while monkeys, parrots and strange butterflies would be much in evidence.

I felt that the glamour of the tropics would be all the more impressive if I were to come suddenly upon the scene I had visualised; so I fixed the ship's position from the morning stars, and then went below to my cabin having told the officer of the watch that I was not to be called to the bridge again until the detail of the trees could be seen.

In due course I was told that land had been sighted; that the lighthouse on the harbour entrance was in sight; that the radar range of the nearest land was one mile.

'But surely you can see the trees now?'

'No, Sir – sorry, Sir.'

Damn it – I'd have to go up. I went on to the bridge. The land ahead of me was quite bare, and strikingly like the Berkshire Downs. There were no trees, and no monkeys. It was one of the most bitter disappointments of my life.

We were to oil from a pipe line on the jetty. The previous

corvette had not yet finished. It was four o'clock in the afternoon before we started to take in the oil, which was fed by gravity from a tank on the hill. At that rate it would take us four hours to fuel.

We decided to call on the local Governor, of whom rumour said that he was rather inclined to side with the Vichy French. The First Lieutenant and I started off to walk the two miles to Government House. When we got there we were told that he was away; but we did not quite believe this as we thought we saw somebody slipping quickly away from a window. We had no option but to retrace our steps, but we had quite overlooked the suddenness with which a tropic night descends. One moment there was the sun, low but bright in the sky. The next it was pitch dark.

The road back to the port was entirely deserted. Hardly had darkness fallen when we heard something patter across the road very fast behind us. We spun round, and something about the size of a small dog crossed quickly. We turned again, and once more there was a dry rustle and a curious clicking behind us. It was all very eerie.

'Land crabs,' I said.

'Are they friendly, Sir?'

'Frankly I'm damned if I know.'

We stopped and they were coming closer.

'I wish they wouldn't make that noise, Sir.'

'Number One,' I said, 'I'm going to run for it. It may be cowardly, but I'd feel happier.'

We pounded down that road as if the devil himself was after us.

We escorted our convoy well south of the Cape, and then were ordered to Simonstown to refuel. There we were told that we would not be going back to Freetown. We were to remain at the Cape to await instructions.

The state of the war in the Pacific was critical in the extreme. The Japs, using a striking force of carrier-borne bombers, had temporarily wiped out the American Pacific Fleet at Pearl Harbour on the 7th December; and a few days later we had lost the old battle cruiser *Repulse* and the new battleship *Prince of Wales*. Except for a few destroyers of the Eastern Fleet we were the most readily available escort ships, and it seemed only too probable that within a matter of days we should be going on eastward.

As senior officer of the four ships I was now faced with a very serious problem. All the ships needed boiler cleaning. We ourselves had 1,500 hours on our boilers when we arrived. Any advance eastward to the theatre of war would mean at least another 500 hours steaming. When we arrived we would have to boiler-clean before we could be used for operations. It therefore seemed obvious to me that we should do so in Capetown, and at once. I could get nothing done. We were told to remain at four hours' notice, and to await instructions. In vain I pointed out that to keep these ships, which had fire tube boilers, at four hours' notice was exactly the same as keeping them at sea; because one boiler must be alight all the time. In spite of all I could do the ships lay there adding hours to their boiler time. We were there for one month 'awaiting orders'.

But it was a month that brought us a great deal of fun. The hospitality committee at Capetown gave us all, officers and men, a wonderful time. We were the first visitors from the real war who had stayed for any length of time, and the local hostesses vied with each other for our company. I found myself lent a powerful American saloon car the better to drive to see my hosts, or to reach the stables where the horses were kept. We organized a wonderful telephone system for recalling the ships' companies in the event of our being given sailing orders, and this system was responsible one day for an urgent recall for me.

Going to the telephone I was told by a horrified Lieutenant Whittaker that he had lost overboard the keys of the confidential safe. He had been inspecting liberty men, and afterwards had walked along the deck spinning the keys round his finger, when they had flown off and over the side. What should he do? Should he report the loss to the Admiralty as was laid down? I told him to do nothing, and hurried back to the ship which was lying in the new tidal dock in Capetown. I knew that the bottom was clean sand.

If only we had possessed a magnet we might, so I thought, perhaps have been able to recover them. I suddenly had a brainwave and took all the magnets from the magnetic compass. I tied them together in a bundle until they looked like a bunch of asparagus, and when we had attached these to a line we began dragging the bottom of the dock. Whittaker and the quartermaster of the watch kept it up all night. Not I – I slept. As I was having breakfast the following morning Whittaker came to me.

'It's no use, Sir. We'll never find them. We'll have to report the loss and get a diver.'

'Go on,' I told him, 'until after I have finished my breakfast. If you haven't got them by then I'll telephone to Simonstown and see if they can send us a diver.'

I had hardly started my second cup of coffee when Whittaker burst into my cabin with the keys in his hand. A board of enquiry had been avoided. Now I had to put back all those magnets in the compass, and re-swing the ship. Fortunately I still had my notebooks from the days when I had taken my navigation examination nine years before. With that help it proved quite simple.

We kept *Verbena's* second Christmas in Simonstown Dockyard. On Christmas Eve I had made a signal to the Naval Store Officer asking for a new boat to replace the one that had been smashed in the gale off the Azores, and had added, 'It would be a nice Christmas present if this boat should be fitted with sails and a centreboard.' But the Captain of the Dockyard had answered that no such boats were available at Simonstown.

On Christmas morning the quartermaster reported that a tug was coming alongside with a boat. The boat had both sails and a centreboard, and on the centreboard case was a note tied with red ribbon 'With the compliments of the Naval Store Officer – A Merry Christmas.'

One sensed a certain coolness between the Naval Store Officer and the Captain of the Dockyard.

At last our signal came. I was recalled and told, 'You are to sail tomorrow afternoon for Singapore.' It was then the 28th of January, 1942. All the ships had over 1,500 hours on their boilers, and *Verbena* had nearly two thousand. I refused to sail unless all the facts were reported to Commander-in-Chief, Western Approaches, as we still considered we belonged to his command. Other authorities were only too ready to use us, but not to look after us.

It was not a pleasant interview. At last when we had reached a deadlock I was told 'Very well, I must tell you in strict confidence – you are going to evacuate Singapore. Now will you sail?'

'Yes, Sir,' I said and left the room.

We prepared to sail and were unexpectedly joined by a fifth corvette, the *Aster* (Commander E. Hewitt R.N.R.). He had been sent down to take over as Senior Officer of the Group. With the difficulties facing us over maintenance I was only too pleased to hand over to him.

We fuelled at Durban and at Mauritius.

Mauritius is a fantastic island. It lies in the middle of the Indian Ocean, and in this the clearest of all seas, the masts of ships whose hulls are below the horizon can easily be seen. The high ridge of mountains down the middle of the island appeared above the rim of the ocean like the spined back of some prehistoric monster; and the tree-covered hills were, at that great distance, an olive green colour such as one would expect from the skin of some giant reptile.

While the ships fuelled their Captains and First Lieutenants were invited to dinner by the Governor and his charming American wife. There, sitting at a long table under the open colonnade of a great porch that ran the whole length of Government House, it was difficult to realise that the war was so near. As I looked down the long line of officers and of ladies, the candles in their little glass bowls cast a warm glow over the diners, who all sat at one side of the table. On the other side, across a lighted fountain in which goldfish swam there was a floodlit gazebo; and beyond it was the dark backcloth of the star-filled tropic night. After dinner there was dancing, and we returned very late to the ships.

At Durban we had been asked to take to Mauritius some soldiers who had been wounded in North Africa, and had been waiting many weeks for a ship to take them home. We had agreed to give them passage. They were black, and proved to be lousy. They were, however, charming fellows, and from what they told us we gathered that the lice were their misfortune rather than their fault. We were able to buy enough sulphur candles to fumigate the mess decks as soon as we got to Colombo, and so the harm they did was not lasting.

We sailed from Mauritius on the 8th February 1942. Singapore fell on the 13th when we were south of Ceylon. As no signal had reached us amending our instructions Commander Hewitt broke wireless silence, and signalled to Colombo for orders. The reply came almost at once. My guess was that our pin had fallen out of the map. We were to go to Colombo. Commander Hewitt and I went to call on Commander-in-Chief, East Indies, Admiral Arbuthnot. Hewitt found himself immediately taken out of his ship, and given a station appointment to a sloop whose captain was sick. He went off at once to pack his things. His own First Lieutenant was put in command of the *Aster*. Once again I was left to deal with a base which had never heard of corvettes, and had no time to spare to come and see for themselves. The staff which had been adequate in the old days was quite unable to cope, if only numerically, with the many big new problems forced upon it. On entering the harbour we had been instructed to secure ourselves in berths which were only suitable for a ship half our size – indeed we should have been aground before we even got to them. They would treat us as trawlers or what was almost worse, would give us jobs beyond our capacity. A complete new staff was on its way from England, but they were not expected until May. In the meantime, the few officers shouldered fantastic burdens, and did the best they could.

Once again I was begging for boiler-cleans; but the ships must run till they burst. During March the Jap carrier force, which had done the damage at Pearl Harbour, appeared south of Java, and in the first week of April they struck at a convoy coming down from Calcutta; and ever since we had been there they kept a submarine at sea off the coast of Ceylon. Our job was to escort convoys from Trincomalee on the east coast, round the southern tip of Ceylon to Colombo, and thence up to Bombay. For this and the many special escort jobs I had only the four corvettes and a little Greek destroyer.

The *Aetos* was a marvellous little ship. At a distance she looked like a modern 'D Class' destroyer; but she was really only a tiny model of one, and displaced little more than 600 tons. She had been built before the first world war and modernized between the wars by Samuel White of Cowes. She was absolutely full of fight, and I had great difficulty with her one night coming southward from Trincomalee when we came across a Jap cruiser. She badly wanted to go in and fight, but we were escorting a very valuable oil tanker which was to fuel our battleships at Addu Atoll. I knew that no other oil was immediately available, and therefore refused *Aetos*' request. Hastily steaming inshore we sought the shelter of the dark hills, while *Verbena* kept between the cruiser and the tanker and made white smoke.

We took our charge to Addu Atoll, which is a wonderful picturebook coral atoll about six hundred miles south-west of Colombo. The four 'R Class' battleships arrived, and while they fuelled from the tanker *Aetos* and *Verbena* kept asdic watch outside the entrance. Round the atoll we experienced the most fantastic ocean currents, and it was nothing to be swept twenty miles off our patrol line between the evening star sight and the morning one. The 'R Class' battleships then left for Mombasa. That was the best place for them, as they were far too old to be used against the Jap aircraft carrier force.

We got back to Colombo just three days before Easter 1942, and were told to prepare ourselves for a boiler clean. Half the ship's company were sent up to the rest camp in the hills. The boilers were opened up on the Saturday night, and I went ashore to enjoy an evening with friends. We had been very fortunate to reach Colombo before the war got too big for the local population to cope with. There was still a hospitality committee when we first arrived, and we had been given introductions and already had friends ashore. Later Colombo was flooded with naval officers, and the small white colony then rather drew into its shell.

In the middle of a very pleasant dinner I was called to the telephone. It was my yeoman Newnes speaking. There was a general recall. Excusing myself I jumped into a rickshaw and was soon aboard. Newnes showed me the signal. 'Anticipate attack by airborne carrier force a.m. tomorrow. All ships should be prepared to counter possible sea-borne attack.'

It was not much later than nine o'clock. I mustered all the ship's company left aboard, and we spent two hours exercising action stations. We had not enough men for the ammunition supply parties, so we brought up as much ammunition as we thought necessary and stowed it near the guns. The attack would be short and sharp anyway. Then, as the ship was not berthed parallel with the harbour wall, we laid out a warp so that we would be able to haul her round and allow the 4-inch gun to cover the sea approach. I went to sleep in my seaberth on the bridge.

At six o'clock we went to action stations, and then sent the men to breakfast in the galley, four at a time. Nothing happened. The sun rose and a great bank of cloud lay to the south of the town. It was this cloud which interfered with the radar defences. At 8.15 we got a general signal from the tower saying that the ship's companies could be sent to breakfast. Newnes showed me the signal. 'We've had our breakfast, Newnes. The men are quite happy, so we'll stay as we are for a bit longer; but I'm going down to get myself a book from my cabin.'

I was half-way down the second ladder when both the bridge Oerlikons and the four-barrel heavy machine gun began firing. By the time I got back to the bridge it was all over, but I did just see the bullets from the port Oerlikon going straight into the nose of Jap plane. We claimed three shot down. The Jap planes came out of that cloud in sections of three planes each. Each section chose a target, and attacked it from three separate directions.

We looked round the anchorage. The *Hector*, an armed merchant cruiser, was on fire. A bomb had exploded inside the depot ship *Lucia*. An 'S Class' destroyer was under water, with only her funnels and bridge showing, and a fleet auxiliary was on her side. We were the only warship in harbour still afloat. The multiple machine gun was manned by its own gunlayer. One bridge Oerlikon was manned by signalman Reeves, and the other by an asdic rating. Each of our attackers took it full on the nose. Two ended up in the sea, and one outside the Galle Face Hotel.

We made a signal reporting three enemy aircraft destroyed, and as we had nothing better to do we stayed at action stations, in case the enemy should return. An hour later the signal tower was calling us. I had expected a congratulatory signal. What I got was, 'Why have I not received your return of church parties for Sunday, 29th March?'

Newnes' remarks almost burnt up the signal lamp. On the previous Sunday we had been playing 'tick' with the Jap cruiser.

'No – you're wrong yeoman,' I told him. 'Don't you see it's the most wonderful signal in the world? It's just the same as those little notices we've seen stuck on the bombed shops at home. It means "business as usual". It's quite true I haven't sent the ruddy form, and I ought to have done so.'

The ensuing scramble on the part of the population had to be seen to be believed. It was estimated that the crowd outside the railway station was over a hundred thousand. The Singhalese were not going to stay if the Japs got busy. They ran for the mountains; but rice was rationed, and their ration cards could only be cashed in their own home town. Hunger, and relations indignant at sharing their rice, drove them slowly back to Colombo.

On that same Easter Day the *Dorsetshire* and *Cornwall* were intercepted by the Jap striking force and sunk south of Ceylon. Four days later the aircraft carrier *Hermes* and one of our corvettes the *Hollyhock*, who was her anti-submarine escort, were sunk together off Trincomalee with very heavy loss of life. *Hermes* had been in Simonstown with us in January, and we knew her officers well. We were particularly 'chummy' ships with the *Hollyhock* whose commanding officer, Lieutenant-Commander T. E. Davies R.N.R., had been a very good friend of mine.

Those of our crew who were in the rest camp were sent down to us, and we were told to close up the still uncleaned boilers and raise steam immediately. The same night the quartermaster came down to my cabin, where I was having a talk with my new First Lieutenant, and told us that a barge had drifted alongside. That night Colombo harbour was full of strange things. I was just about to tell the quartermaster to give it a push and get rid of it, when my new officer suggested we look inside it first. We did. Under the cover were Oelikon guns. We turned out the ship's company, and we had two of those hoisted aboard within half an hour. Then we gave the barge a push and sent it clear of us. We had only two breast drills to pierce the necessary holes in the steel deck and they blunted very quickly. Every man in the ship, officers included, took a fifteen minute spell on the drills and we had those two guns bolted down by sunrise. After a lick of paint no one would know that they had not been there for months. We now needed ammunition for our new trophies, and as the chief had reported steam available for the engines we took the ship over to the ammunition store. There was still a considerable panic ashore, and we filled ourselves up with ammunition for the asking. We even had it stowed in my cabin and under the wardroom table.

The new Number One whom I have just introduced had come to me through a 'station appointment'. He had been at Singapore when it fell. If the reader blames us for thieving, he should hear the tales of the Singapore disaster; how after using the ammunition to the last round they were unable to draw any more, although there was plenty in the Fortress. Riches did not intend the same thing to happen twice in a lifetime if he could prevent it.

He was quite a different type of man to his immediate predecessor. Before the war he had been in business in Singapore, and was used to the East. He was a Lieutenant in the Singapore Division of the R.N.V.R., and was well grounded in service customs. He was a real go-getter, and knew just how to go about the East getting things. As a matter of fact that was the one point on which we did not quite see eye to eye. His limit of how far it was allowable to go in order to get something for the ship was considerably in advance even of mine. He acquired a real motor boat from Bombay Dockyard by means which can only be described as dubious; but perhaps he reached his high water mark of devilry a week or two later.

I had always disliked the plain iron hand-rails on the ladders leading from the wardoom to the flat where my cabin was, and thence upward to the deck. We had tried to cover them with canvas on which neat 'turks-heads' had been worked, but there was too much traffic up and down those ladders for the canvas to last. I had often asked various bases for teak rails to be fitted, but always without result.

At this particular time we were lying in Bombay outside the big fleet destroyer *Nubian* (Commander D. E. Holland-Martin R.N.) I came aboard one night, and as I was passing over her deck the captain met me and asked me into his cabin for a drink. There amongst other things he talked about the awful thieving that went on in the dockyard.

'Damn it, Rayner, this afternoon my First Lieutenant put the new teak accommodation ladder ashore right alongside the ship – within full view of my quartermasters; and do you know it's gone – and no one knows where or how? It's just been spirited away, and the dockyard can't make me another in time.'

Naturally I expressed my sorrow at this disaster, because I knew how terribly difficult it was to get anything nice for your ship in war time.

It was dark when I crossed over to *Verbena*. As I went in through the blackout screen, I put out my hand to grasp the well-known iron rail – but my fingers closed on substantial wood. I struck a match, and there was a teak rail. I looked upward at the other ladder. It too had miraculously grown a similar rail since tea time. The match burnt my fingers.

'Number One,' I called out to the dimly lit flat below, 'Come out you bloody thief.'

He came out grinning and stood looking up at me.

'Number One, I presume that these are all that are mortal of *Nubian's* new accommodation ladder.'

'That's right, Sir – very careless ship that, Sir. Leaves her gear all over the jetty.'

'Careless or not, her captain's coming to drink with me tomorrow night.'

'That's fine, Sir,' (he sounded really pleased). 'He's never been aboard us before. He'll not know, Sir.'

'Perhaps not – but it's devilish awkward for me. I wish you'd learn where to stop.'

I started for my cabin, and then curiosity got the better of me. I went back.

'How did you do it?'

'I gave some Indian "dockyard maties" a couple of tins of tobacco. They picked it up quite easily as if they were taking it away, put it on a barge and brought it round to our starboard side.'

An over-zealous First Lieutenant can be a nightmare, but he did my ship a power of good; for he was a first-class officer, and the men liked him.

We did not get our boiler-clean at Colombo after all. We went to sea again to take a convoy round to Trincomalee with three thousand hours on our boilers. On the way back to Colombo we received a signal.

'Embark one hundred sheep, one hundred goats for Addu Atoll.'

The First Lieutenant looked at it dubiously. I laughed.

'Don't worry it can't mean what it says. It's some silly code. Sheep for soldiers, goats for marines. They can't really be turning us into a Noah's Ark.'

But they were. Apparently units of the Indian Army had been put on the island with anti-aircraft guns. Being Mohammedan they needed fresh killed meat. We delivered the goods, but we stank to high heaven.

A fortnight later we were taking a convoy up to Karachi.

It was a big convoy, and for once we had one of the other corvettes, the *Heliotrope* with us.

Passing Bombay the engineer came on the bridge. Sorry Sir, I've had to draw the fire in Number 2 boiler. The water's running out of the firebox doors.'

'What is it, chief? Tubes gone?'

'Araid so, Sir.'

I made a signal to *Heliotrope.*

'Take over convoy; I have serious boiler defect and must go into Bombay.'

It was quite impossible to keep up with the convoy on only one boiler. It was the constant high speed work as much as the lack of boiler cleaning which had proved *Verbena's* undoing.

We limped into Bombay. As we manoeuvred the ship to go alongside the jetty in the Naval dockyard the telephone from the engine-room rang on the bridge. I picked up the hand-set. The engineer was telling me that the other boiler had gone too, and that he must stop the engines. 'Just five minutes, chief,' I begged.

'I dur's'n't, Sir.'

'All right we'll anchor.'

I leant over the fore side of the bridge.

'Number One, I'm going to anchor. The chief's bust his second kettle.'

I never handled *Verbena* again. We were towed the remaining two hundred yards.

Examination proved that we needed eight hundred and sixty-four new tubes. They could not be made in India, but must be shipped out from home. The first consignment was in a ship that was torpedoed. We put into Bombay in May, and in August we were still there. My lovely *Verbena* was only an anti-aircraft guard-ship lying off the Taj Mahal Hotel.

I did not waste my time. I arranged as well as I could for the comfort of the men. We kept two-thirds of the ship's company up country in a rest camp, and one-third aboard. I took leave as often as I could. I explored India from the jungles south of Belgaum, through the fantastic Mount Abu that rises sheer from the plain of Rajputana, to the North-West Frontier where I made a trip of two hundred miles on horseback into the Harboi hills; and I stayed at Kalat as a guest of the Khan. There, as I was the first naval officer ever to visit Kalat, I was pressed into inspecting the whole of the Kalat state force – all 2,000 of them. I arrived on the parade ground after a ride of some thirty miles on a lovely chestnut mare wearing my number one white uniform, which by the grace of heaven I had with me, and surrounded by an escort of hill tribesmen on their ponies. It was magnificent fun – but it was not war.

I longed for the North Atlantic convoys, and there was still no news of *Verbena's* boiler tubes.

The trouncing which the United States Navy had given to the Jap aircraft carrier force at the Battle of Midway Island in June 1942, had removed the threat to India of a sea-borne invasion direct from Rangoon and Singapore across to the Madras coast. The Japanese U-Boats were obviously of very inferior calibre to the German craft, and had shown a very different spirit to that of the Jap airmen. As there could be no general advance into the eastern Indian Ocean until Germany had been dealt with, it was plain to me that advancement in any chosen anti-submarine profession could only come from service in the Western Approaches.

A chest complaint could turn to anything, and as the doctors wanted to invalid me home, I allowed them to do so. I stepped on board a troopship early in September 1942.

The ship docked in Liverpool on Christmas Eve. I went straight home, and then immediately after Christmas up to London to see the Admiralty. To my surprise I was asked if I could handle a destroyer. Naturally I said that I could, and I walked out of the Admiralty with an appointment to command the 'S Class' destroyer *Shikari*. I could hardly believe my own senses, for I was the first R.N.V.R. in the history of the Navy to be appointed to a destroyer.

I went back to Liverpool to call on the new Commander-in-Chief, Western Approaches, Admiral Max Horton. I had heard all sorts of things about this new Admiral. Some people swore by him, other people swore at him.

It is impossible to be a very efficient senior officer, and at the same time to be universally popular. The actions which such officers must take for the good of the service will almost certainly cause trouble and heartburning to a number of perfectly decent human beings, who do not happen to measure up to their standards of super-efficiency; and to climb in any service sometimes involves treading on the toes of one's contemporaries. It is enough that Max Horton's own staff regarded him as something less than God but more than Man. If they had not done so they would have found themselves relieved.

The staff that he had built up was very good indeed, for he certainly had a flair for picking men. He had more personal charm than any man I have ever met, but he could be unbelievably cruel to those who fell by the wayside. There is a picture by Goya of a 'Grand Inquisitor' which suggests much the same characteristics. Quite by chance I was later to discover the key to his character. He loved, and I really mean loved, the things which he himself had built; the Northern Patrol Command which he held from the outbreak of war to December 1939; the Submarine Command from January 1940 to November 1942, and the Western Approaches from November 1942 to the end of the war.

These great commands, in all of which he was outstandingly successful, were wife and children to him. Is it too much to suppose that when the last closed down the man himself could no longer live? At any rate he only survived his last command by six years. No one seeing him on the eve of victory would have believed that he would last for such a short time in the retirement that he sought as soon as the Western Approaches ceased to exist.

Max Horton's achievement in Western Approaches was tremendous, but he was more than fortunate in those who had gone before him. He took command at a time when a great many vital reforms initiated by his brilliant, if less well known, predecessors were coming to fruition. By any standards the Western Approaches command was already extremely efficient. Admiral Sir Percy Noble had succeeded in creating a first-class organization before ever Max Horton arrived, and before him Admiral Dunbar-Nasmith had started from nothing to build the broad foundation on which the whole edifice was to rest. It is profitless to venture an opinion as to what the ultimate position would have been if these three great officers had taken over the command in a different sequence. For what it is worth my guess is that the final outcome would have been much the same under any one of them. If I came to know Max Horton better than the other two, it was only because in their day I was very small fry indeed.

There had been great changes in the Western Approaches in the fifteen months that I had been away. All the old Escort Commanders had been replaced by new, for there was a limit to the point to which flesh and blood could be driven. Howard-Johnston was now Anti-U-Boat Officer at the Admiralty, and had been promoted Captain. The new Commander-in-Chief brought in a number of new officers, many of them ex-submariners like himself. His new tactical school, under the direction of Captain H. G. Roberts, R.N., had already set about evolving a general tactical system for dealing with the U-Boats. At this time of the war they were hunting in packs, and had been doing enormous damage if they succeeded in breaking through the escort screen. I believe that Max's secret was no more and no less than this. He saw that some groups whose team work was excellent achieved results, and that others were less effective. Being himself strongly biased towards the offensive, he concluded that it was in the tactics of offensive-defence that success would be gained.

Here we should note that the lack of trained ships would have prevented either of his predecessors from passing from the defensive to the offensive, however much they may have wished to do so. Basically Max's achievement was, with the help of his tactical school, to co-ordinate the best of each group's tactics, and to provide the punch to get his new 'Convoy Instructions' carried out. When he had done this and protected his convoys, he could then organize the destruction of the enemy by creating from the new ships coming forward the Support Groups, whose work reached its zenith in the hands of the greatest of all Escort Group Commanders – Captain F. J. Walker, R.N.

I went to call on Admiral Max Horton. He told me that *Shikari* was in Belfast refitting, and that I was to do a tactical course and join her in a month. He told me also that he was collecting all the 'S Class' destroyers into one fast escort group. Naturally I was interested, for I wondered who the Senior Officer would be. I had opportunity for wondering, because my interview was interrupted by an officer of the Free French Navy. This officer had produced a chart, and there had been a certain amount of leaning over tables looking at it. When he left the Admiral turned to me.

'Rayner, had that man really a revolver in his hip pocket?'

'Yes, Sir,' I answered. 'He obviously hasn't learnt the difference between British and French Admirals.'

The interview continued, and I was kept wondering just when I should take my leave. I can only assume that Max was sizing me up, for when I did see a chance to go he said, as I got up from the chair, 'You realize that you will be Senior Officer of the 21st Escort Group.'

I left him in a complete daze. This was something that was beyond even my wildest dreams. I would have not one 'S Class' destroyer, but all six under my command. I could see them already – six long pencils of ships – the bow waves level with the fo's'cle as they manoeuvred at speed. I tried them in line abreast, and I tried them in line ahead. They looked wonderful whichever way I tried to see them. I fell down the stairs on the way out, and was picked up by an astonished Wren officer who obviously thought that I was drunk.

CHAPTER 6

SHIKARI AND THE ROSEGARDEN

I joined *Shikari* in Belfast. She was lying in the dry dock, the beautiful hull a delight to the eye. Before going aboard I walked around her admiring the cunning of the draughts-man who put her lines on paper. It was only a pity that she had not been built on a bigger scale, for then she would have been the perfect escort vessel. It appeared to a sea-man's eye that she was carrying far too much gear on the upper deck – as indeed she was; for she had been designed in the first world war as a small fleet destroyer to deal with German torpedo-boats in the North Sea. It had never been intended that she should work in the wilder weather and much bigger waves of the North Atlantic, and certainly her designer had never meant her to carry 110 depth-charges on the upper deck, with all their heavy throwing gear. Looking at her in the graving dock I could see that her present waterline was eighteen inches higher than the designer had planned.

It is almost an inevitable fate that the Navy should ruin the plans of any ship designer. During the comparatively long life of a ship, the weapons she carries are bound to develop and change; but her hull remains the same as when it was built. This is no new problem. Henry VIII had exactly the same trouble with the *Great Harry*, when he had hopelessly over-gunned her. Pepys mentions similar problems, and we find Captain Cochrane in the Napoleonic Wars complaining bitterly that his ship was 'crank' because the Admiralty had replaced his 32-pounder carronades with the new long gun.

The changes in armament nearly always mean added top weight, and so reduce stability. I daresay that there are few commanding officers, at any rate of the smaller ships, who have not on some occasion had their hearts in their mouths for this reason. *Shikari*'s designed metacentric height was eleven inches. This meant that her centre of gravity should have been eleven inches below her centre of buoyancy. I had a stability test taken before we left dock, and found that alterations and additions had reduced the metacentric height to four inches, which was far too little for a ship of her size.

As I was walking round the dock I noticed the officer of the day keeping an eye on me. I could imagine the poor man's feelings, waiting for his new commanding officer and wondering when the fellow was going to come over the gang-plank.

I went aboard. The sub-lieutenant who was officer of the day showed me round. A new after funnel had just been lowered into position by a gigantic crane.

'You lost the funnel overboard?'

'Yes, Sir.'

'Do you often lose a funnel over the side?'

'Not often, Sir – not funnels.'

We went on along the upper deck.

'Where's the motor boat?'

'Don't carry one, Sir.'

'Why ever not?'

'Not worth it, Sir; we lose 'em. N.S.O. got fed up with replacing them, so we have two whalers now instead. We don't often lose both and, you can get whalers off the hook.'

We went on forward.

'What happened to the bridge, Sub?'

'She stuck her nose into a big one and it flattened the Captain's sea cabin – just like that, Sir. Luckily the Captain wasn't in his bunk at the time.'

I agreed.

'We'd have needed a tin-opener to get him out.'

In bad weather I never slept very soundly in that sea cabin.

It appeared that my latest pride and joy was going to be a 'problem child' – and so she turned out to be. A few pertinent questions revealed the astonishing fact that she had not re-commissioned since 1938. At least sixty per cent of the ship's company were long-service ratings, and there were Petty Officers in the ship who had joined her as able seamen. Enquiries as to why this party of old shellbacks remained year after year in an old, not too seaworthy and terribly congested ship (for the asdic, radar, and depthcharge crews added nearly forty men to the number for which the messdecks had been designed) elicited the opinion that the men liked her because she spent so much time in harbour having weather damage repaired! Such a reason for staying in an uncomfortable ship did not sound too promising from my point of view. As Senior Officer of the group it was absolutely essential for the ship to go to sea whenever she was ordered to do so. The attitude of the officers and the ship's company can make a great difference in this respect. Defects of a marginal nature can either be overstated or understated. In war time in the Western Approaches the commanding officers had a good deal of control over this problem. I had always taken the view that even a half efficient escort was better than no escort at all.

Her First Lieutenant came back from leave that night. It was my first experience of having regular officers of the Royal Navy serving under me, and I was disappointed in the extreme when he appeared to be of the opinion that *Shikari* was a good appointment because one got so much leave. The next day I took a car from Belfast Naval Base and motored the sixty odd miles to Londonderry to see the new Commodore (D). If *Shikari's* views were to be altered I wanted a First Lieutenant whose outlook was the same as mine.

To ask for a new First Lieutenant on a first call on your new Flag Officer is not an easy matter. It is never an easy matter. However great your justification in your own eyes, there is the danger that you may be damning yourself as one of those men with whom it is impossible to get on. I had never met Commodore G. W. G. Simpson, and had no idea what I should find.

I was fortunate. I found a sympathetic ear, and as a result three days later a new First Lieutenant arrived aboard – Lieutenant G. Blackwood, R.N. There was never any question about him from the moment his stocky figure appeared in my cabin. He was a terrific worker, a first class seaman and came from a family which had the Navy in its blood for generations. Nelson had a Captain Blackwood amongst his 'band of brothers' and if he was anything like our 'Blacky' I am sure his ship was both happy and efficient.

All the time we had her *Shikari* went to sea exactly when she was ordered to do so. It was true that on one occasion she nearly let us down when the dynamo failed to 'excite'. It went round and round perfectly, but no current came from it. The base engineer officers were called in and a galaxy of talent was fiddling with the machine, trying this and that. I joined the party in the engine-room to ask how much longer they would be. When I got a vague reply I remembered the old stoker's precept for dealing with recalcitrant machinery 'Give it one with the sledge, mate'. So I picked up a heavy hammer and gave that dynamo three sharp blows. Immediately it sprang to 'life' and we sailed on time.

We left Belfast for Londonderry at the end of February. Twenty thousand horse-power in two steam turbines was a joy to handle after *Verbena*'s twelve hundred horse-power.

We went down Belfast Lough at ten knots, with the engines turning at one hundred revolutions each minute. As soon as we were at sea I rang down for two hundred and thirty revolutions and was amazed at the way she leapt forward. The powerful engines seemed to thrust the very deck from under my feet.

It was blowing hard from the north-west, but the sea was calm under the land; and even when we got to Rathlin Island sound the wind and tide were going the same way, so that the seas were remarkably small.

On our way round we took in a signal from the Commander-in-Chief, Western Approaches, 'Fuel at Moville and proceed to a position 200 miles south-west of Iceland where a tank-landing craft with survivors has been reported by aircraft.' The position was about five hundred miles from the north-west corner of Scotland.

Moville was the name of the anchorage at the seaward

137

end of the River Foyle, which leads to Londonderry. The tide was approaching the turn as we neared the oiler, and the strong westerly wind had swung her stern towards the shallow sandbank on the east side. There was barely room to turn up to the oiler and, to make matters worse, I had to berth on her downtide side. Finally, and just to round off the problem, a destroyer was already lying alongside, and her commanding officer was *Shikari*'s previous captain.

As I made my approach I could see the new commanding officer of the *Duncan* leaning over his rail, watching his old ship approach. To the uninitiated bringing a ship alongside in a sluicing tide often appears far more difficult than it is. So long as the tide is steady and flowing parallel with the jetty or stage it is a simple matter, because one has plenty of steerage way even though the speed of the ship over the ground is small. *Shikari* with two propellers and her enormous horse-power was much easier to handle than the single-screw *Verbena*.

After fuelling we got away to sea just as it was getting dark. It was blowing nearly a full gale from the west, and there was a big sea running. I was at once reminded of what I had thought when I first saw her in dry dock. She was terribly wet, and her motion, on a course that was forty-five degrees from the direction of the waves, was awful. She was just not big enough for the weight she was being asked to carry. Head-on to the sea she did very well; and beam-on to it she rode quite nicely, even if she rolled like a log. It was obvious that humouring her would greatly reduce the weather damage she would suffer.

My course to the position of the aircraft's report was north-west, and that was the course she did not like. If I went up through the Minches where I could use my speed, and then went out into the Atlantic, I would be going a long way round but I would get there faster. Our course from the Butt of Lewis to our destination would then be almost straight into the sea.

So up through the Minches we went, doing twenty-five knots in the smooth water inside the Hebrides. The sensation of power was terrific. She vibrated all the time like a live thing. I began to forgive her for her failings and I was reminded of the remark of that great horse-lover John Jorrocks, 'Be to their faults a little blind and to their failures ever kind.'

I made a signal to Commander-in-Chief, Western Approaches, to tell him what I was doing and got back the reply, 'Is your journey really necessary?' To that I answered, 'For the continuance of my funnels, yes.'

We shot round the Butt of Lewis before dawn, and had to reduce speed to fifteen knots. All that day we ploughed into the lonely green waves that rolled out of the west beneath a heavy layer of grey cloud. After the hard light and the brilliant, sun-flecked waves of the Indian Ocean, I felt at home once more. This was the Western Approaches, and it was here that the U-Boat battle was being fought and won. It was not a great fleet action like Jutland or Trafalgar. It could not suddenly produce spectacular results as happened after the battle of Midway. It was a long, cold, hard death-grapple, fought against the most cunning of all enemies, under an almost continuous waterfall of salt spray. I still do not think that the nation realizes what went on in those vast wastes of sea when, from mess decks in which six inches of water washed from side to side as the ship rolled, the watch would come on deck in wet clothing only to go back at the end of four weary hours wetter still – and like as not find that their dinner had been flung from their mess table. Nor were the officers in better case. The Navy has always stowed its officers aft, and to get forward to the bridge to stand their watch they had to cross the long slippery length of the destroyer's main deck, across which the seas would often be swirling two or three feet deep. True, life lines were always rigged and if one kept a tight grasp on them one was unlikely to be washed overboard. It was not however good to start a watch soaked to the skin. Yet even in such conditions a ship was always ready to attack a U-Boat, or to rescue survivors.

I was the only man in the ship who had a fair chance of staying dry. I had a sea cabin – a small slit just big enough for a bunk – under the bridge, and from it I could get directly up to the bridge. I only got wet if I could not duck my head quickly enough when she put her nose into a sea and sent the spray flying in sheets over the bridge. As I did not leave the bridge at sea, all my food had to be carried along the upper deck by my poor steward in a sling made from a dish-cloth held at the four corners. It could be quite exciting to see it coming. Coming? – would he? – he's going to be caught – he has been. Damn! there goes my lunch!

At dawn the next day we reached the eastern edge of the area of sea I intended to search. It was then forty-eight hours since the aircraft had reported the tank-landing craft. Assuming that such a machine – for it can hardly be called a ship – would blow down wind at four knots, I had reckoned its position to be no less than 192 miles from the place in which it had been reported. I had been told that aircraft from Iceland would co-operate, but I had heard nothing from them; nor was I surprised, for they could hardly have flown in that weather, or seen anything if they had done so.

I started the search on a line two hundred miles from the sighting position. It was like looking for a needle in a haystack. The only thing in our favour was that the wind had remained steady for the past two days. On the second leg of the thirty mile zig-zag which I had plotted, and at ten o'clock in the forenoon watch, a look-out raised the cry 'Submarine on the surface!'

At first glance his report seemed to be correct, and I hastily pressed the alarm bell for action stations. Through my binoculars I could see the object plainly. It certainly had the characteristic outline of a U-Boat – the long bow parallel with the water, and the conning tower. But it rode the seas too buoyantly. Whatever it was it was no U-Boat. I realized that it was the tank-landing craft!

We closed it rapidly, but could make out no sign of life. As we got closer we could see that it was much smaller than we had expected, and afterwards learnt that it had been part of the deck cargo of a torpedoed American merchant-man. At its after end was the armoured conning tower below which would be its engine. It was closed with a heavy hatch. Before laying off to sink it by gunfire we thought we had best knock on the door by firing at it with a rifle. A very astonished face appeared as the hatch was flung back. We apologized through the loud hailer for disturbing them, and asked if we could be of any assistance. We got them aboard quickly, and then lay off while the gunnery department had a good practice. Then we started for home.

As each 'S Class' destroyer came in from sea she was ordered to join the new 21st Escort Group. Very smart we considered ourselves too, for were we not the fastest group in the Western Ocean? All the other ships were commanded by senior Lieutenants, Royal Navy. They had been put into these craft to learn their trade before taking over the new 'Hunt Class' destroyers which were now coming forward in numbers. We therefore had a strong Navy (as distinct from Western Approaches) bias, and would go everywhere very fast and in close order, carrying out manoeuvres that could not be carried out by the escort groups, because of the wide differences of speed and turning circle between their individual ships. High speed manoeuvres are only safe when all ships have a similar performance. With destroyers, frigates, corvettes and trawlers all serving in the same group one could only carry out the simplest of movements.

As soon as we were formed into a group we were put to work escorting the fast convoys of big troopships which were bringing the American soldiers from their training grounds in Iceland to the build up for D Day in England. It was certainly a fairly responsible job, but as the convoy speed was only fifteen knots we had plenty of excess speed in weather when a submerged attack was probable, and could give the troopships good protection. A surfaced attack on a fifteen knot convoy was not very likely. If a surfaced U-Boat came in from before the beam he would be detected by the radar of one of the escorts, while if he came in abaft the beam his own maximum speed was so little in excess of the convoy's that he would certainly 'lose bearing' (i.e. drop behind) his target and never get into a firing position. For the Senior Officer of the escort these fast convoys were fairly simple, and, as I always had at least four destroyers to escort three troopships, the asdic screen could be really effective. By comparison with an ocean convoy of anything from sixty to a hundred merchantmen our closely packed little party, carrying out a permanent zig-zag would have deterred any but the most determined of U-Boat commanders. We never saw the enemy. Satisfactory it is true, as our job was to deliver the soldiers; but we badly wanted a U-Boat for the group. Often, talking it over in harbour, we would plan methods of enticing one into our net. But we always had our convoy with us, and for weeks we never got an opportunity.

At last our chance came – at least to lay the bait we hoped the fish would take. The group was due to sail on a Saturday with a convoy to Iceland, but when *Shikari* was 'duty destroyer' on the day before, an urgent job took us down to Liverpool. This was no less than the delivery of a new type of German magnetic mine, which someone had discovered when Bizerta fell. It had been rushed home in a frigate, and the wooden box in which it was packed was only to be spoken of in a hushed voice as 'Parcel A'. Unfortunately for us, the frigate had returned home so fast with its precious parcel that her engines had developed a defect, and she had crept into Londonderry. *Shikari* was then told to take the package on to Liverpool. There we could expect to be met by a lorry specially sent from London, with a party of very experienced mine-disposal officers. We duly lashed the beastly box down, and started off gingerly for Liverpool. We had been warned not to shake it, because the mine people in Bizerta only 'thought' that it had been rendered safe. We arrived in Gladstone dock, Liverpool, at one o'clock on the Saturday. Everyone had gone to lunch. When it was time for them to come back we discovered that it was 'Saturday afternoon', and no one knew about 'Parcel A'. Nor did they want to find out about it until Monday morning.

It was, of course, nothing to do with Western Approaches. They knew nothing about the matter at all. It was purely the business of Flag Officer, Liverpool. All Western Approaches wanted was that *Shikari* should go back to her job of escorting as soon as possible. We landed the wretched parcel ourselves, and put it on the dock wall, telling the crane man who had helped us that the case contained the embalmed body of a houri who had been the favourite concubine of the Bey of Tunis.

At last I got through to the Flag Officer himself.

'It's about "Parcel A," Sir.'

'I don't know anything about "Parcel A". What's in it, anyway?'

'It's a mine, Sir, a new German magnetic mine. And no one knows whether it's really safe . . .'

'Where is it now?' he interrupted me.

'On the jetty by the dock gates at Gladstone dock, Sir.'

'Good God! I'll see to it.'

And he did. There was a bomb-disposal lorry alongside within an hour. But *Shikari* had missed her convoy, and we went up alone to join the group in Iceland.

All the U-Boats coming from Germany to work in the North Atlantic, and all the U-Boats at Brest going back to Germany to refit, had to make the passage between the Faroes and Iceland. As we were on our own for once, without a convoy, we decided to bait our trap. In the old days B.12 Group had used barrels of tar to decoy the enemy, and the Naval Store officer at Londonderry had been only too pleased for us to clear what he considered redundant stock. All the other groups were slaughtering U-Boats, and we had never been given a chance. On the way north we prepared our decoy. We buoyed the barrel to make certain it would float and fitted an ignition system to set it alight. On the second night out when we were just about in the right position to find a U-Boat if one were about, we set fire to our toy, and set it adrift. At the same time we fired a few rockets into the air to entice any customers who might be below the horizon. Then we lay off to await results. We watched it burn right out and then as no inquisitive U-Boat appeared, we turned towards Iceland. But we had overlooked the efficiency of Coastal Command. They reported our tar barrel as a ship on fire, but they reported it twenty miles south of where it really was. Commander-in-Chief,

Western Approaches, sent us to investigate, and of course we had to go. As we expected there was nothing there and I had to report, 'Reference aircraft report, nothing found, suspect it was tar barrel fired by me in position——.'

On our return to Londonderry I was told to go over to Liverpool to see the Commander-in-Chief.

I must admit that I was frightened. Max had a certain reputation.

As I was ushered into his office he looked up from the pile of reports on his desk.

'What the hell do you think you are doing setting my ocean on fire, Rayner?'

'Trying to catch some flaming U-Boats for you, Sir.'

He grunted and getting up from his desk led me into the big operations room.

'See that bit of sea between the Faroes and Iceland, where the minefields are? The Germans call that the Rosegarden. All deep mines there. Coastal Command are putting the U-Boats down. We hoped the mines would catch them, but they don't – at least not often enough. I'm going to put your group in the Faroes. When the 'Met' people say it's going to be fine, you'll stay at sea on patrol. When the weather's bad you'll lay in Halfiord at two hours' notice. As soon as there's a sighting report you'll go to the position at full speed and sink the U-Boat. Coastal Command damage more than they sink. Captain Walker's doing wonders on that system – you can do the same. Commander-in-Chief, Home Fleet, will provide three fleet destroyers to help, and I'm basing the 10th Escort Group on Iceland to support you that end. You've the same chance as Walker.'

'Not quite, Sir.'

'What do you mean, "not quite?"'

'The weather, Sir – it's terrible. Captain Walker has got smoother water and wonderful air co-operation, and he picks them up much nearer to the coast of France than I can get to the coast of Norway. But I'm terribly grateful for the chance, Sir.'

'Don't forget I commanded the Northern Patrol. I know

all about the weather there. Do your best.' He led the way back to his own office.

'That's all I can promise you, Sir.'

As I was going I said, 'I hope, Sir, that the three fleet destroyers will be picked with regard to my seniority.'

He looked at me. 'You can leave that to me. You've one more trip to Iceland, haven't you?'

'Yes, Sir.'

We took a convoy to Iceland and were lying in Reykjavik waiting for the merchantmen to load their cargoes of soldiers. As usual in that harbour the fish were plentiful, and the sailors were fishing over the side for a 'fry' for tea.

The officers had been discussing the question of fishing over lunch and the gunnery officer had put forward the theory that the proper way to catch fish was to use a demolition charge fired from the surface by an electrical contact and immured in a basket full of fish guts which would act as bait.

So as not to spoil the sailors' fishing the officers took the motor boat some distance away from the ship. The charge was now in the wardroom waste paper basket, and securely packed with fish guts. I had insisted on carrying a motor boat in *Shikari*, not only because it was necessary for me to visit the other ships of the group, but because I felt that now we were all 'S' boats together the chances of looking after them in heavy weather were better. They would no longer be at the beck and call of a Senior Officer of an ocean escort group who was probably in a larger and very much more modern destroyer.

When the motor boat had gone some distance from the ship, we lowered our noisome basket over the side. We were just about to 'touch it off' when someone, I think it was the doctor, noticed that *Shikari* was flying the motor boat's pennants, indicating that she was recalled. Glancing towards the ship, and cursing the luck that had interfered with our fishing, we could see much activity on the upper deck. Then a signalman jumped on to the top of the bridge and began to semaphore.

'Number One, read it if you will, while I fire this basket

of guts. Guns,' – addressing the gunnery officer – 'what do I do? Touch this end on the battery?'

'Yes, Sir.'

I did so. There was a muffled explosion below the surface, anxious faces peered over the side. For a moment nothing happened then, with a hurrush, a hugh bubble broke surface – bringing back the fish guts.

Four filthy faces were raised to the First Lieutenant who was still reading the signal from the destroyer, and the doctor was desperately trying to catch the one small dab which was all we had to show for the officers' fishing party.

'Well, Blacky,' I asked as I washed my face with water, 'what is it this time?'

'You've been promoted. Half-yearly promotions, Sir.'

'Promoted what?'

'I presume Commander, Sir.'

'Nonsense I'm only thirty-five. Even if I was R.N. I'd still have to serve another year before I would be in the zone; and as far as the R.N.V.R.'s concerned there's a very small establishment of Commanders and I haven't heard of any of them dying. If it's the half-yearly promotions it can't be acting rank.'

We got the motor going and the doctor having retrieved his fish we went back to the ship. The ship's company started to cheer as we came alongside – filthy and dirty, and with only our one small fish. But it was true. The seniority problem for Operation Rosegarden had been solved, for it was most unlikely that the Commander-in-Chief, Home Fleet, would detach a flotilla leader carrying a commander for such an operation.

A little more than a month later I was sitting in the heather on a shoulder between two mountains in the Faroes. Below me the fiord, never more than three-quarters of a mile wide, stretched its six-mile length. The half which was to the south shimmered golden with the reflection of the midday sun. The northern half was vividly blue, and reflected the brilliantly clear northern sky. There was absolutely no sound but the wind in the heather; for as usual it was blowing hard. Every now and then a cumulus cloud, torn by the north-west gale would flick over the mountains on the other side of the fiord, and drift in long streamers across the sky, throwing bars of shadow on the water below.

Far below me my ships lay at anchor. *Shikari* was at the head of the line, then the three fleet destroyers, *Meteor*, *Oribi*, *Opportune*, followed by the remainder of the 'S Class' *Sardonyx*, *Sabre*, *Saladin*, *Scimitar*. These were the eight destroyers taking part in Operation Rosegarden. Probably nearly one thousand eight hundred men – what a command! But my heart was heavy. Operation Rosegarden was a failure, and it was my duty to tell the Commander-in-Chief, Western Approaches, that no further effort should be wasted upon it. I had climbed the mountain the better to find the seclusion I needed. The weather had beaten us, not the enemy. How to tell the Admiral that I had failed? Before getting out the pencil and paper to draft my letter, I lit a pipe and allowed myself to think over the events of the last few weeks.

Three weeks ago we had entered Halfiord, five destroyers slipping confidently into harbour, sure that they could do the job that had been given to them.

As we swept in line ahead through the narrow entrance we could see the three fleet destroyers already lying at anchor, and my yeoman of signals was bending on a small blue and white flag. This was a flag, or more correctly a burgee, not normally used in the Western Approaches. It brought back nostalgic memories of pre-war training, when the sea had been all fun, and U-Boats did not lurk within its clean waters.

'What's that you've got, Yeoman?' I had asked.

'Senior Officer's pennant, Sir.'

'But you know we don't use that in the Western Approaches.'

'The "fleets" won't know that, Sir. Made it myself last night, seeing we haven't one aboard.'

'All right, Yeoman, we'll wear it while we're here.'

It made me think. The 'fleets' would not know that in the Western Approaches it was usual to allow ships to anchor independently. Not only were our anchorages so crowded that only rarely could a clear enough stretch of water be found for a whole group in line ahead, but the different size of ship, and their different anchors and cables, made it a rather hazardous operation. In addition there was a technical reason against anchoring as a flotilla, because when the anchors were let go simultaneously the ships would still have a little headway on them, and the cable running out might have caught the delicate dome in which the asdic was housed. Unlike the frigates, corvettes, and trawlers, the destroyers could haul the asdic machine within the hull. With our retractable domes there was no reason why we should not anchor as a flotilla, so long as our domes were housed.

'Yeoman, I'll anchor the group as a flotilla. Pass it down the line, and tell them to check that their domes are up. Better send the bosun's mate to get another signalman on the bridge. You'll need him.'

Soon the bright coloured flags were climbing up to our yardarm – the signal on ours, the answering pennants on the ships astern. In addition to the anchoring signals, the signalmen were busy with equal speed signals, telling the ships astern *Shikari*'s speed, so that they would keep perfect station. We swept round and approached our chosen anchorage. Slow now. Hardly a ripple spread from our bows. Stop engines. It was strange how quiet everything seemed. There was only the steady hum of the big fans that supplied air to the boiler-rooms, and to that one was so accustomed that it remained unheard. At a sign from me the signal flags dropped to the deck, and five anchors fell simultaneously into the deep, clear water.

'Yeoman, make a signal to *Meteor* and ask her how tall her Captain is.'

Reply : 'About six foot.'

'May I borrow your cabin for conference? Headroom in mine is only five foot nine inches below the beams.'

'With pleasure and relief.'

That day was the last which had given me any pleasure. The very next day had come our first aircraft sighting report of a U-Boat, and as we had ourselves intercepted the aircraft's report *Shikari* had led the group to sea even before we had received the signal from Commander-in-Chief, Western Approaches. In the smooth water under the land we had been steaming at twenty-five knots. Astern of *Shikari* was *Meteor*, looking to our eyes enormously big. Rounding the headland *Shikari* almost drowned herself in the first wave from the open Atlantic. We had to reduce speed immediately, fearful lest the *Meteor* should run into us. But she too was easing down already. As she lolloped over a big wave, I could see her keel plates almost as far aft as her bridge. The eight destroyers, which a moment before had been a compact orderly force in perfect station, were now spread out. Their masts swayed dizzily as they rolled and plunged, throwing sheets of solid water over their backs. When they were in the troughs of the waves you could only see their masts, and perhaps the top of a bridge and the funnels. Then suddenly they would climb into view, dragging themselves from the sea until their whole fore part was as naked as in dry dock, and solid water poured from their decks in arched lines of foam.

The position where the aircraft had sighted the U-Boat was a hundred miles away. We should have been there within five hours from the aircraft's signal, and we could still hear him homing us on to him with his wireless. It took us twelve hours to get there. I had told the 'fleets' to go on and leave us to follow, but they could go no faster than we could. After six hours the aircraft could stay no longer. We had searched fruitlessly for twenty-four hours in a gale, and then returned to Halfiord.

And so it had gone on; or rather it had got worse, because on that first day communications with the aircraft had been quite good, and they were never good again. For some reason wireless communication in that part of the world was deplorably bad.

It had, I thought, best be a personal letter.

'DEAR ADMIRAL HORTON,

'I am very sorry to tell you, Sir, that bad weather and bad communications prevent me obtaining any success with Operation Rosegarden. All I have achieved in three weeks is, in spite of taking the greatest care of them, to reduce all five Western Approaches destroyers to a state where not one of them is seaworthy. I have sent details of weather damage to Commodore (D) Londonderry.

'I have considered transferring to one of the fleet destroyers, leaving Lieutenant Blackwood in command of *Shikari*; but although the big destroyers are more comfortable for the men, they cannot really go much faster than the "S Class". Besides it is our Western Approaches ships that we must get to the enemy. The "fleets" only fire a five charge pattern of depth-charges, they have no heavy charges (for deep U-Boats), and they do not handle well in the heavy seas at hunting speeds.

'The officers of the fleet have given me magnificent co-operation and the "S Class" destroyers have been beyond praise. We have nearly a foot of water in the mess decks every time we go to sea; but never a grumble.

'All this would be more bearable if only the wireless communication were better. There seems to be something peculiar in the atmosphere here. Quite frequently we have been unable to establish wireless contact with an aircraft flying overhead, but must pass messages to it via Iceland. Two days ago we had to ask Quebec (Canada) to pass a message to an aircraft six miles away; and my last signal to you, Sir, was routed via New York, as we could raise no station in U.K.

'It is my considered opinion that with these ships and in the prevailing conditions, the continuance of Operation Rosegarden cannot be justified.

'Naturally I am terribly sorry and disappointed that I must make such a report.'

I put down my pencil and looked at the ships. *Shikari* caught by a different air stream had swung round and, by reason of the drift of her cable, looked out of station and apart from the others. The local soldiers had asked us to co-operate in a field day, and we had landed a number of men from each ship that morning. The boats had just returned and were lying alongside the ships. *Oribi* had taken the opportunity to paint her topsides, and had men over the side on the painting stages.

A sudden roar of powerful engines made me look up. A Heinkel passed over me. As he shot between the hill tops the German plane was so low that I could have hit him with a twelve-bore gun. I could see his nose go down following the slope of the land. Almost at once he was below me going down – going down to the ships. I could tell the exact moment when he made up his mind to attack. His wings dipped as he turned away to give a longer run to his bomb aimer. Now his other wing dipped, and he turned to run in down the line of ships. He would bomb *Shikari* and strafe the others. I prayed and cursed alternately. The decks were crowded with men. As our own ships' radars were useless under the high land, we had been relying on the local radar for air raid warnings. The plane was going in fast. 'Oh God! – Oh *Shikari*! Do something.' It came – dear God it came! First one red ball of a tracer bullet rising from *Shikari*'s port Oerlikon, then a burst. Now the starboard Oerlikon – a steady stream poured from both guns. How slowly the little red dots climbed to meet the black plane! I could see the Hun pull up, as a pheasant will do when a charge of shot passes ahead of it. His bombing run was spoilt. He banked steeply, his wings intensely black against the golden water. A puff of white smoke showed abaft *Shikari*'s after funnel. Oh lovely! Someone had brought the 3-inch high-angle gun into action. The plane was pulling out, it was climbing, turning away, going. Only then the rattle of the first shots reached me. The 'fleets' opened up with their two-pounder pom-poms. A long triangle of scarlet tracer bullets tore after the retreating plane from the whole line of ships. I shall never forget the way the shadow of the plane swept up the mountain on the opposite side of the fiord. He was gone in a burst of gunfire, and then silence dropped like a pall over the lovely scene. But if *Shikari* had not been just in time there would have been men swimming down there, and men dying.

I knelt in the heather and thanked God – and the men who had died in Norway, that we should learn.

So now we were observed. That Hun would certainly have photographed the anchorage. Even if it meant nothing to the pilot, the German staff would see from our camouflage, white and green, that an escort group lay in wait for their U-Boats. Only the Western Approaches groups carried the light camouflage, and it was as definite a sign as writing 'Beware' in white letters on a blue ground. The boats would make the passage of the Rosegarden submerged. Sighting reports would be fewer, and autumn was only just round the corner.

In the month of June Captain Walker had slain three U-Boats off Brest, and in July a further two. In the Rosegarden none had been accounted for. I folded up the letter and put it in my pocket. Then I went down to where the motor boat waited for me.

It was a very peculiar team that had fired *Shikari*'s guns – cooks, sick berth attendant, and a stoker. The stoker had been the gunlayer of the first Oerlikon to open fire. Cookie had rushed out of his galley and laid the 3-inch high-angle. When the proper gunlayer arrived he was very upset to find that pastry had been smeared all over the trigger.

I sent Max Horton my letter. A week later we were withdrawn. The 'fleet' destroyers were ordered to Scapa. *Sardonyx*, *Saladin*, *Sabre* and *Scimitar* were sent to Londonderry to be patched up, and I was ordered to take *Shikari* to Scapa where a plane would be waiting at Hatston to take me to a conference at Rosyth.

It was then August 1943. In the three years since I had left Scapa there had been fantastic changes. Where there had been miles of muddy roads and open fields there were now hard roads and serried ranks of good huts. There were canteens for the men and there was also a giant mess for the officers. A busy town had sprung up in the salty wilderness, and there were even Wrens about on roads where before only the male of the species had been seen.

We berthed alongside the depot ship and I was asked to dine with the Commander-in-Chief, Home Fleet, Admiral

Frazer, in the Flagship H.M.S. *King George V.* Naturally I was considerably put out at the failure of Rosegarden. It would have been bad enough if the news could have been confirmed to my own Western Approaches Command. As it was all the northern Commands, the Home Fleet, and even Rosyth, which had operated some of the aircraft, had been concerned. Admiral Frazer could not have been more kind and sympathetic, and his kindness did much to revive my spirits. At least he understood what we had been up against; and I was sure that our own Admiral would do that too, however disappointed he might be in the result.

The next day I went to Hatston for my aircraft. It was a vile day with visibility not much more than two hundred yards, and in the rain and mist the plane, an Airspeed Oxford, looked a most dreary conveyance. Meeting the pilot in the mess, he told me that he did not want to fly. I could not have agreed more profoundly. We had lunch together instead, but during the meal he was called to the telephone. We were told that we must fly down because very important people were coming up from the Admiralty to meet us.

We climbed reluctantly into the plane, and could see only a little more than half-way down the runway. The pilot turned to me and said that he hoped these very important people would stay up for the funeral. They would lend tone to the proceedings. He then let in the clutch, or whatever you do with an aircraft, and we shot off savagely into the mist.

After a minute of seeing nothing I said to the pilot, 'When do we get off the ground?'

'We are off.'

'Oh.' It did not seem reasonable. I could still see nothing. In quick succession we nearly hit a lighthouse, a ship in the Pentland Firth and then the cliffs of Duncansby Head. This last was too much. I wanted to know why we did not stay at a safe height and go by navigation instead of sight; but apparently there was no navigation equipment other than our eyes. I began to realize why the smaller aircraft were always so unsure of their position, but was not enamoured of the method of learning. We followed the cliff edge all the way down the coast of Inverness-shire, and then along by Nairn to Peterhead.

Peterhead proved a headache because the local barrage-balloon people, who had been told that there was no flying, had got all the balloons up; and we nearly stopped there for ever. However after Aberdeen we ran into clear weather, and landed at Donnibristle just before three o'clock. Here, because there was 'no flying', they had dug a trench across the runway, and we had to hop over it.

After that the conference was rather an anti-climax. There were all sorts of high-ranking officers, and I found myself the only representative of Commander-in-Chief, Home Fleet, and Commander-in-Chief, Western Approaches. I was too tired to be polite, and spoke my mind about what I had been trying to do. No one seemed surprised or to disagree; and that was the end of Operation Rosegarden. I never heard it mentioned again.

It was interesting to see how the theoretically perfect plan had fallen down in practice – particularly in waters which must always be vital to the defence of these islands. If war should come again to Britain it seems certain that submarines will once more be used to cut off our sea-borne supplies; and almost all of them will have to pass through that same Rosegarden. There are only two places where U-Boats can be met with any degree of certainty. One is when they are nibbling at the bait, which is the convoy, and the other is when they are forced to take some particular passage to their base. How to kill in this area was a problem we never solved in the last war. It is to be hoped that improved aircraft co-operation and improved, and much larger, hunting vessels will be available next time.

After the conference I was offered the same aircraft in which to return. I declined hastily, and went back by train and the Scapa Ferry. I am not a birdman.

We rejoined the group in Londonderry, and after our more serious cracks and leaks had been welded up we all sailed to Rothesay at the entrance to the Kyles of Bute, which is the first turning to your left after passing Cumbrae Light on the way up the Clyde.

The British submarine service had been giving a very good account of itself up and down the Mediterranean, particularly in attacks on fast shipping off the Italian coast. The Italians had a number of small high-speed destroyers, and in order to defeat our submarines they had learnt to create a physical barrier around their small convoys.

The torpedo is like the shell in only one way. Both are fired out of a tube. Beyond that the similarity ceases, for the shell travels at hundreds of miles an hour, and does its journey in a time that is measured in seconds. The torpedo on the other hand travels at a speed little more than twice that of a fast merchantman, and its time is reckoned in minutes. The position from which a submarine can launch a successful attack is very restricted. It lies roughly one mile from the target at an angle of forty-five degrees to its course. If destroyers are zig-zagging at very high speed on either bow of the convoy, it is very difficult for the submarine captain to carry out his attack, because he must not only raise his periscope to see the target, but must also do so in order to keep a lookout for the destroyers. The more he raises his periscope the more likely he is to be seen. Our business at Rothesay was to pretend to be Italian destroyers escorting a merchantman, while our young submarine captains learnt their business.

It was a wonderful period from the point of view of ship handling. We would steam up and down Loch Long in close order at thirty knots, by night as well as by day. We learnt to carry out all the usual evolutions, and a lot of new ones especially asked for because the Italians employed them. We achieved a standard of handling rare even in peace time, when the need for economy prohibits continuous steaming at high speed.

We learnt to carry out the most intricate of the zig-zag diagrams together and in close order. We could even maintain a continuous weave. It was exhilarating work, and lovely to the eye, for no more beautiful ships than mine were ever built. The design of the *Hood*, of the heavy cruisers *Hawkins* and *Frobisher* and of the 'S Class' destroyers all came at the same time. These ships represent a period when beauty of line coincided with the dictates of efficiency. In my opinion, no modern ships, with the possible exception of certain destroyers of the immediate pre-war period, were so beautiful; and the later craft lacked the flowing lines of their predecessors, and were less feminine in appearance. The 'S Class' were at their best at high speed. The five bow waves level with, or spread out like wings, above the five fo'c's'les. The ships would lean over in unison as their rudders bit into the water. Sterns would swing in a wide arc, smoothing the crisp curls of the sea to a sheet of satin. Slowly the narrow hulls would right themselves as the ships settled to the new course; and the group would still be in perfect station.

I don't know how we avoided a fatal accident to the submarines we were teaching. There were many narrow escapes, and the danger was a real worry to the commanding officers of the ships; for even if you are only carrying out your instructions it is not pleasant to run down one of your own submarines. The strain began to tell on some of us, and I know that for this reason alone I heartily wished myself elsewhere.

The whole place bore an air of tension, for the depot ship near which we moored when in harbour was the school for these submariners. When we met them we were impressed by the strain to which these young men were being subjected. However well they carried it off, one could see it fixed permanently upon their brows. I suppose each branch of the many services thinks that it carries the brunt of the stress of war. The truth is that it falls on all – not continuously, but shifting first to one branch, then to another. What the airman achieves one day is matched the next by the sailor, and on the day after that by the submariner. Lastly all are saved by the foot-soldier who walks into the enemy country and says to the rest of us 'You can go home now, chaps. We've won.'

We went back to Londonderry for a boiler-clean and I took the opportunity of going to see Max Horton again. It was the first time that I had seen him since Rosegarden closed down. He promised me something better. There

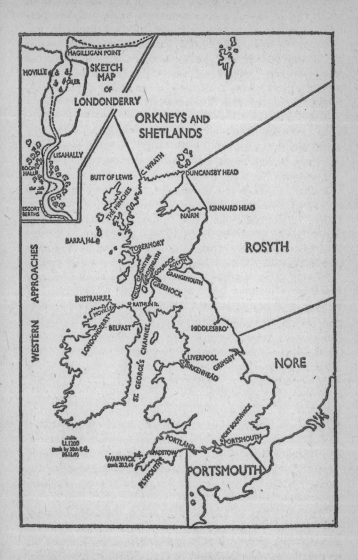

would soon be big changes in the groups, as the new 'Captain Class' frigates were coming across from the American yards and the 'River Class' frigates from our own.

He ended by saying, 'In any case I look upon you as one of the spare Senior Officers. Wherever I may send you temporarily you can be sure of another group of your own one day.'

Before I left the group I was to have the pleasure of welcoming another R.N.V.R. officer, Lieutenant-Commander E. Playne, who had been appointed to *Sardonyx*. I heard also that Lieutenant-Commander Norman Wood (like myself from the Mersey Division) had been given a 'Hunt Class' destroyer. The Volunteer Navy was justifying the faith of those Naval officers who had championed our cause. They had not always been many, for there had always been some who thought that the R.N.V.R. could never be employed afloat, except as junior officers. Fortunately our supporters had been powerful, both in debate and in authority.

I had hardly got back to *Shikari* when I was told to take her round to Grangemouth to dry dock; and when I berthed her there I found a letter appointing me to command of H.M.S. *Warwick* to relieve Commander McCleves R.N.R.

I went down to Liverpool to join the *Warwick* in October 1943.

CHAPTER 7

WARWICK

The destroyer *Warwick* had been Admiral Keyes' flagship on St. George's Day, 1918, at Zeebrugge, and on the wardroom bulkhead was a plaque commemorating her service there. Because of the effect on my life of the reproduction of the attack which I had seen at the Wembley Exhibition, I always felt a special bond of sympathy between the ship and myself. Some people may hold that it is impossible for an inanimate object either to feel sympathy or to possess an atmosphere; but with this I disagree. Admittedly a ship, of herself, can have no human qualities; but the men who have lived in her leave behind them either an aura of happiness or the gloom of unhappiness, either of which becomes as much a part of the ship as her own steel structure. *Warwick* had so happy an atmosphere as to be almost startling. As soon as your foot touched her deck you became aware of it. She radiated a human warmth from the whole of her slim figure.

She was the first ship I had taken over in a state of full efficiency. *Loch Tulla* and *Verbena* had been empty hulls before commissioning, and *Shikari* had been peculiar as far as the crew were concerned. By contrast *Warwick* was a proper ship. Her previous captain, Commander McCleves, was one of the very best of R.N.R.s – and that is high praise indeed. Everything in the ship was as I would have it. She had just returned from ocean escort, and was lying alongside the wall in Gladstone Dock, Liverpool, looking trim and smart. I walked down to the dock, the better to savour the taste of the first encounter with my new command. I know of nothing quite so exciting as the first meeting between a captain and the ship which will be his own as soon as he has climbed the narrow gangway to her deck. So rapidly is the enigma of her character resolved, and by so many little things will he judge her, that by the time he reaches the shore end of the gang-plank he will know a very great deal about her, and will even have hazarded a guess at her seakindliness and how she should be handled.

As our weapons became more and more complicated and numerous it became ever more difficult to house all the new ratings in the older ships. *Shikari*, whose original complement had been just over one hundred men, was carrying one hundred and forty. The *Warwick* originally had called for one hundred and twenty men to fight her; but when I joined her she had one hundred and seventy.

To accommodate this increase she had been converted to an escort destroyer. This had involved taking out the forward funnel and boiler-room. In the lower half of the space thus cleared an additional oil fuel tank had been built to increase her range, and above this was a new mess-deck for the stokers. To make more room in the fo'c's'le, the galley had been brought outside and placed where the forward funnel had been.

This conversion only reduced her speed from thirty to twenty-five knots, and she really would have been a very fine escort vessel if the hull had not been so old and leaky. It might be thought that small leaks would not be very serious, because any water that came in could easily be pumped out again. But a large proportion of a destroyer's bottom is lined with the oil fuel tanks, and a very little sea water in them will so contaminate the fuel that it is extremely difficult to burn.

After *Shikari* my new command seemed immense. For once I could stand upright, my comfort was assured. The Captain's harbour quarters stretched right across the ship, and unlike *Shikari*'s the sleeping cabin was separate from the day cabin. Although I would never see anything of either when the ship was at sea, this would make a great difference to my time in harbour. At sea too I would be much more comfortable for my sea cabin was close enough to the upper bridge to enable me to get there instantly if called. As the whole bridge was much higher than *Shikari*'s I would no longer suffer from the continual slop of water that had always swirled about the floor of my last sea cabin.

As my favourite recreation in harbour was to hold dinner parties, both to repay the hospitality of the many friends I had made, and to enjoy the pleasure of good wine in good company, it was a great boon to have a home that was adequate for entertaining. I had always taken with me my photographs, and some good pictures, and had collected a number of 'objets d'art' in my wanderings. My greatest prize was my collection of old Arab and Persian horse-bits that I had made on my trip to the North-West Frontier of India. Much to the amusement of my 'bearer' I had combed the bazaars of little towns which had not seen a European for years, in search of these trophies. 'And why does the Commander Sahib pay four rupees for a broken old piece like this when he can go to the blacksmith and buy a new one for three? the bearer had asked me; nor did my enthusiasm over an exquisitely worked piece, at least two centuries old convince him.

Because I could never see why fighting a war should make one less appreciative of the better things in life, my steward had orders to keep a constant supply of fresh flowers in the big vases. I took great pride in the appearance of my cabin and even after all my things had been lost with the ship, I never regretted that I had taken them with me. There were of course officers who thought that a spartan simplicity was the proper way of life in war-time. I myself could never see why anyone should make themselves less comfortable than they had to be, nor could I believe that stoicism in any way added to efficiency. Rather did I find that if I made a pleasant home of my cabin the ship's company realized that I wished to make a home of the ship herself. A ship is a strange place, and your sailor the strangest of mortals. Although he himself is forbidden to take alcohol aboard, or to have lady visitors except on special occasions, there is nothing he likes better than to see his officers having a party – so long as it is kept within bounds. The sailor at heart is a prude. So far you may go, and he will spare no trouble to see that your guests enjoy themselves; but if a party is allowed to go too far there will be serious trouble at once. If you invite no friends aboard and live like a recluse, he will think that you are unnatural and be unhappy because of it. He wants you to behave as you would in your own house and with your own family.

Commander Y. McCleves, D.S.O., D.S.C., R.D., had been of the original Unit Commanders. He had graduated, as I had done, through command of his own group to a corvette, and then to the *Warwick*. Out of all the original Unit and Group Commanders there were now only two left in the Western Ocean, Commander Wemyss, R.N., then serving in the *Wild Goose*, and myself.

I found that *Warwick* was due for refit, and was only waiting for a signal to tell her where she could be dry-docked. In a day or two came the order for us to sail for Grimsby, and at the same time a telephone message from the Chief of Staff to Commander-in-Chief, Western

Approaches, calling for me to see him. He told me that the Tactical School had just put forward a theory that each group should have two senior officers – one on the bridge of the group leader and the other down in the plot. As soon as I had seen *Warwick* safely into the dockyard hands at Grimsby he wanted me to join Commander R. C. Boyle, R.N., in the destroyer *Havelock*, and to make a trip with him to Newfoundland and back. If I would go he wanted both of us to make a report on how the idea worked in practice. Commander Boyle was the senior officer of my own B.5 group, but because *Warwick* had been taken away to refit before I joined her I had not yet met him. On paper it seemed a reasonable idea, but I thought that both Boyle and I would have to exercise a lot of self-control if we were to avoid a quarrel. As however there seemed no way of avoiding this 'trial by experience' I said that I would go.

When I had taken *Warwick* round to Grimsby I went straight across England to join *Havelock*, and we sailed within an hour of my getting aboard. As I feared the scheme proved quite unworkable. In the last chapter I explained how in a U-Boat attack the 'plot' could tell exactly what was happening, and could judge what should be done. Commander Boyle on his bridge was in the same position as the reader before the purpose of the plot was explained; whereas I, from the plot, was controlling everything, including the movements of Commander Boyle's own ship. Not even a saint could stand having his own ship moved by someone else, far less the Senior Officer of a group of ships. It would have been bad enough if we had possessed similar temperaments, but in fact we were poles apart. Boyle was slow, accurate and very meticulous. Everything he did must be weighed up and considered most carefully; and he was very neat and tidy. I am impetuous, and inclined to be slap-dash; and no one has ever said that I am tidy. We disagreed about every mortal thing, even about the type of sherry we should drink. There was only one point on which we were united – that the scheme of dual control was the craziest idea we had ever been asked to try. That we never quarrelled is a tribute to our background, and to the discipline of the service. In separate ships we would have been complementary to each other, and could have made an excellent team; for he was my senior officer and I would then have carried out the orders I received. If I learnt anything from this strange interlude it was that 'he who controls the plot controls the whole battle.'

After this abortive effort the next idea from the Tactical School was to put the senior officer of the group in the plot, and give him a captain to look after the ship. Although this was better than the scheme which Boyle and I turned down it was still not the ideal solution, because the ships were not big enough to carry a Senior Officer and a Captain. The obvious answer, which was the one finally chosen was to give the Senior Officer a very experienced First Lieutenant who could handle the ship in action. The former then retired to the plot, and dealt with the problems as a whole.

Although we passed through waters where U-Boats were known to be working in quite large numbers, no attack was made on either convoy. This, though possibly fortunate for our friendship, was unhelpful in the matter of gaining experience. However, there were enough sighting reports from our aircraft, and enough manoeuvrings by the escorts to keep the enemy down, for us to form a reliable opinion that the scheme was unworkable. On my return I went to see the Chief of Staff to ask his advice about my report, because I felt sure that it was going to be very much against the idea we had been trying out. He told me that Boyle had already sent in one sulphurous document, and he saw no reason why I should have to write another. I rather think the result was only what he himself had expected.

We sailed again eastbound from St. John's, Newfoundland, on Boxing Day, 1943. As soon as I was back I spent one night at my home, where I arrived with two frozen salmon, and then rushed over to Grimsby to get *Warwick* ready for a convoy due to sail early in January.

We should have left Grimsby on the 11th, but delays occurred and we did not get away until the 13th. which was the day on which the convoy left Liverpool. However, by dint of pushing her along at her best speed we managed to catch up while the merchantmen were still forming up off the north coast of Ireland.

The convoy was a fast one, and was supposed to make nine knots; but already a westerly gale was rising, and the ships were having great difficulty in getting into their stations. It had been blowing hard from the west for the last fortnight, and a very big westerly swell was running. January 1944 produced the worst weather of the whole war. For escort we had *Havelock* (Senior Officer), three more destroyers, *Warwick*, *Vimy* and *Volunteer*, and two Belgian-manned corvettes, the *Buttercup* and *Godetia*.

That convoy never formed up. We could not get them into their stations that night, and by morning we were all virtually hove to. In the first twenty-four hours we made eighty miles to the westward. The second day we were down to fifty-two miles; and on the third we made only forty – a fraction over one and a half knots. The weather showed no improvement, and the seas got steadily worse. *Havelock* sprung her mainmast, and went off to Iceland for repairs. This left me as Senior Officer of the Escort. Ten of the merchant ships had returned to England with cracks appearing in their superstructures, and fifteen were straggling we knew not where. The convoy was reduced from about fifty to twenty-five ships, spread over miles of sea; and the escorts were more or less out of touch with each other.

As the seas were breaking over the upper deck and green water, two and three feet deep, was sweeping across *Warwick* between the after-house and the 3-inch H.A. gun, I brought the watch-keeping officers forward to sleep in the sick-bay under the bridge, and closed the upper deck to traffic. At the very slow speed which the convoy was making my ship was unmanageable. I had to go faster, and this meant making a broad zig-zag if I was to keep station on the convoy. We were thus constantly altering course, and steaming at an angle to the mountainous seas, instead of heading more comfortably into them. Soon after the upper deck had been closed the motor boat was swept clean out of the davits; half an hour later the whaler on the other side went the same way. We then discovered that all the drinking water was in the fore-part of the ship, and all the bread in the after-part. We solved that one by using a rocket gun to get a line from the bridge to the stern of the ship, and rigging a breeches-buoy. We then exchanged water for bread.

Soon after daylight on the following morning the engineer officer telephoned from the engine room to say that he thought something on deck must have carried away, because a lot of water was coming down through holes in the deck above him. I went to the after end of the bridge and looked over but could see nothing wrong. When I got back to the compass platform, the First Lieutenant was just being re-lieved for the forenoon watch. Before he went below for his breakfast I said :

'Number One, the Chief thinks something has carried away abaft the funnel, as water is pouring into his engine room. I've had a look but I can't see anything missing. You might have a look yourself and see if anything has gone, because I think that he's imagining things.'

I watched his oilskin-clad figure as he moved cautiously aft, clinging to hand-holds as she rolled, until he disappeared from view behind the asdic hut. Soon he was coming back again, excitedly, and much less carefully. Above the wind he shouted :

'The 3-inch gun's gone – platform and all.'

It had too – whipped clean out of her. The gun and platform had been carried over the side without even bend-ing a guardrail to show where they had passed.

The following morning, our fifth at sea, both *Vimy* and *Volunteer* reported weather damage and as the convoy was reduced to about twenty ships I ordered the destroyers back to England. The two corvettes were much better suited to this weather than the destroyers, and could still manoeuvre fairly easily. I therefore sent them round to count how many children remained in the bed, and to find out if the escort oiler was still with us. One corvette came back with a count of twenty, and the other with twenty-one – but the escort oiler was not among them. As we did not carry enough fuel to cross the Atlantic without replenishing, this was a serious matter.

The following night was, if anything, even worse than its predecessors; and at dawn we had only eight ships of the convoy in sight. I made a signal to Commander-in-Chief, Western Approaches.

'Convoy scattered by continuous gale. Have only eight merchant ships with me. *Warwick* will have to be dry docked on return as all fuel tanks are leaking. No U-Boat can operate in this weather. Request permission to return.'

That afternoon I received the answer, 'Approved'. Having collected the two corvettes we put our stern to the wind and with revolutions for seven knots on the engines, but actually making ten through the water, we started for home. The Belgians had put up a very good show indeed. Their mess decks might smell peculiar to our Anglo-Saxon noses, but they were both very efficient little ships, and very anxious indeed to please.

Although landsmen may imagine that it can be done, it is of course impossible for an ocean-going ship to travel faster than the waves. A big wave travels at forty-five knots, which is faster than the speed of any such ship. Even if you could steam at, or near the speed of the waves, the down-drag of your propellers would be so great that a following sea would break aboard instead of lifting the stern.

Now at last we could open the upper deck to traffic, and the ship rode much more easily. But as the enormous waves came up astern and passed under us, the hull was bending so much that the steering rods from the wheelhouse to the steering engine were continually jamming; and the big watertight bulkheads between the engine and boiler rooms were popping like biscuit tins. The noise could be heard even on the upper deck. After supper I was standing wedged in the port after corner of the bridge. The seas were quite stupendous. They would roar up astern of us, huge mountains with a curling crest five or six feet deep in foam. Up would go our stern and down went the bow; as the wave passed under us the stern would sink until, looking aft the following wave appeared twice as high as it really was – and its true height was quite enough to be frightening. It was the first time in my life that I had ever felt the wind to

166

be distinctly less when we were in the troughs than on the crests. By any standard it was thrilling to see the way this slim craft would cock up her tail to mock the elemental fury that the westerly gale flung at her.

As I was watching I became aware of a sudden change. The sky behind me to the north-west had blackened to an intensity that was appalling. Even in the darkness of the gale the seas had been plainly visible. Now, against that new and unearthly blackness they were becoming startlingly light in colour, so that the ship herself showed up ever more clearly against the pale waters. It was while I was considering this phenomenon that I first saw the line squall. It can then only have been about a mile away, and coming down from the north-west at something over eighty miles an hour. From the many old books about sailing ships which I had read I was aware of the terrible power of these squalls. They could catch sailing ships aback and whip the masts clean out of them; for they brought with them a sudden shift of wind of anything from forty-five to ninety degrees. I had seen minor squalls, but never one like this. It was plainly marked by a single foam-topped wave, as high and as fierce as the westerly ones which we were riding. As I waited I realized that one of the old seas would meet this new one just at our stern. Breathlessly I watched. The stern went up and up – and then she broached to, just as a dinghy will do when landing on an open beach. She slewed right round to take the foaming wall of water full on her side.

I had felt her start to swing, and realized instinctively that the helmsman had lost control of her. Before she went over I was already half way down the weather ladder to the wheelhouse deck. For a sickening minute while I struggled with the door she lay right over. I did not know it then, but learnt afterwards, that water was pouring into the forward messdecks, and that our elderly bos'n – a most God-fearing man – was nearly drowning in the lavatory. 'Up to his neck in water and swearing most horrid, Sir,' as it was reported to me later.

I got the door open, and there in the centre of the wheelhouse was the untended wheel. In the far corner was a muddle of legs and arms, which was the helmsman and the bridge messenger. I launched myself towards the engine room telegraphs, and more by good luck than good management succeeded in getting a toe and hand hold that would support me. I rang down for full astern on the starboard engine and stopped the port engine. As I did so I heard the cry of 'man overboard'; but I could do nothing. My first duty was to the ship. I could feel her vibrating as the starboard engine began to run astern. Glory be – she was coming up! The compass bowl, which had been jammed, was swinging freely in the binnacle again, and slowly the compass card began to creep round as she brought her head to the eastward. She took one more sickening roll and then seemed happier. I took the wheel and rang down for seventy revolutions ahead on both engines.

'Wheelhouse – Forebridge,' I called up the voicepiece.

'Forebridge.'

'I'm down here, Mac, at the wheel.'

'Thank God, Sir. We thought it was you that was overboard.'

'I'll stay down here and steer her myself.'

'What about the man overboard, Sir? Don't yet know who it is – but someone was certainly seen to go.'

'Sorry – I dare not risk it. I'm afraid the men won't like it, but I can't jeopardise the whole for one; and we'd never find him now. I'll keep the wheel until the sea has settled down.'

I steered her all night, and found that by putting on the wheel I needed before the rods could jam I could keep her pretty well on her course. With the dawn at last came signs of the wind moderating. The wheel was jamming less and less, and the quartermaster of the forenoon watch was a helmsman I could trust. I handed over the wheel to him, and had my breakfast.

As I feared, the men were grumbling. I sent for the coxswain. He was a fine man, and did not like having to tell me what he must – if I pressed him. In the end he told me that the men felt that I should have turned back and searched for their shipmate. I wrote a notice and gave it to the coxswain to put on the ship's notice board.

'Decisions are mine – not yours. I shall have to answer for my decision to the Board of Enquiry that will certainly be called. Until the decision of the Board is known you must refrain, for the good of the ship, from criticizing. I will say only what I shall say to the Board, "That to have turned the ship at that time and in that sea, would have been hazardous in the extreme, and I would not place 170 men in such jeopardy to save one who, even if found, would I am sure have been beyond our aid." I would have preferred to have said this to you personally but I cannot leave the bridge.'

Half an hour after this notice had been on the board the coxswain, bos'n and chief stoker came on the bridge to see me. They were a deputation to say 'thank you', and to tell me that the ship's company wanted to apologize for any hard words that I might have overheard.

Later that morning we came across a large tanker, which, damaged by the heavy weather, was going home. She had been torpedoed previously, but the repair was giving trouble. As she had already started to break in two, we signalled for a tug. We stayed with her until off Barra Head, where we were met by the ocean tug to whom we handed over the merchant ship. We had not left her half an hour when she broke clean in half and sank. The tug picked up all her crew.

We were ordered to Londonderry, and then to Ardrossan to dry-dock. We had only left dock on the 12th January, and it was then the 22nd. B.5 Group had been pretty well decimated by that gale. All four destroyers were weather-damaged, the three older ones badly. Only the two corvettes were left. I went down to Liverpool as soon as we had docked to see the Admiral.

'I'm afraid those old destroyers are no longer fit for the western ocean,' he told me and added, 'I've got a number of new escorts coming over from the United States; and I am being asked to provide some destroyers for the Plymouth Command to help with the invasion, and to beat up the

German E-Boats which are working out of the Channel Islands against our traffic along the south coast. Our own M.T.B.'s cannot compete with the weather there, and the E-Boats need a lesson. You'll have one or two more "F & W's" (such ships as *Warwick*), and all your old "S Class". It should be quite a party.'

With business in the U-Boat trade so slack just then, and the invasion obviously planned for that summer the idea had attractions.

'Shall we still be in the Western Approaches Command?' I asked.

'Yes, you'll still belong to me. You'll just be loaned to Plymouth.'

'And can I have the hedgehog taken out of her, and the forward 4-inch gun replaced, Sir?'

'You can have anything you can squeeze out of anybody.'

I went in search of a 4-inch gun. The most likely place to start seemed to be the Admiralty. So I went off down to London. I was wrong. After wandering round many passages, and seeing a number of very serious-minded officers who obviously considered that I was a dangerous lunatic, I went north. After a day or two searching round Glasgow I at last found a gun that had actually been taken out of a 'V & W' destroyer. To get a gun that does not belong to you was, I discovered, one of the most difficult of undertakings. All sorts of people had an interest in it, and most of them wanted me to 'put it in writing,' and they would 'put it up' to someone else.

'My dear man,' I would exclaim, 'the ship sails on Sunday, and it's Tuesday now. Do you really think we've time to exchange "billets-doux" on the subject of a cannon that must be delivered alongside by Friday afternoon?'

The gun arrived in a contractor's lorry at two o'clock on the Friday, and we sailed on Sunday, 13th February. There is an old sailor's saying that you should not sail on a Sunday, and the meaning of the 13th is always clear. We swung our compasses, carried out firing tests on the new 4-inch and on the 3-inch high-angle gun which had been issued to replace the one lost overboard, and sailed for Plymouth on the 17th. We arrived on the afternoon of the 19th, and I went ashore to call on Captain (D). His office overlooked the river, and from there he could see everything that went on.

'I must congratulate you on your ship. I've not seen a destroyer enter harbour like that since the early days. I like to see things done smartly. Of course you've been here before.'

'Only up here once, Sir, when I got *Tiger*'s whaler foul of the ferry.'

'Oh well, I'll be seeing a lot of you I don't doubt. Just at the moment the Commander-in-Chief wants to see you. There's a car outside.'

As a matter of fact *Warwick* did look very smart. Not since *Verbena* had painted herself from truck to waterline three years before in Gibraltar, had I ever been able to paint my ship all over at the one time. In Ardrossan we had the whole crew aboard, because they had only just finished refit leave; and it had been the obvious job to give them.

I called on the Admiral and was told that I was to take *Scimitar* with me, and intercept a U-Boat which was expected off the west coast of Cornwall. As I told him that my asdic set had not been behaving in a very satisfactory way, the staff anti-submarine officer, Commander J. W. Heath, R.N., was sent for in a hurry and told to go to sea with us to look after it.

We rounded Land's End about ten that night with the 'S Class' destroyer in company, and started to patrol the beat. This was a new sort of war for us. Convoys in long lines of two columns were passing up and down the war channel, and the sea was littered with fishing vessels of all sizes. As our radar screen was confused with the echoes from the small craft a determined U-Boat could have done what he liked.

Next morning we were still sweeping in a line abreast. It was a lovely clear morning with bright sun, but bitterly cold. After 'Sunday Morning Rounds' I spent an hour practising radar control of the guns, and painting the arcs of fire of each gun on the gyro-repeater compass on the upper bridge. If we were to tackle E-Boats we must shift our main interest in life from asdics to guns. At midday I sent for the Engineer Officer and the First Lieutenant to protest about the state of the stokers' messdeck at 'rounds' that morning. I also sent a message to the asdic officer of my own ship and to Commander Heath to say that I was not satisfied with the asdic, and would they please do something about it. As all these officers had gathered in the wardroom before lunch I unwittingly saved their lives when I brought them forward. Then the anti-submarine officer telephoned from the asdic compartment to say that he would like to shut down the set for half an hour, and I agreed. I then turned to the First Lieutenant and the Engineer Officer to discuss the messdeck problem.

The sky suddenly turned to flame and the ship gave a violent shudder. Then the flame had gone, and as far as I could see everything was strangely the same. Looking ahead, I could see something floating and turning over in the water like a giant metallic whale. As I looked it rolled over further still and I could make out our own pennant numbers painted on it. I was dumb-founded. It seemed beyond reason. I ran to the after side of the bridge and looked over. The ship ended just aft of the engine room – everything abaft that had gone. What I had seen ahead of us *had really been the ship's own stern.* There were small fires all over the upper deck. The First Lieutenant was down there organizing the fire parties. He saw me and called, 'Will you abandon ship, Sir?'

'Not bloody likely, Number One. Get those fires out, and then all the life-saving equipment over the side and secured by boat-ropes. We'll not get out till we have to.'

I went back to the compass platform.

'Signalman.'

'Sir?'

'Make to *Scimitar* – "I think I've been torpedoed." Then get down to the main deck. Yeoman, you go too – but first take all your books down to the wireless cabinet. Collect all the charts you can lay your hands on, and push them in there as well, and lock the door.'

The officer of the watch was still standing by the compass. I wondered how much longer he was going to stand there.

'Must have been hit in the magazine – the stern's been blown clean off,' I told him.

He leant forward to the wheelhouse voicepipe and called down 'Stop both.'

'Both wizzers have been blown to glory.' I could not help laughing. 'Better get down to the main deck and give Number One a hand.'

When he had gone I was all alone on the bridge. It was strangely quiet. I took off my sea boots and tried to blow up my inflatable life jacket. It would not fill with air. I put my hand behind my back and found that both the rubber tube and my jacket had been cut, I supposed by some flying fragment. I had often complained that life jackets were left lying about the wheelhouse, so perhaps there would be one there now. I went down to see. But no, my recent words had taken effect. I seized a 'sorbo' cushion, and tucked it into the jacket of my battle dress. It gave me a feminine silhouette, but it could be a help if the worst was to happen. I went out on to the wheelhouse deck. The ship was upright and apparently floating well. The carley-floats were by then all over the side, and secured by boat-ropes. The First Lieutenant had all the small fires out. We might save her yet.

I could hear a high windy sort of noise that I could not place. The deck began to take on an angle – suddenly – so suddenly. She was almost on her side. I was slithering, grasping all sorts of unlikely things. My world had turned through ninety degrees. I just caught sight of Harries, the navigator, going over the high side of the main deck. He had a polished wooden box in either hand, the chronometer and the sextant. I wished that I had someone to laugh with over that one. I jumped for the galley funnel which was now parallel with the water and about two foot clear, and flat-footed it to the end. I could see water pouring into the main funnel. It made a guggling sound, like an enormous bath drain. The sea around me was covered with bobbing heads.

I paused at the end of my small funnel to look at the faces. They were laughing as if this were part of some gigantic fun fair. The men called to me.

'Come on, Sir. The water's lovely.'

'I'm waiting for the *Skylark*,' I shouted back. But the galley funnel dipped, and I was swimming too – madly. The man beside me turned to look over his shoulder, 'She's going!'

I turned to look. He was right. Her bow was pointed at the sky. 'Swim like hell – suction,' I shouted back. We swam like hell. I turned once more, but now there were very, very few bobbing heads behind me. I swam on. The destroyer of my old group was passing through us. I could see her men at action stations. They were attacking. They were attacking the wreck of the *Warwick*! I screamed at them in my frenzy. Wherever else the U-Boat might have been it could not have been there. The depth-charges sailed up into the air. Funny how they wobbled from side to side, I'd never noticed that before. When, I wondered, would they explode? It was like being punched in the chest, not as bad as I had expected. I swam on. Things were a bit hazy. I was not as interested in going places as I had been. I could only see waves and more waves, and I wished that they would stop coming. I did not really care any more. Then I felt hands grasp my shoulders and a voice say, 'Christ, it's the skipper. Give me a hand to get the bastard in,' and I was dragged into a carley-float which was more than crowded to capacity.

'Is there an officer here?' I gasped.

'Yes, Sir. MacIndoe.'

'Then for God's sake get some of the men over the side and lashed in the beckets, or this thing will capsize. Put me back again if you like. Take charge, I'm all in.'

I had always feared that the smaller carley-floats would capsize for I had experimented with bathing parties and found them remarkably unstable. They are so easy to get away from a ship, and appear to offer such a good chance of rescue, that they nearly always end by being overcrowded. I had evolved a plan, and had always seen that all the

174

carley-floats in the ship were fitted with a number of lengths of rope, about six feet long, which were spliced at intervals to the jack-stay running round the edge of the float. If it should become overcrowded, a number of men could then stay in the water, pass the ropes round their bodies under the arms, and tie them again to the jackstay. In this way the whole balance of the float was greatly improved, and almost double the number of men could be carried.

MacIndoe went over first, and found it much warmer in than out. A number of others followed his lead, and soon we were riding the waves very easily. About two hundred yards away we could see another laden float. They had not followed our example, and it looked hopelessly top-heavy. It must in fact have capsized, and then no one could have found the strength to climb back again. It was empty when we ourselves were picked up by the steam fishing vessel *Lady Luck* and taken to Padstow.

In the tiny bunkroom of the fishing-boat twelve men and a red-hot bogey stove were tightly packed, while the cook handed round cups of scalding tea. It was almost an hour's steaming to the harbour. By the time we were half way there we were getting some heat back into our numbed bodies and I, for one, had taken off my wet clothes. When we got in the captain of the drifter lent me a mackintosh in which to go ashore. Admiral A. G. Crauford, Resident Naval Officer, Padstow, met us as we berthed. As we walked across the quay to R.N.O.'s office, three other trawlers were rounding the headland. We looked for more, but could see none. He lent me a MacDonald tartan rug with which to cover my nakedness, and an ancient cap which he had worn in World War One. It had a very small peak, and set on my head above the rug must have given me a very odd appearance; for my legs and feet, bare and brown as a nigger's from the fuel oil, were sticking out below. I suppose it was this oil film which saved my life, because it was two hours before I could go up to the Air Station myself. The wind was from the east, and it was only just not freezing. After I had telephoned to Captain (D), Plymouth, we went back to the jetty. I wanted to meet the men as they came ashore, and to make a list of names as soon as possible. As the tide was falling, the other three fishing boats had been unable to get alongside, and so we had to have the men brought ashore in a motor boat. I could not believe at first that the three trawlers held all the survivors, but the skippers told me that four trawlers had gone to the scene of the torpedoing, and that no boats had been seen making for other ports. There was no other conclusion but that the ninety-four names I had was the sum total of survivors.

The explosion of *Warwick*'s magazine had been seen by many people, including a number of naval aircrews from St. Merryn Naval Air Station. When we landed we found that transport had been arranged, and everything organized for our comfort. The men were put straight into the buses and taken to the Air Station. When we had seen them all off Admiral Crauford and I went round the four trawlers to thank the skippers; and he then took me up to the wardroom mess in his own car.

They gave us a wonderful reception at St. Merryn. The Commander helped me to try to get the oil fuel off. We tried everything – Vim, soap, even high octane petrol. The last was the most successful, but it stung terribly on the tender parts of my body. After a meal I heard that our bos'n was in hospital nearby, so borrowed a car and drove over to see him. He was a reservist, and an elderly man – too old for the rigours of that day. He was in a very low state, but could recognize me. I was glad that I had come. He slipped his moorings peacefully in the night – just shock. In the evening the Padre held a special service for us. It was entirely voluntary but every man was there. That night I sent a telegram to my wife, 'Rumour is a lying jade.'

Sub-Lieutenant D. H. Harries, R.N.R., the navigator, survived but neither the sextant nor the chronometer did so. He trod water for twenty minutes holding both, and then decided that one would have to go. After considerable thought he let go the chronometer because he reckoned that, although a more expensive instrument, it would also cost more to repair. After another spell of keeping himself and sextant above the waves, he was forced to the unwelcome conclusion that it too would have to be jettisoned. But the moment his fingers relaxed their hold a hand grasped his shoulder and he was hauled into a raft, madly trying to get at the sextant, which was then sinking into the depths. The seaman who had hold of him thought he had gone 'nuts' and knocked him out.

The next day we were taken by bus to Plymouth. It was extraordinary how the ship's company remained a crew. Discipline was perfect, and they sang all the way. It was not bawdy tunes they sang, but old west country songs, Widdicombe Fair and The Jolly Plough Boy, and a lot I had never heard before. They might have been an excursion party. Or was there something more behind the singing, a something intangible and utterly remote – a spirit of companionship born of a common experience? As we drove through the sunlit Cornish lanes I remember thinking, 'I am sorry for the Hun. I should not like to have to fight against men like these.' With the coxswain getting the men fallen in, we were still 'Warwicks', still a ship's company when we tumbled out of the buses on the parade ground at Devonport Barracks. The men were coming to their own officers for help too. I remember one man, a very small and rather elderly reservist, who took such a very small size in boots, that even the resources of Devonport Barracks were defeated. We telephoned to the local Superintendent of W.R.N.S., and she had a pair of Wren's shoes sent down within half an hour.

A Board of Enquiry was held in the Captain's cabin of H.M.S. *Glasgow*; for service custom dictates that this should be done, not only to ensure that all the safety precautions were carried out but as a check on the discipline of officers and men, and to learn any lesson. There was only one other query. Could it have been a mine from our own minefield? Fortunately Harries remembered the bearings of a fix he had taken a few minutes before, and this removed all doubts on that score. Also the German wireless had claimed us as a sinking. There seems no doubt that the U-Boat we were looking for had fired a homing torpedo at us. It had hit us just forward of the propellers, and exploded the after magazine. *Warwick* would have continued to float had the after engineroom bulkhead not collapsed.

When the President of the Board had told us that he would not require any more evidence, we were free to go on our survivors' leave. That evening for the last time we mustered the Warwicks. The coxswain came to me, 'I've twenty-three requestmen, Sir.' He was fingering a bundle of request forms.

'Requestmen, Coxswain? I can't possibly deal with requestmen now. Anyway I don't believe I've the power to do so – even if there was time. What on earth do they want?'

'They all ask to be drafted to your next ship, Sir.'

The men's request was of course fantastic, but their thought kept me warm on the long journey home. I arrived back the next evening, and the following morning went to Liverpool to see the Admiral. He rose from his chair when I was shown in, 'I'm sorry about this, Rayner.'

'So am I, Sir. Can you give me another ship?'

'Of course if you want one. But I thought you could do with a shore job for a bit. You've had a long spell.'

'If you'll trust me with another, Sir?'

'Certainly.' He sat down and waved me to the other chair. 'You'll be a better commanding officer for having lost one ship. You can go over to America and take a Captain Class Frigate. Work her up in Bermuda, and have a good rest while you are over there.'

'A Captain Class Frigate !' There was horror in my voice.

'Why not? They're wonderful ships.'

'But I don't want to go round the Atlantic with "U.S.A." stamped on my backside, Sir.'

He looked at me from those queer eyes, which however bright they might seem, always hid what he was really thinking.

'What *do* you want?'

'A destroyer with two funnels.'

'Good God, Rayner, I've only got very few of those left, and the R.N. fellows are after them all the time.'

'Anything that can sink a U-Boat's good enough for me, Sir. But destroyers with two funnels are what I really like.'

I left him and went home. I had hardly got inside the door when the telephone bell rang. I answered it. I knew at once it was from Commander-in-Chief's office. I could hear the operator saying, 'The Admiral's secretary wants you, Sir,' and then her announcing my name. A voice addressed me,

'Rayner?'

'Yes.'

'Could you be at Troon by tomorrow night?'

I did a bit of quick thinking.

'If it's got two funnels, yes,' I answered.

'It has' – pause – 'it means giving up your survivors' leave.' The soft voice tempted. But I was ready for that one.

'I bet it's in dock for repairs or refit, and I'll take my wife with me.'

'I can tell the Admiral you'll take her then?'

'You can tell the Admiral from me that he knows damn well I will.'

'Right. You are appointed *Highlander* in Command. A signal will be made to the ship, and you'll get confirmation in due course. Good luck to you.'

I was on the jetty at Troon the following night. There before me lay the dream that had come true. Not a relic from World War One but a powerful modern destroyer completed in 1940. There were only three of them left now, *Highlander*, *Havelock*, *Hesperus* – for *Harvester* had been sunk by a U-Boat two months before. What ships they were! At the beginning of the war there had been nine similar ships already commissioned for our own Navy and six more, slightly modified, were building for the Brazilian Government. The latter had been taken over and completed as British ships. *Highlander* was one of the six. They had just a little more headroom than their sister ships, because the Brazilians had insisted that they should have big 'punka' fans in the living spaces. She really was the most beautifully fitted warship I had ever seen. She had been built as the 'leader' of the six ships, and her cabin fittings, if a little old fashioned to our eyes, were quite exceptional. The Captain's day cabin was about eighteen feet by fifteen, and panelled in mahogany; and there was a green-tiled bath-room and lavatory for his own use, and beyond that was a sleeping cabin with a polished brass cot. The Brazilian Navy certainly did itself well. As a 'leader' she carried personal crockery for the Captain's table, white fluted china with a thin rim of gold round the edge of the cups, saucers and plates. She was fitted out almost like a yacht. At sea, too, I would be much more comfortable than in any previous ship. My sea cabin was big enough to stow an easy chair along-side the bunk, and there was a knee-hole desk and drawers. It may seem curious that I should consider my personal comfort so much, but few people are so spartan that they would not have been as pleased as I was with my new ship.

As a matter of fact I had not brought my wife up with me at first, as I had discovered that the ship could not be ready for three weeks. We had decided that I should go on alone and spend three or four days getting the reins into my hands. She would join me as soon as I was settled.

I had wondered why there had been so much insistence on my getting to Troon that night if the ship was not sailing for three weeks. The first thing that the Officer of the Day told me when I went aboard was that the new First Lieutenant had joined half an hour before, and he added that the new Engineer Officer was expected at any moment. So that was the way of it. There was a general reshuffle, and we were to be given the chance to get to know each other. I often wondered how much Max Horton knew about what went on in the individual ships of his command. Once his personal assistant said to me, 'Max knows every-thing.' Sometimes I believed he did – even down to things you would not think an Admiral would trouble his head about. And yet I wonder whether such matters are so small? A little cog that sticks may stop a vast machine. So too in a Naval Command; and the Admiral is there to see that his machine never stops anywhere.

CHAPTER 8

HIGHLANDER

As I was shown to my quarters I could see the First Lieutenant unpacking in his cabin next door. He came in at once
to introduce himself, and together we went round the ship.
It did not take me long to learn that I was very fortunate
in my Number One – Lieutenant H. E. G. Atkins, R.N.
Some men, like some ships, remain a doubt in your mind for
days and weeks, even in the close association of shipboard
life. Others at once make an indelible impression – favour-
able or unfavourable. With Atkins there was never any
doubt. He was tall, smart and almost too good-looking to be
true, but without any trace of effeminacy. He had the same
wild charm that I had known so well in *Verbena*'s First
Lieutenant and, because I remembered Jack Hunter's smile,
I felt that I had known Atkins for months.

I think we both fell in love with the ship when we went
round her; but I think we both came back to my cabin a
little worried at the atmosphere we had encountered, when
we had stopped two or three of the men to ask questions.
There had been a noticeable lack of interest in us, and after
all the pair of us were going to be rather important to them
for the next few months. I thought this decidedly odd, and
was just wondering whether I should say anything to Atkins,
when there was a heavy knock at the door. In answer to my
call a tall and elderly Commissioned Engineer pushed the
curtain aside. Our new 'Chief' came in very slowly, for he
was a big man in every way.

At that first meeting I saw only the outward appearance.
Garner was slow of movement, and chary of speech. Had he
been a Scot one would have used the word 'dour' in speaking of him. But we very soon discovered that it would have
been a most unsuitable word to describe a character which
was so open, and which became ever more charming as our

friendship grew. I use the word friendship carefully and deliberately, for even if love of *Highlander* was the common bond which was to join the three of us together as partners, there did grow up between us a very real friendship.

'The 'Chief' was a good twenty years older than the average age of the wardroom officers. More than thirty years ago he had joined the Navy as a boy, and he had retired on pension before the outbreak of war with the rank of Commissioned Engineer. This he told us was his first sea-going job since recall, and we were to learn that he was at heart a seaman. I was soon to discover that he shared with me a veritable passion for handling the 2,000-ton ship in a way which would have been considered reckless had anyone else been in charge of the engines.

At sea he was always to be seen wearing such spotless white overalls that one wondered how many times a day he must change, and how many of his stokers were kept busy washing the extraordinary number of those garments that he possessed. Even when we borrowed half a dozen to clothe the chorus of the concert party it had no visible effect on the capacity of the 'Chief's' wardrobe.

When entering or leaving harbour I could see the flash of white overalls as he stood in his favourite vantage point abaft the after funnel. From there he could look down through a convenient hatch to the 'starting platform' of his beloved engine room, and he could also watch how I was handling the ship. No wartime Captain ever had a more exacting audience. He had seen much service in destroyers of the Mediterranean Fleet, and nothing short of a faultless performance on my part would satisfy his craving for perfection. As I ran down the bridge ladder after berthing the ship and hurried along the upper deck to my harbour cabin in the stern, I would see him waiting for me.

'Well done, Chief,' I'd say, knowing full well that it was really for this that he was still standing there. The little commendation meant everything to such a perfectionist.

'Ah, I don't know, Sir. My lads are still just a little too slow in getting those engines astern for my liking.'

'Damn it, Chief, I felt them going astern immediately the telegraphs had rung.'

'Ah, but it's the seconds that count handling a ship at that speed. You know, Sir, if only my lads had got her astern just a second or two earlier, and if we'd given her just a few more revolutions, say 180 instead of 150, you wouldn't have needed to give her that extra little kick with the wheel hard over – we'd have been right alongside and secured, Sir.'

'Are you suggesting I alter my standing orders to use 180 revolutions instead of 150 for "half ahead" and "half astern"?'

'Well, we could try it, Sir.'

'You'll get me court-martialled for hazarding the ship. Bring your copy of "Captain's Orders" to my cabin, and I'll initial the alteration.'

So he made me 'drive' *Highlander* as a destroyer should be handled. But I could not have done it with anyone else.

At first he had said that he was too old to join in the wardroom parties, but I do not think it was really his age which made him say that. He was a very moral man, and I fancy that he feared our parties would be a little wild. When he discovered that there was no vice in us, and that our enterprises were only the result of high spirits, he would easily be persuaded to leave his cabin for a corner chair in the wardroom. Like Mr. Badger in the 'Wind in the Willows', he would sit the whole evening through with an avuncular smile on his lips, watching the children at play. He was guide, philosopher, and friend to all of us – a very fine engineer, a first class officer and a delightful companion.

Happily before I left the ship I was able to recommend him for, and to see him given the promotion he so much deserved, and which would make so great a difference to his pension in the future. When the last handshake came and he said to me 'I have so much to thank you for,' I was able to answer from the bottom of my heart 'And I to thank you for, Chief. I shall never forget our partnership in handling *Highlander*.'

But when we first met in Troon all this still lay in the future. All I knew when I climbed into my cot that night was that I was happy enough with all my officers, and my ship – but the men were a question mark.

It was worse than that. The following day we discovered there was something wrong. The defaulters' list was as long as your arm, and there were twenty or more requests for 'permission to change to another ship.'

We waited for two days and then the three of us – myself, the First Lieutenant and the Engineer Officer, held a conference in my cabin.

'You know,' I told them, 'I think it's just something that's been allowed to grow up between the officers and the men. They are thoroughly "browned off". After all the poor beast has had a new Captain almost every quarter. You can hardly expect her to be a happy ship. Let's tear up everything and start afresh.'

The Engineer Officer goggled at me 'What, Sir? Tear up the defaulters' list?'

'Yes, Chief, the whole damned lot. And pardon all men under punishment.'

'But we've two or three who are second class for conduct. (Meaning men who have lost certain very valuable privileges for continual misbehaviour.)

'But you can't do that, Sir,' from the First Lieutenant.

'Of course I can – so long as they remain in my ship. And of course the whole thing is dependent on their allowing me to tear up these ruddy requests for draft.'

Next morning I 'cleared lower deck'. The whole ship's company was mustered closely round the 4-inch H.A. gun, so that I could use that as a platform.

'I want to speak to you. I'm used to having a happy ship. There's something wrong in this one. I don't know what it is. I want to put it right. I want to see you chaps with smiles on your faces. I haven't seen one since I came aboard. Now I'll tell you what I'm going to do. There's a defaulters' list here which is quite fantastic. I think ten per cent of the ship's company are waiting for my first "Captain's Defaulters" and there's another ten per cent under punishment. I've got the list here. At the present time one man in five of the ship's company is either under punishment or waiting to see what I'm going to give them. We can't run a ship that way. Now I'll tell you what I'm going to do. Of course I can't do anything where pay has already been stopped; but this I can do. I can tear up these lists, and we'll start afresh. That goes for the second class for conduct boys too – but there's a tag to it.' I could see that I'd got their interest, and I could see the curiosity in their faces. 'Well you didn't think I was such a fool as to do that for nothing, did you? There are two things I want from you. To hear no more about draft chits. In future the only way out of *Highlander* will be by promotion. We'll start classes for leading hand as soon as we leave Troon, and I want to see you make this ship the happiest out of 'Derry. Now can I tear up these papers?' I held out the bundle of request forms and looked round. I had them guessing. They did not know what to make of it, but the tension was easing. There was something almost tangible growing between officers and men while I stood there. Laughing, I was able to tease them.

'Come on, what shall I do with them?'

They were laughing too.

'All right, I won't make you say it. I can see the answer. Number One, take these and stuff them where they belong. No, on second thoughts don't do that – you'll block it up. Give 'em to the Chief. He'll burn 'em in something or other.'

I got a roar of laughter then, but held up my hand for silence.

'Now, before I get down I just want to say this. There are two things I won't have. One is missing the ship on sailing. I want you back whatever state you're in. The other is inefficiency. And just one thing more, you must remember that a very important part of an officer's job is to look after his men. If you want anything go to your divisional officer, and he'll sort it out for you – and if he can't, I will. I don't care how long "Captain's Requestmen" takes, so long as "Captain's Defaulters" are non-existent.'

We had found the trouble. There had been too many changes. She had been a senior officer's ship, carrying a senior officer's staff, for so long that no one had spared the time for her own men. We turned up the most extraordinary tales; men who had muddles over pay that had not been cleared up for years; medals and clasps not applied for; promotions not made. The twenty odd requests for draft were replaced by a pile of chits for all sorts of things. We set up a special 'bureau' for requests, and we badgered everyone we could think of to get matters put right. One Stoker Petty Officer got £94 back pay, and there were many smaller amounts. One result was that the next quarter's punishment returns were almost nil. As there were practically no defaulters the coxswain (who is also the ship's policeman), now had time to spare. We put him in charge of the ship's concert party.

The town of Perth had 'adopted' the ship, and while we lay in Troon we sent an invitation to the Mayor to bring some of the city notables over to lunch, and to see the ship. When they arrived they produced three bagpipes as a present. Apparently some previous Commanding Officer with a musical ear had asked for them. I accepted the gift as gracefully as my astonishment would allow. I fear though that they must have seen the look of consternation on my face when the gigantic parcel – it was almost a four foot cube – was opened on the upper deck because it was too big to go down the hatchway to the wardroom. Then they asked me what *I* would like for the ship, and I plumped for a silk ensign to use on Sunday mornings. An old Naval custom, now more or less extinct. *Hood* had been the last ship I had seen with one. In due course it arrived, thanks to the kindness of the citizens of Perth. It proved to be just one of the many little things which made *Highlander* into the ship she was to become.

We always seemed to be in trouble with musical instruments and the wardroom hatch. It was never big enough for the curious selection, varying from a piano to a harp, which the officers brought aboard from time to time.

In the middle of March we were sailed to Tobermory for a week's 'refresher' course. With a crew already trained we had no trouble with the 'Terror of Tobermory' and having passed successfully, we went to join B.4 Group in Londonderry.

We had decided that, as we could not learn to blow our bagpipes ourselves, we would put three sailors to stand on the searchlight platform holding them in what we hoped was the correct 'blowing position'. With a powerful loud hailer rigged on the searchlight playing pipe tunes, they gave a most realistic performance. This had been exercised with good effect in Tobermory.

It was a lovely spring afternoon when we steamed up-river to Londonderry. Boom Hall with its green lawns falling down to the river, had been taken over for the Wren ratings, and there were quite a number sitting outside on the grass. We gave them the chance to hear our pipes as we passed. The reception was so enthusiastic that we thought we would provide them with an encore. Shutting off the loud hailer we turned the ship round and went silently down river, made another turn, and then went past once more with the pipes playing and the pipers on the searchlight platform – and a great deal faster than I had ever taken a ship up there before. *Highlander* was excellent for entering harbour with plenty of speed, because until she was travelling about fifteen knots she made almost no wash. The encore performance really did bring the Wrens out by the hundred.

It is difficult to say at what moment something which has been going wrong will suddenly be found to be going right. From some point or other the *Highlander* never looked back. It was as though the lid had been removed, and all the frustrated good ideas bubbled out at the same time. Although these ideas seemed to spring spontaneously from the messdecks, an officer was always somewhere roped in to help. Football and hockey teams came into existence and played regularly. The boats were always in the water in harbour. Ship's company dances were held when we were in Londonderry, and to these a large wardroom party would go, quite sure that we could 'let our hair down' without affecting tomorrow's discipline. At sea we had quiz teams competing over the 'intercom' in the dog watches. A debating society flourished, and there always seemed to be re-hearsals going on somewhere for the coxswain's concert party, which included two excellent 'tap dancers', or the ship's 'comb band'.

My own contribution was to organize a gunnery competition with the 4.7-inch armament. No less than twelve teams from various parts of the ship took part. The officers' crew, who had won their first and second rounds, got a bye into the final; and their opponents would be the winner of either 'B gun's' proper crew or a crew from the stokers' mess. The crew of 'B gun' really thought themselves first-class. It was quite a shock to them when the stokers won after a re-fire, and even more of a shock when the officers beat the stokers in the final – which was all as it should be. The method of holding the competition was this. A smoke shell was fired from the forrard gun to burst at about 8,000 yards, and the competitors from the after gun then had to fire six fused rounds against a time limit. On the bridge I fixed up a ring sight which I kept trained on the smoke target, and marked the bursts of the fused shell as one would a rifle target. With the ship travelling fast and beam-on to the sea it was a very good practice, and soon after we had fired the last competition a German aircraft showed up and got the shock of his life.

The Germans had just developed a small V.1. 'buzz bomb' which could be steered by the parent aircraft until it was close to the target, when a radar device in the bomb's nose took over and brought it down to hit. Either the Hun had misjudged his distance, or he had not allowed for an escort having the 4.7 inch guns of *Highlander*. He launched his toy at us out of the sun one evening, but we gave him such a shaking that he lost control of the bomb and it fell into the sea half-way between us and the aircraft. One of his friends was back again the same night, but our radar picked him up and we opened fire. Although we could not see him we must have shot pretty close, because once again we frightened him off. These aircraft were working from Bordeaux, and once they had got their fingers on a convoy they could be quite a nuisance. They not only carried the miniature 'buzz bomb' but also a float which they dropped some miles ahead of the convoy. This float sent out wireless signals, and the U-Boats would 'home' on to it. Bordeaux sent another attacker the next morning, but our escort carrier had its aircraft up in time for that one, and they shot him down. *Highlander* was sent to pick up the pieces, but there was very little to find.

The ship's improvement was not all in the entertainment line. Results came too. We won the group regatta, and headed the group football league. Twelve of the seamen who passed a group board for leading seamen were *Highlanders*, out of a total of fourteen. Six of our leading seamen passed for Petty Officer, and I started fifteen 'C.W. papers' to set those young men off on the road to becoming officers.

I now entered a period of idyllic existence. My ship was thoroughly happy and efficient, and I could do things with her that I had never attempted, even with the very much smaller *Shikari*. No heaving line dared fall short when we were going alongside, or if it should there would be another in the air even before the first fell to the water. We comfortably broke the time record for oiling at sea, thanks to the First Lieutenant's excellent work on the fo'c's'le. The only thing missing were the U-Boats.

In February and March the U-Boats from Brest had taken a severe caning from Captain Walker's 2nd Support Group, and thereafter they were very much on the defensive. In the summer many of them were withdrawn, to take up their anti-invasion stations, or to have the new 'Schnorkel' fitted. There were just enough at sea to make us feel that we were doing a worthwhile job, but with constant air cover from our own escort carriers, and the long-range patrols from shore-based Coastal Command, the U-Boats were a beaten team.

Commander C. W. McMullen R.N. was the Senior Officer of B.4 Escort Group in the 'River' Class Frigate *Helmsdale*. *Highlander* was second in command, and our job a regular trip to Gibraltar and back, with a convoy each way. The route had now been greatly shortened and we went down about the meridian of 15° west, thus taking only ten days on passage. In 1941 the distance and time had been twice as long. This gave us ten days at sea and five in harbour at Gibraltar. The weather was kind, and at both ends we had excellent ports. There were bathing and parties at Gibraltar, and parties and more parties at Londonderry. I had always been fortunate in our North of Ireland base, since on my first visit I had met a very charming family from whom I could always be sure of a welcome. To amuse my officers there were now plenty of Wrens. The Western Approaches Wrens liked to think that they were a hand-picked selection, as I suppose in some respects they were. They certainly provided the officers with a great deal of companionship, and contrary to what some war novels would have us believe, there was almost no 'boy-girl' trouble at all. For one thing there was not time, and for another each girl had so many 'beaux' that when one sailed away for three or four weeks another would be steaming up the river. The girls all knew exactly when the various ships could be expected, and would arrange their schedules accordingly. It really was an astonishing tribute to the men and girls at Londonderry that, in the whole history of the base, there was, as far as I know, only one incident that should never have happened – and that was not in a ship of the Londonderry Escort Force, but a stranger who did not know the rules.

Commodore Simpson and his staff had hammered out a most sensible routine. If the wardroom wanted to give a party, they would make a signal to the Commodore repeated to the First Officer W.R.N.S. requesting the pleasure of the company of so many W.R.N.S. Officers, and giving the date and time. When an 'approved' signal had been received, you would telephone up the First Officer W.R.N.S. and tell her whom you had arranged to invite. In due course they arrived aboard, and although they had to wear uniform aboard the ships, they were allowed to wear long frocks in the Allied Officers' Club. One imagines that the W.R.N.S. Officer in charge had her side of the situation pretty well organized, and that any Wren showing signs of losing control was hastily removed to some other base. I suppose too, that she had a pretty good idea of the behaviour of the various wardrooms to which her charges were let out. In any case the men and girls would have got together. To acknowledge this fact and provide an organization to control it, was a most successful psychological manoeuvre. Our base was fortunate in that, being so isolated it could, and did make rules to suit itself. I know that its ships were the envy of less fortunate ones, based on other ports.

Londonderry base had always been first-class ever since the early days, when Captain Ruck-Keene had built it out of nothing. It had the advantages of a foreign station in its freedom to go its own way, and also the advantage of being near enough to the storehouse of the United Kingdom to get adequate supplies for the ships. Under Commodore Simpson a really remarkable series of training devices had been built. There was a dome-shaped construction on whose white walls, and by the use of a cinematograph machine, enemy aircraft could be made to come in at all angles of attack; while the men under training handled a gun fitted with a light. Pressing the trigger produced blobs of light just where the bullets would have gone in practice, and by a cunning mechanism both the time of flight of the bullet and the speed of the target were allowed for. It was a most realistic toy, and great fun to use.

Another booth in 'Simpson's Fun Fair' offered even more exciting attractions. This piece was called 'A Night Attack Teacher.' It consisted of the bridge of a ship, built in the centre of a hall which could be made completely dark. You went to it with your entire bridge staff, officer of the watch, look-outs, signalmen, yeoman of signals. Down below was a model wheelhouse where your coxswain was stationed, and in a cabin behind was the automatic plot manned by your own Plotting Officer and his crew. At the word 'go' you would probably be given a radar range and bearing, and when you had turned your ship's head in that direction you would give the order to fire star shell. Immediately a flash of magnesium powder would be touched off just below the bridge, for all the world like the flash of a real gun. Then a little light would appear gently sinking in the darkness, and if you were lucky you'd see a surfaced U-Boat in the camera-obscura that surrounded the hall. Everything that ever happened in the Western Ocean could be put on that machine. If you got your ship too near the convoy the directing officer would give you a radar range and bearing, and on looking that way you would dimly discern a line of merchantmen. It came quite fantastically near to producing the real effect.

In yet another booth, the asdic game was played. Here complete asdic sets, coupled to the inevitable automatic plot produced all the effects of an attack. Days in harbour with the ship to look after, and parties going off to this or that instruction, were never idle ones. About once every two months the group as a whole would go to *Philante*, the training ship for the Western Approaches. Before the war she had been Mr. Tom Sopwith's steam yacht. She was now based on Belfast Lough, and had with her a British submarine to give our asdic and radar ratings practice in detecting submerged or surfaced U-Boats. By that time Admiral Sir Percy Noble's dictum of 'training and more training' was really bearing fruit. Now behind the front line of sea-going ships was a vast array of training officers and their staffs. Most of these training devices were under the management of officers who had served at sea in the earlier years, and really knew what they were talking about.

All the summer of 1944 we ran the convoy to Gibraltar without interference from the U-Boats. *Highlander* did have one little expedition of her own. Two days from Gibraltar at the end of June we received a signal detaching us from B.4 Group to 'proceed with all despatch to a position fifty miles north of Cape Finisterre'. Full of excitement we bustled off without the slightest idea why we had been sent. It appeared unhealthily close to Bordeaux and the German air force. When we arrived in position about ten o'clock at night we found a cloudless sky and a brilliant moon. We had hardly been there for half an hour when the radar office reported an aircraft circling us at five miles. In that moonlight we should have been a sitting target, if it had chosen to attack. The radar operator reported that 'it was not one of ours'. That did not, of course, necessarily mean that it was a German. It could have been a Spaniard although that seemed unlikely as it did not appear to be burning navigation lights. To prevent the pilot getting a view of *Highlander* I kept her bows always pointing at him, so that even when upmoon of him he would only see a triangular blob in the moon path, and would not be able to recognize our unmistakably British silhouette. Because I had only an anti-surface vessel radar which gave only a very rough idea of the target's height, and only our own makeshift radar control of the guns, I would rather not fight an enemy aircraft in the dark. For some reason the Admiralty wished *Highlander* to be in that position. Presumably not to be sunk there.

It was a silly situation. He wanted to know what I was, and I was most curious to find out what he was; and neither of us could do a thing about it. He was the first to lose patience, and the radar reported him closing rapidly. As he came from the down-moon side he had me full in the moon path. He also had my bows pointing towards him. When he was about a mile away I switched on the mast-head and side lights at full peace time brilliancy. He roared over us and no bombs fell. My experts told me that it was a four-engined Junkers 290, and that his bomb doors were open. I confess I am not too good at telling one aircraft from another. I only know that he was much too low to be pleasant. He seemed satisfied with our lights, and winged away towards France.

Recognition from air to ship is always difficult, and I was reminded of a tale told in the early days of the war when four British destroyers were carrying out a sweep into the Skagerrak between Denmark and Norway. As one of the ships had developed a defect they were rather late coming back. Some British Blenheim bombers saw them by daylight, and went in to bomb. As they did so the party were sighted by some patrolling German Heinkels, who thought the British planes were bombing German destroyers, so came down from the clouds and obligingly chased the Blenheims away.

We settled down to wait for our appointment, but nothing came. Midnight passed and we still had no orders. One o'clock, two o'clock, and then at last a signal to return to Gibraltar 'with all despatch'. We heard afterwards that H.M. the King had been flying home after reviewing the army in North Africa, and that destroyers had been stationed every fifty miles along the route. I was glad we had played no longer with that Junkers.

I called the Engineer Officer in the engine-room.

'Return to Gibraltar with all despatch. Do you hear that, Chief? You've been moaning for long enough that you've never had an opportunity to see how many revolutions you can get out of your engines. Here's your chance to flash up the third boiler and try. I'll put three hundred revolutions on the telegraph but you can do as many as you like.'

Our course was straight up the moon path, in a dead calm sea, with a long lazy swell coming up from the south. From the bridge the water ahead looked like corrugated glass. The ship began to tremble. The electric log ticked faster as the speed increased – a metronome of speed. She leapt from the top of each swell and sheets of golden spray shot out as she flung herself into the trough.

From the engine-room, 'Third boiler connected, Sir.'

'Good show, Chief. Let's see what you can get out of her.'

I put down the hand-set and turned to the Officer of the Watch. 'You know old "Chiefy" is like a boy. I swear he loses thirty years every time he goes down the engine-room hatch.'

'Yes, Sir, and he's beginning to lose 'em down the ward-room hatch too. How the Wrens love the old boy! He's always got one on each arm of his chair when we have a party now.'

I laughed. 'Yes I noticed that. You'd better get the First Lieutenant to order an extra Wren next time, if the Chief is always going to appropriate a couple.'

The engine-room phone buzzed again.

'Yes Chief. . . . Three three o. That's fine. What is her record? Do you know? . . . Oh, she's never been any faster, but you hope you'll be able to squeeze her up another ten. . . . No I'm not going to turn in – far too exciting. When you're happy down there come up here. We have cocoa in half an hour.'

I replaced the hand-set telephone.

A few minutes later he was calling again.

'Just holding three four o, Sir.'

'Well done you! . . . No, I'm sorry I've no speed for three hundred and forty revolutions on the speed board. The last figure is three hundred and thirty, which gives her thirty-six knots. I'd say that another ten revolutions should give her another knot. Come up and feel what it's like.'

Very soon his tall white figure showed round the edge of the asdic hut just as the ship hurled herself over a wave, and two great wings of water were momentarily poised on either side of the bow. The plunge had sent him tottering forward to clutch at the binnacle. He stood there with a rapt expression of sheer delight on his face. We gave him cocoa, and then he had to hurry away to see how 'his lads' were treating the two whirring monsters that were almost like children to him. When he had gone, I went down to the fo'c's'le deck, took a line from the bos'n's locker and fastened it round my waist. I then went forward as far as the capstan, where I made the other end fast to a link of the anchor chain. Then I crawled forward on hands and knees until I could grasp the bull-ring in the eyes of the ship, and look down the stem to the water rushing below me.

I do not think I have ever been in a position so thrilling, and so utterly beautiful. Behind me, startlingly white in the moonlight, rose the tiered outline of the destroyer. I could look from the fo'c's'le deck to 'B gun' deck with its flaring blast shields, and to the signal deck and the high forebridge, where the armour-plate glass windshields reflected back the moonlight. Ahead of me stretched a golden pathway, and below were gleaming pits into which the ship rushed. The bows were plunging until the surface of the sea was barely twelve inches from my face. The next moment, as she rose out of the swell, I could see almost down to where the stem turned into the keel. At one moment I was only a foot above the sea, which was rushing to meet me at forty-two miles an hour, at the next I was suspended thirty foot above it.

Woosh! – and she would plunge her throbbing stem into the wave. A pause, and then she would fling herself forward, dripping golden moonlit water. I could have lain there content for hours, watching her bow tearing the waves apart, while behind me the air was filled with the steady whine of the boiler-room fans.

While I was in the very eyes of the ship we ran through a school of porpoise, and I was amazed to see that even at the speed we were travelling they could make some attempt to gambol alongside, although they could not hold us for long. It was the best chance I ever had to gauge the speed of these fish with the lovely movements, and I put their maximum at fifty miles an hour with an endurance of barely a minute. At forty-two miles an hour they seemed capable of holding us for about five minutes before they dropped astern, so that their capacity for maintaining maximum speed is about the same as that of a racehorse.

As the examination for leading seamen was due to take place the first day after arrival we were very keen to reach Gibraltar not far behind the rest of the group. Actually we found the convoy just entering the Straits, and we stormed through them at full speed. We entered harbour before they did.

We also had a new toy to play with in the shape of a seine net. Looking through books I had discovered that a destroyer was entitled to one, and had promptly ordered it for use in Gibraltar and also at Moville at the mouth of the Foyle. Of course we had only the very vaguest idea how to use it, and when it arrived there appeared to be much more of it than we had expected. We had no chance until the following Sunday. There was only one possible place on 'The Rock' from which it could be used. That was the bathing beach on the Mediterranean shore, which was reached by a long tunnel. We could not carry the net through the tunnel, and we hoped that our catch would be too big to carry back that way. So we decided to take the ship herself round, with any of the officers of the other ships of the group who wanted to see the fun, and towing the *Helmsdale*'s and the *Foley*'s motor boats. We thought that we should need at least three motor boats to haul such a big net out to sea and back to the shore. So *Highlander* asked for permission to go to sea for exercises, and towed the motor boats round the point to anchor off the bathing beach.

We put a large picnic party ashore in the afternoon, and the net. The first haul was not a success as the net fouled some obstruction, but the second was a great improvement. We took hundreds of beautiful fish, ten laughing Wrens and three Paymaster Commanders livid with rage. They were not caught separately, but all bundled up together — fish, Paymasters and Wrens; and the fish scales stuck like glue. The ship's company enjoyed a fish supper; the wardroom officers enjoyed the Wrens; and the three Paymasters reported me to the Commander-in-Chief. Of course no one could do anything about it, because there was no rule against seine netting from the beach; and after all it was an exercise.

But I fear that the Staff decided to black-list the whole of B.4 group, and from that time onwards we were continually in trouble at Gibraltar. We were going through one of those periods when everything that the group did would turn into an escapade of some sort or other, and the more the Staff looked down their noses at us, the worse were the things that happened. We had a wonderful crowd in that group, and *Highlander*'s big wardroom was always a seething mass of officers. To avoid the strain which so much entertaining would have thrown on the purses of our own officers they had, at my suggestion, made their friends honorary members of our mess. This made a lot of work for our doctor, who was mess secretary, and had to render and collect the many mess bills, but it made our wardroom into a sort of club for the group. Consequently most of the wild parties started in *Highlander*, and I got the blame.

On the way home the Chief had much trouble with the amount of fresh water that the ship's company was using. With tropical whites to wash after leaving Gibraltar, and no time for washing them in harbour, we were using far more water than the ship's evaporators could produce.

Notices on the ship's board had no effect at all. The Chief came to see me on the bridge.

'It really is desperate, Sir. We shall be out of fresh water before we reach Londonderry.'

'How much,' I asked, 'must be saved to satisfy you, Chief?'

'We must cut the consumption down by half, Sir.'

'Signalman.'

'Sir.'

'Give me a signal pad, please.'

I wrote out yet another notice and handed it to the Chief who, with a broad smile on his face, took it away to the ship's notice board. But the water situation did not improve. Two days later in the forenoon watch the bos'n's mate could have been heard piping round the ship, 'Messdeck sweepers muster abreast the whaler with all buckets from their messes.'

There the Chief, with a party of grinning engine-room artificers, waited for them. Armed with punches and heavy hammers they cut a neat round hole half-way up each bucket, and the water consumption was restored to a level with which our evaporators could cope. I had wondered just how the sailors would take it, but I need have had no fear. They were intensely amused at their mutilated buckets, and were even seen to show them with pride to other ships. For ever afterwards anything which was not a great deal of good would be referred to as being 'as much use as a *Highlander*'s bucket.'

On the way home the great invasion of D Day began, and we all wondered whether the U-Boats would show their teeth in retaliation. But they remained as quiet as ever. We were all amazed at the surprise achieved in this great operation, because when we were in Gibraltar and a number of the Captains had been in Commander McMullen's cabin, someone had raised the question where exactly it would be staged. We had sent for the Channel charts, and had decided that there was only one place which we could conceivably recommend. It was there that the landing was actually made. One can only remark once again that the

German is essentially a land-based animal, or he would undoubtedly have protected the eastern side of the Cherbourg peninsula much more heavily.

For the next convoy to Gibraltar *Helmsdale* was away for boiler cleaning, and I was Senior Officer of the group. We had a very uneventful passage down, and all tied up together in the harbour – *Highlander*, the 'Captain' Class Frigate *Foley* (Lieutenant-Commander Charles Bird, R.N.V.R.), and four 'Castle' Class Corvettes.

Charles was a particular friend of mine. He was a long-service R.N.V.R. from the Bristol Division, and ran a very efficient ship. Among many idiosyncrasies – for he was by way of being an individualist – was his fixed determination never to alter the time in his ship, but always to keep British double-summer time, however far west he might go. There was some point in this, because the constant changes of one hour daily did mean shuffling the watches round to keep them fair for all. Charles decided against such nonsense, with the result that once, when we had been diverted a long way further west than usual, his ship's company would breakfast at noon and have their evening meal at midnight local time. Of course what he did in his own ship made no difference to the rest of us, but one received some very queer signals from the *Foley*. After tea in the dog watches was a very good time to experiment with new radar plotting techniques, but one had to remember what time it was aboard the *Foley* before asking him to co-operate. Otherwise a signal asking for a 'radar-run' might bring the rather plaintive reply, 'If you say so; but can't you let a fellow have his afternoon sleep in peace?'

I have introduced Charles because he figured largely in the events during the five days in Gibraltar, when the group reached its high-water mark of unpopularity with the Admiral's Staff.

We berthed there on a Wednesday, and as our concert party's first major performance was to take place the next day, we reberthed *Highlander* in the morning between two of the corvettes. We thus created more vantage points overlooking the stage, which had been built on our main deck.

By the time the concert was due to begin our own decks and the ships on either side of us were crowded with men, and a large number of copies of *Highlander*'s song had been distributed.

From the stage curtain came repeated blows with a hammer on some metallic object, and when the curtain went up a caricature of myself was seen to be busy with a hammer and punch and pile of buckets.

A policeman came on the stage.

'Hoh ! and what are you a-doing of ?'

'I'm making buckets for the *Highlander*.'

'The *Highlander* – what's the *Highlander* ?'

'What – you never heard tell of the *Highlander* ? – Oh ! we'll sing you a song about her.' He signed to the chorus who came on singing the song which had been chosen in a competition open to all the crew. It was the combined work of the four quartermasters and they had shared quite a substantial prize between them for their effort.

SHIP'S SONG

Now there is a Ship in the British Navy,
She's nifty, she' sturdy, she's always at sea.
For the boys that are on her
Are good to the core,
For they are the lads of the H.44 [1].

Chorus : *All together please* !

Highlander, Highlander,
I ain't said a word about half what's occurred,
What yer say, what yer say?
The aircraft and U-Boats get out of our way.

Now whenever you see her she's always in trim,
Out of the harbour or whether she's in.
When she's on manoeuvres the boys don't get sore,
For they are the lads of the H.44 !

Chorus all together.

1. *Highlander*'s pennant numbers.

Sometimes in harbour the boys have to paint,
Some are all for it and some of 'em ain't;
But when they are finished they all step ashore.
For they are the lads of the H.44!

Chorus all together.

I'll give you an outline of some of the crew
Some of them old hands and some of them new:
I'll start with the Skipper, and his word is law.
But he's one of the lads of the H.44!

Chrous all together.

Now he's a Three-Ringer and he's got a set,[1]
If he got a draft chit the lads they would fret.
He's been with the Ship now just three months or more.
He's one of the lads of the H.44!

Chorus all together.

Then comes our Jimmy,[2] he's a bit of a lad,
And he's a lot better than others we've had.
He joins in our sports when we have tug-of-war,
For he's one of the lads of the H.44!

Chorus all together.

Now next we have Shorty, young Lootenant Grieve,
When he's got the middle he'll always relieve
His oppos[3] on time and never before,
For he's one of the lads of the H.44!

Chorus all together.

Now next comes the Gunner, his name's Mr. Bray.
When he goes on leave, how he'd like to stay.
He'd stay for a week, for a fortnight or more,
For he's one of the lads of the H.44!

Chorus: *All together please*!

1. A set is Navy slang for a beard.
2. 'Jimmy' is another term for the First Lieutenant, really 'Jimmy-the-One'.
3. 'Opposite number', in this case the previous Officer of the Watch.

Highlander, Highlander,
I ain't said a word about half what's occurred,
What yer say, what yer say?
The aircraft and U-Boats get out of our way.

It was a very good concert. It is surprising how much real talent can be found among any body of men, once their natural shyness has been broken down.

The next day, Thursday, we moved the ship back to our usual shore-side berth, and that night I dined ashore with Charles Bird. When we got back to the ships we found an enormous party in progress in *Highlander*'s wardroom. The night was hot, and the atmosphere down below was almost unbearable. A number of Wrens from the Cypher Office were aboard, and someone had suggested taking the motor boat away for a breath of fresh air. The boat was just leaving the ship's side as Charles and I got back, and I was persuaded to jump into her at the last minute, and to take the wheel. Somebody unknown had brought along some thunderflashes (small fireworks), and that person slipped one over the side. It went off underwater with quite a bang, and made the girls scream. Even more interesting, it produced the most wonderful circle of phosphorescence. The girls were quite enchanted by this – so we fired some more. We then went on round the harbour admiring the sudden activity on the part of the soldiers, who seemed to be having some sort of 'field day.' Searchlights suddenly sprang up all over the place, their long pencils of light searching the night. It really was a wonderful sight. We had never realized how many searchlights were hidden about the fortress.

When we got back alongside and the quartermaster had taken our boat-rope, a signal pad was handed down into the boat for me to read. It was from Commander-in-Chief, 'Am informed your motor boat firing charges in harbour. Report name of officer concerned forthwith.'

The girls had already left the boat. I stopped the men and showed them the signal. I looked round. In the boat were most of the Captains of the group, and at least half the First Lieutenants. I made a list of the names. 'What about the girls, Sir?' I waved the list. 'I've got eleven names here and my own, no one will believe that there were at least eleven girls aboard as well. I'm going up to the Staff Office to hand in the list personally.'

I went up to the Office. The Staff Captain on duty administered one of the biggest 'dressing downs' I had ever received. It made me feel like a whipped schoolboy. Apparently the whole garrison had 'stood to' or as we should say 'gone to action stations'. Even the Governor and Commanding General had been 'alerted.' The soldiers had mistaken our underwater explosions for an attack by the enemy, and the Admiral had ordered the arrest of the officer concerned. However they could not arrest all the Commanding Officers of an escort Group, and half the First Lieutenants as well. I was told that Commander-in-Chief, Western Approaches would be informed of every detail, and that he would deal with us on our return.

When I got back to the ship it was to find the Commanding Officers in my cabin. 'Anyway I've kept the girls out of it', I told them. 'They wanted to put whoever was responsible under arrest, but they can't lock us all up. Apparently the whole garrison went to "action stations", and even the Governor was "alerted".'

'How do you alert a Governor?'

'Probably by giving him a shot of Benzedrine.'

'Or a shot of his own excellent sherry.' This last was an allusion to a case of Governor's sherry that I had wangled from the cellars of Saccone and Speed.

'Anyhow, go away all of you. You cause me nothing but sorrow.' I turned all but Charles out of my cabin.

'Is this serious?' he asked.

'Very serious for me. I was the Senior Officer in the boat, and for my sins I'm in charge of the lot of you. Pity McMullen is boiler cleaning, or he'd probably have been there too.'

'What about this wedding tomorrow? Shall we go?' One of the staff was marrying one of the cypher Wrens, and there was to be a big reception at the Yacht Club. We had both been invited.

'Of course – unless you feel like throwing thunderflashes at the bride, in which case I won't take you.'

'As we arranged – by boat?'

'Of course. We'll use mine – not that American thing that you use for a boat. I can make our motor boat as smart as a "barge". Do you know they told me that we didn't know how to behave like Naval Officers? At any rate we'll turn out the smartest boat in Gibraltar.'

The next morning, Saturday, I had to carry out one of the periodic inspections of a ship in the group. Because the men were generally on leave when we were in Londonderry, one ship was inspected each time we visited Gibraltar. Before I left I had told Atkins that I wanted the motor boat to be quite perfect by three o'clock.

And she was. The wartime coating of paint had been scraped off the brasswork, and it shone with pre-war brilliance. Boathook-staves and floorboards had been scrubbed to a wonderful whiteness. The heads of the boathooks shone like gold. In the stern-sheets were white canvas cushions piped with blue, and a little fringe of canvas hung from the after canopy.

It was a wonderful present from the ship's company, who of course knew all about the trouble. I don't know how many men had laboured at her, but she could have lain off the starboard ladder of a fleet flagship, and no one could have found a fault in her. As I followed Charles down into the boat I wondered how many more times I should hear the side 'piped' for me. It was a sobering thought. Standing amidships at the wheel was a burly and familiar figure, his hand raised in salute as I stepped into the boat. 'Cox's'n, what are you dressed up like that for?' *Highlander*'s chief petty officer coxswain was dressed as a leading seaman. 'Well, Sir, I couldn't trust any of these young fellows to handle the boat properly, Sir. They haven't the experience you see. They may be all right for ordinary work; but we don't want anything to go wrong, Sir, not today, Sir.'

'That's terribly nice of you, Cox's'n.'

'And I've got Petty Officer——, Petty Officer——as bowman and stern-sheetman, and Stoker Petty Officer——is at the engine.'

'In other words the Petty Officers' Mess is having an afternoon out?'

'Yes, Sir.'

'Well, I hope you'll all come to my cabin at six o'clock for a drink, and since you've taken to impersonation, you can bring the motor boat's proper crew along with you. Carry on, Coxswain.'

As we crossed the harbour to run into the Yacht Club jetty we could see boats from the many other ships discharging guests. Good, bad and indifferent boats. We lay off waiting our turn. At last it came. The bowman was standing with his head and shoulders through the flap in the forward canopy. The stern-sheetman had clambered aft, and was in the stern. Boathooks had been tossed right up out of hand – and caught again. Sitting under the canopy I could talk through the open flap to the coxswain.

'You take her in fast, Coxs'n.'

'You used to scare me with the ship, Sir.'

'Did I?'

'Yes, Sir – not now, Sir.'

There is a special bond between Captain and coxswain. It is he who takes the wheel in action, and when entering or leaving harbour. One of the most comforting sounds I know is the voice of your trusted coxswain coming up the voice-pipe, 'Coxs'n at the wheel, Sir.' It is a guarantee of efficiency. He is the man who turns your orders into fact – the projection of your own personality.

The engine gong in the boat sounded three times. The propeller churned in reverse, causing a flurry of white water to appear under the stern. The tinkling sound of the gong, and the propeller stopped. The boat lay rocking gently as our wash overtook us. The two boathooks dropped as one, to catch the ring bolts in the jetty. I jumped ashore, followed by Charles.

'Thank you, Coxs'n – an excellent alongside. Lie off for me, please, I'll be about an hour.'

Our arrival was observed all right. Eyes followed the motor boat as she went astern.

Commander G. O. Symonds, who had been Anti-Submarine Officer to Howard-Johnston in the *Malcolm* hurried to meet us.

'Quite worthy of B.12 – but for God's sake be careful. The Staff Captains want to shoot you, but they can't think how.'

'They are going to pass the gun to Max Horton, and let him do the shooting,' I told him.

With only the Sunday left before we were to sail, we thought that we must have seen the last of trouble, but it was not to be. We held our Sunday morning Divisions on the jetty alongside the ship, and after I had inspected the men I went back aboard leaving the First Lieutenant to muster the church party and march them round. Before entering the Cathedral they had to march past the Admiral who, with Captain (D) and a number of the staff, took the salute. The Captains of the individual ships were meant to be there as well, and those from our group were all going to cross the harbour in *Highlander*'s motor boat to save the walk round. Suddenly I heard Atkins run down the ladder and go into his cabin. I hurried after him.

'What's wrong, Number One?'

'Fell over a wire and sat in a pool of oil – I've got to change my shorts, stockings and shoes, Sir.'

'All right – I'll send the men off. You can run after them.'

I had then rushed on to the jetty, seized the party nearest to the road and ordered 'Left turn – quick march!' – and off they had gone.

As I got back to the ship Atkins was rushing down the gangway. He took one horrified glance and wailed, 'Oh, Sir, you've sent the wrong party. We're only supposed to send forty men and there's at least a hundred and fifty in what you've sent – Roman Catholics and all sorts.'

'Well it's too late to change now. You'll have to run like a stag to catch 'em up.'

We took the motor boat across the harbour and hurried to our vantage point outside the Cathedral. Already ships' companies were marching along the road. Small parties of thirteen file – perhaps double that size from the cruisers. Then came a number from other destroyers, each of forty men. *Highlander*'s came into view. They were the last party. The men were obviously enjoying the joke hugely. It could be seen in the way they swung along, making those that had gone before look like the 'detailed' parties they were. For this parade the *Highlanders* considered themselves volunteers. They went by with a wonderful swing – but there were four times as many as there should have been. Captain (D) turned to me.

'That's a hell of a big church party.'

Fixing my eyes on some point in space and hoping I could keep a straight face I answered:

'Yes, Sir. Very religious ship, Sir.'

As one of the corvette Captains said afterwards, 'It sounded as if Captain (D) had suffered an underwater explosion.'

So the *Highlanders* marched into the Cathedral, the believers with the disbelievers. But they jammed. Half in and half out of the west door they stopped, while harassed vergers rushed to fetch more chairs to put in the aisles.

As a matter of fact there was some justification for referring to her as a 'religious' ship. On our first Sunday at sea Number One had come to me and suggested holding a Church service. I had never before had a ship where we had either the room or the proper atmosphere, and in any case I have always believed that such things should be voluntary. I had answered Atkins that we would certainly try it out, but that it must be understood by the men that attendance was not obligatory. An hour later, when church had been 'rigged' in the big messdeck, I went down to conduct the service, and was amazed to find there almost every man who was not on watch. It was such an obvious success that on the following Sunday we drew upon the concert party to form a choir; and from thence-forward was added another sound that might be heard aboard in the dog watches at sea – the ship's choir practising the hymns for the following Sunday.

I heaved a sigh of relief when we sailed on the Monday;

but we had not yet finished with Gibraltar, nor they with us. We had hardly been at sea for an hour, and were waiting off Europa Point for our convoy from the Mediterranean, when our gyro-compass developed a serious defect and we rushed back into harbour to get a gyro-engineer to repair it. We had arrived back before our signal explaining the position had been delivered from the signal tower. Without waiting for a berthing signal we went alongside, so fast that a crowd ran out from Captain (D)'s office, which overlooked the jetty, to see the crash. However, by the time his Staff Officer arrived to enquire what was the matter, I was already ashore telephoning to the Engineer's Office. We finally left for good two hours later, and caught up our convoy. Half-way home we received a signal ordering the convoy to enter St. George's Channel from the south-west instead of going the long way round the north of Ireland. Brest had fallen, and there was no longer any need to fear U-Boats in the Bay of Biscay. On arrival at Londonderry I was not surprised to hear that I was to report to Commander-in-Chief, Western Approaches, at once. I left for Liverpool that night.

First I called on the Chief of Staff, who looked up from his papers and said, 'Admiral wants to see you.' I was afraid so. A little further on I came across a secretary who said joyfully, 'Oh come in and wait here, the Admiral wants to see you.' It was getting monotonous. I met the Admiral's Personal Assistant, a very charming W.R.N.S. Officer. She said, 'The Admiral wants——'

'Yes I know that one, "the Admiral wants to see you." I've a very good mind to run home to mother. I don't like your school, and I haven't padded my backside.'

'Why, what have you been up to?'

'Don't you know?'

She laughed and answered 'Max knows everything. Come on – your turn now.'

I went in to the Presence.

'Rayner, the U-Boats are coming inshore. The "Castle" Class Corvettes have been out with the various groups, and they should be efficient units by now. I'm putting the first six into a Support Group – the 30th. I want you to be the Senior Officer. Well, what is it?'

'This letter, Sir – the one Commander-in-Chief, Gibraltar, has written to you? He has sent me a copy.'

The Admiral looked across his desk at me and said rather testily and without a smile, 'Oh that. I don't take any notice of that. Where was I? And don't interrupt me again.' He continued, 'They are the finest anti-submarine vessels we have. They have everything, the squid, the new radar, the new asdic, a special echo-sounder, and the new wireless navigational machine which will fix your position to fifty yards any time of the day or night.'

Relieved as I was about my own position, I was sure that there was a catch in it somewhere.

'I can keep *Highlander* as Senior Officer's ship?' I asked.

'You can *not*.' His mouth was set to bite, but seeing my consternation he paused, and I blurted out,

'I think I'd rather have *Highlander*.'

'You're crazy – these are the finest anti-U-Boat ships in the world.'

'But I love *Highlander*.'

He looked at me angrily, and then suddenly his face softened, and for a moment I saw a Max Horton that I did not know existed. I have said earlier that quite by chance I should discover the key to the enigma of that great man's character. He lived mainly for those things which he had conjured into being. At any rate he understood my desire to cling to *Highlander*.

'Don't make it harder for me. You've got to go.' It might have been a father talking to his child.

'All right, Sir – and thank you.'

'Good luck to you. Let me know as soon as the group is ready for sea – I need you.'

I was half way to the door. 'Was it a good party, Rayner?'

'A bloody good party, Sir!'

Max's eyes twinkled.

I went back to Londonderry and called on Commodore (D).

'So you're going to leave *Highlander* and have a group of your own?'

'Yes, Sir, I hate doing it, but I suppose it's inevitable.'

'If you ask me it's a damn good thing you're not going to Gibraltar again. I've got a letter from Captain (D) about you.'

'From Captain (D), Sir!' I exclaimed. 'I knew you'd have a copy of a letter from the Admiral.'

'Oh yes. I had that one too, but that was to Commander-in-Chief, Western Approaches. This one was just to me – something about your entering harbour at twelve knots.'

'It's not true, Sir.'

'What speed were you doing then?'

'One four of revolutions, sir – fifteen knots.'

'Well you see what I mean? You've made Gibraltar too warm for you. Get some leave, and join your group in a week's time, and you might like to know that Commander-in-Chief has recommended you for your qualified status as a Commander. You'll be the first Volunteer Reserve officer to get that.' (I had lost my status on promotion for one could quite logically be only given equality in the rank you held at the time.)

Highlander gave me a wonderful send off. When the taxi arrived to take me away it was fitted with drag ropes. Half the ship's company towed it down the main street of Londonderry, with the rest running behind. It should have been one of the happiest moments of my life, but it was the saddest.

CHAPTER 9

PEVENSEY CASTLE AND SENIOR OFFICER 30TH ESCORT GROUP

After I left *Highlander* I was never happy at sea. I had given her everything that I had, and my first impressions of the 30th Escort Group did nothing to mitigate the deep sadness I had felt when I left my *Highlander*. I there found a different world of officers and men. My three destroyers all had a very big percentage of long-service naval ratings in their crews. *Loch Tulla* had been manned by a crew of reservists, and *Verbena*'s men had been half long-service and half reservists.

The 30th Escort Group was manned almost entirely by 'Hostilities Only' officers and ratings. Of the officers I could make neither top nor tail. Although they were the legatees of the robust tradition of the Western Approaches, they were totally different from their forbears in background, outlook and training. This does not mean that they were inefficient, for they certainly were not. They were merely the products of the Radar Age. As I looked round the ward-room table at my new Commanding Officers, I realized just how much we had changed during five years of war. The ages of the Captains in the original escort groups had spanned more than twenty years; I doubted if two years separated the youngest from the oldest of these young men. Responsibility sat rather heavily on shoulders not yet broad enough to bear the weight. They were terribly serious, and inclined to be worried over such matters as the correct way to fill up forms and make returns. In some measure this was justified, for at that stage of the war the long fingers of bureaucracy were reaching out to the front line, and the burden of 'form filling' was increasing every month. One could no longer bring a gale-damaged ship into harbour and write-off everything that could not be accounted for as 'lost in bad weather'; nor could one explain a deficiency in the rum return by merely noting 'supplied to survivors' against the amount short. In the years that now seemed so long ago a corvette had done just that to the tune of ten gallons, only to discover the missing jars some weeks later stowed under the towing hawser in the tiller flat. As they could not re-enter these in the ledger they had no option but to distribute the rum round the various wardrooms in the group.

In 1941 our eyes may have been red with salt water and heavy with lack of sleep; but at least we laughed. It was obvious that one would never receive from these new ships signals such as had set us all rocking with laughter years before. I remembered a day in a full Atlantic gale when a corvette had approached close to *Verbena* to pass a long visual signal. She had been flinging herself half out of the water as she came round the corner of the convoy, and we had made to her 'I can see your dome,' (referring to the asdic dome which was fixed to the ship's keel almost beneath the bridge). The reply came back like a flash, 'How indelicate of you to mention it.'

Perhaps in fairness to my new group I should admit that the fault may well have lain equally with myself, for already I was beginning to look backwards to a time when I imagined that things had been better. We had all been living at such a pace, burning ourselves up, that perhaps we were already developing some of the characteristics of the elderly. There were, however, one or two deep and fundamental differences between us. I doubt if any of the officers in the 30th Escort Group had ever kept a watch without radar. This device had certainly been largely responsible for the destruction of the enemy's U-Boats, and it had greatly relieved the strain on officers; but its arrival marked a rubicon in our lives. Either you had experience of the Western Ocean convoys before radar – or you had not. Those who became officers after this revolutionary change took place could never know the satisfaction which their fore-runners had experienced when sound judgment and good seamanship – helped perhaps by a slice of luck – brought success. Never would they have the thrill of closing the position where they hoped to find the convoy after a night spent on extended patrol, and hearing the look-out cry 'Merchantmen on the starboard bow, Sir,' just when they were expected. Even the science of navigation also had suffered the same war-change, for the 'Loran' wireless navigational system had destroyed much of the artistry in a sailor's work. His business of finding his way across the great waters had been reduced to a matter of twiddling dials and looking up the answer in books. True, his life was made easier; but how dearly he paid for his ease! He could never know the joy of making the correct landfall after days without sight of sun or stars.

It was more efficient – but I defy anyone to argue that it was more fun.

The men too were very different. They were all much of an age; and the Petty Officers and Leading Seamen were distinguished mainly for their greater intelligence and education than for having stronger or better characters. I do not think there was anyone in the whole group who, like my two ratings in *Verbena*, would have crawled back to the ship on their hands and knees rather than miss her on sailing. They would either never have been in such a state or, if they were, would probably not have bothered to return. In my former ships I had always known every man aboard by name; but in my new job I doubt if I ever knew more than a score of names. One circumstance in particular helped to put me out of touch with the men. I had a Captain in the ship in which I was living as Senior Officer. We were back to the old Unit Commander-Skipper problem and, with both in the same ship it could never really be made to work. It was not fair to either side, if only because the ships themselves were not big enough to house the two in comfort. After years of having my own steward, sea cabin, and chart table, and losing my own rubber or pencil on the bridge, I would now lose the Captain's pencil, or find that he had carried off my rubber in his pocket. To make matters even more difficult there was a ship's navigator as well as my own staff navigator. All four of us who had an interest in the ship's position had to use the one chart table. It is curious how the Navy always seems to lean towards the Senior Officer living in a ship commanded by someone else. I suppose it all springs from what one might term 'The Admiral complex'. But while the group commander of anti-submarine trawlers and the senior officer of a group of escorts did perform some of the functions of an Admiral in a minor key, I feel that authority may have overlooked the fact that the working quarters of a real Admiral and his staff are wholly separated from those of the Flag Captain and the ship's officers. If the two of them had to live and work cheek by jowl, as we had to do, friction would surely occur. I was just as sorry for my captain as I was for myself.

None the less, and no matter how deep were my regrets at the changes, it is beyond doubt that without radar and navigational wireless we could not have won the upper hand over the enemy; for we now had to face up to the new U-Boat, which was working inshore with the aid of its Schnorkel. One impudent devil had actually torpedoed a merchantman right on our own doorstep, and within sight of the entrance to the River Foyle. The 30th Escort Group went to sea to try to find it.

Working close to the shore gave us a very busy time. Not only was it necessary that every manoeuvre should be safe for all the ships of the group, but we were also continually investigating asdic echoes. There were hundreds of 'contacts' around the coast – old wrecks, rocks, and tide rips. If we declared them 'non-submarine' then they had to be accurately charted. If we found something new in waters which we had worked over before, we might reasonably suppose it to be a U-Boat. Unfortunately where the tide runs fast a lot of contacts were caused by tidal eddies; and as they all changed with the tide they caused great confusion.

During this first patrol we attacked, with our 'squid', a very likely contact, which proved to be the wreck of a tanker carrying high octane fuel. The petrol was ignited by the bursting of our charges, and the ship was surrounded by flames two or three hundred feet in height. The Captain fortunately rang down for full ahead, and we got out just in time; but the paint was burnt from the ship's side as if it had been taken off with a blow lamp. This episode scared me much more than the loss of *Warwick* had done. I had now been in continuous command for more than five years, and I began to wonder if I was getting tired. But I was looking for a U-Boat to pay me back for *Warwick*. Until I got one I would manage somehow.

We patrolled the north western approaches to the St. George's Channel for a fortnight, and then went back to Londonderry. I went to see Commodore (D) about the difficulties over my command, and found him full of sympathy. I asked him to allow me to be my own Captain, and to give me a secretary to help with the paper work. He agreed to this, and as a new corvette was in need of a captain *Pevensey*'s was sent to her. I did not therefore feel that he had lost his command on account of me. The new plan was quite a workable one. I had a staff navigator to help with handling the group, and a writer who could take down what I said in shorthand and quickly produce a reasonably accurate report. Unfortunately for my happiness the ship was a brute to handle. She was underpowered, and so a bad seaboat; her radar and other new toys made her windage excessive; and she blew down-wind like a rubber ball whenever speed was reduced to investigate a contact. It was then impossible to keep her bows to the sea, and she would lie beam-on rolling like a pig, with her asdic crew as much concerned in remaining on their stools as in classifying the echo with which they were in contact. Had she had the two engines for which I believe this class of corvette was originally designed, she would have been a very fine little hunting vessel. Unfortunately they were all built with only the one engine. Although she was half as big again as *Verbena*, she had only the same 1,200 horsepower. To make machinery taxed the manufacturing power of war-time Britain much more than building ships' hulls. Her anti-submarine equipment, however, was first class.

The U-Boats were then operating south of Ireland, looking for our convoys at their point of greatest density. By saturating that focus of shipping with hunting vessels and aircraft we were preventing them doing much damage; but we were not succeeding in killing many of them. One felt that with just a little more determination they could do a great deal of harm, for no matter how hard we all tried, our efforts reaped very little reward. These U-Boats with their Schnorkels and homing torpedoes were just about as different from the early boats as *Pevensey Castle* was from *Loch Tulla*; so the final result was about the same. Only the great benefit of unlimited airpower kept the balance in our favour.

Our next assignment was a patrol off the south coast of Ireland. The trip started badly in the first week of November 1944. We had hardly gone two miles down river from our berth when the coxswain handed over the wheel without telling me. I was in the habit of taking a pilot for the passage of that difficult river, although I would never allow him to berth or unberth the ship. As we passed down the tree-lined glade below Londonderry I heard the pilot give the order 'starboard ten', and saw the bow start to swing to port. He increased the wheel to starboard twenty, the ship took a sudden sheer across the channel to port – and she struck. I jumped on to the compass platform, and rang down for full astern. With the strong ebb tide under us she heeled over as she swung round, quivered for a moment, and then slid off into deep water. I stopped the engines, and sent the First Lieutenant down to see if she was holed. He reported by telephone from the asdic cabinet in the bottom of the ship that she appeared to have suffered no damage.

A very shaken voice, 'Coxswain at the wheel, Sir.'

'Where the hell have you been?'

'Heads [lavatory], Sir.'

'I'll deal with you afterwards.'

I turned her round, went alongside the oiling jetty at Lisahally, and telephoned to Londonderry for a diver to inspect the stem. By the mercy of providence it appeared that we had hit the only soft spot between Londonderry and the oiling jetty. Even the river pilot had not known that there was a patch of mud there. Investigation proved that the coxswain, a very young petty officer, had handed over the wheel to the quartermaster, and the latter had put it the wrong way.

We arrived in our patrol area off the south coast of Ireland on the 9th November. Our instructions were little more than to 'seek out and destroy the enemy wherever he may be found.' We were told when convoys would be passing through and were expected to sweep the seas ahead of them, and to be on the spot in case of attack. We also had to co-operate with the air patrols, in case they should want anything investigated. Beyond that we were left free to go and look round our beat, and to smell out the U-Boats. If we spent time investigating every possible asdic contact, we found that we moved so slowly over the ground that even the most sleepy of U-Boats would have got out of our way. I had a theory that they would generally be doing something, rather than just drifting aimlessly; and that if they were moving they would give a good asdic contact. We therefore concentrated on keeping the group steaming as fast as we could through the water. If any ship obtained an echo which was doubtful that ship alone would stop to classify the contact. The rest of us closed our ranks and moved on, leaving the investigator to catch up afterwards.

By the night of the 10th November we had swept through our beat once from the westward, and shortly after dark we had turned to a westerly course. At ten o'clock I was lying down in my sea cabin. On the bulkhead above the foot of my bunk was a repeater from the radar scan. I had only to turn over on my back to see the relative positions of all my ships. By night at sea we were, of course either in complete darkness in the wheelhouse and sea cabin, or had only the smallest of red lights. The group, of four ships, was disposed to port and starboard of *Pevensey Castle*; one ship to the north, two ships to the south of her. On the radar scan the bright little blobs which were the ships glowed brightly, as the pencil of light that represented the ever-searching beam of the radar caught them. They faded slowly when the beam had passed and were rekindled as it came round again, just before they became difficult to see. Round and round swept the beam. Fascinated and half asleep I watched. The night was very calm, and the ship rolled slightly and steadily. I was mesmerized by the revolving beam, and lulled by the gentle motion of the ship. Suddenly I thought that beyond the wing ship I could see a little spot of light. Yes, there it was again – a momentary flash as the beam passed over it. Thoroughly awake now I picked up the telephone to the radar office.

'Is that an echo about 145 degrees, I should say about 10,000 yards beyond *Porchester Castle*?'

I watched the beam sweep round investigating it, probing the night like a finger.

'Yes, Sir. It's a very small echo, but quite distinct. Never seen one like it before, Sir. Conditions are very funny to-night. Anomalous propagation, Sir.'

'What's that? For God's sake don't blind me with science. Tell me in simple words.'

'Well, Sir, you might detect an echo tonight much further than you would normally expect to.'

'Will that apply to all ships?'

'Can't say, Sir. I believe it varies from set to set.'

'What you really mean is that although we normally reckon that a surfaced U-Boat would be picked up at five miles, for some odd reason your set might pick one up very much further away tonight. Is that it?'

'Yes, Sir.'

'Thank you. Watch that echo. It interests me a lot.'

'Watch the echo, Sir.'

I took up another telephone. It was the short wave 'inter-com.' set for talking to the other ships.

'Calling *Porchester Castle*. Can you get a radar contact bearing around 100 degrees from you about 10,000 yards?'

I waited for the reply.

'Sorry, no.'

'I've got it very clearly on my set. I'm going to watch it. Will you keep a special look-out on that bearing please? I'll let you know if anything further happens.'

I sent for the staff navigator to plot the echo. Very soon he reported back, 'Target is on a slightly converging course to our own. Its speed seems about the same as ours, possibly a little faster.'

I called *Porchester Castle* again, 'Can you pick it up yet?' Reply : 'Sorry, not yet.'

I called all commanding officers and told them to 'stand by'. 'I have very interesting echo, bearing 147 degrees 19,000 yards.'

I settled down to think. The target was a single unit. It must be a small one, or *Porchester Castle* would certainly have picked it up. We had met no fishing vessels, and if it were a fisherman it would be burning lights; and again *Porchester Castle* would have seen it. There seemed no answer but that it was the U-Boat for which I had searched for five years. What was more it was a most accommodating one, and was actually engaged in stalking us in the belief that we were a convoy.

I picked up the 'intercom' again.

'Ships are to form very slowly on to line of bearing 105 to 285 degrees. Course 240 degrees speed 10 knots. Manoeuvre to be completed within thirty minutes.'

Previously they had been disposed at right angles to our course. When they had taken up the new disposition the axis of the group would lie at an angle of 45 degrees to the direction of our advance.

I lay back and watched the radar. The little echo was by now quite clear, and I could see my ships begin to form on to the new bearing. This was the way to fight a war, lying on my back in a warm cabin. Some minutes later the navigator called me from the plot.

'That echo is hunting us.'

'I agree absolutely. His captain probably thinks we are a convoy. You know his radar is very good for "range", but very bad for "direction". All he will be able to see is five little blips on his scan. With this very low cloud layer he is probably banking on there being no aircraft about. If only one of the other ships could get him too. Watch him and let me know the moment he makes an alteration of course.'

Yes I would be much happier if only one of the other ships would confirm it. I called up the radar office again.

'What's the range now?'

'16,000, Sir.'

I called the navigator in the plot.

'What speed do you reckon he's making?'

'A fraction over fourteen knots.'

Porchester Castle called me, 'Confirm your contact – very small echo but firm. Shall I investigate?'

'No. Stay in bed until I tell you to get up.'

I called all ships.

'My appreciation is that the target bearing 150 degrees 15,000 yards from me is a U-Boat. I intend to hold this course until target bears 180 degrees then turn together by blue turn to 180 degrees. This will put him in the middle of our sweep. Tally-ho, chaps! Tally-ho!'

Signal from *Porchester Castle* : 'He is stalking me.'

I replied : 'I agree. One bait is as good as another.'

From *Launceston Castle* : 'I confirm your contact.'

From *Kenilworth Castle* : 'I've got him too.'

I signalled to the group to reduce speed to six knots. This might catch the enemy unawares, because his plot would not detect the reduction of speed for some time and his bearing from me would draw very quickly forward to 180 degrees, which is where I wanted it to be.

His bearing was indeed altering fast – from 165 to 170 degrees. If I altered the group then he would be inside the net. Oh, I was going to catch this one! I called all ships.

'Stand by for blue turn. If you have not already done so your ships should be at action stations. Target bears 178 degrees 10,000 yards from me.'

I made to *Porchester Castle* : 'How does target bear from you?'

Reply : '230 degrees, 3,000 yards.'

He's in the net! I made to the group, 'Blue 180. Speed 12 knots. Forrard on – Forrard on!' and to my own bridge, 'Port fifteen. Steady on 180 degrees. I've made Blue 180 to the group.'

The staff navigator called me, 'Are you coming to the plot, Sir?'

'I think not. I'm very happy here, and I want to watch this. I'll be up as soon as he dives.'

Looking at the radar, I could now see the little dots that were the ships start to change shape as they altered course. The target was still there – or was he? I knelt on the bunk. It was fading – it had gone.

From *Porchester Castle* : 'Lost contact. Reckon he's dived.'

From *Launceston Castle* : 'I've still got a very small target in the same position. – Could be a periscope – 180 degrees, 2,500 yards.'

From *Launceston Castle* : 'Very strange roaring noise on asdics.'

I made to her, 'Probably a torpedo. Am keeping fingers crossed.'

From *Launceston Castle* : 'Have asdic contact 182 degrees range 1,500 yards. Shall I attack?'

I replied, 'Yes, please. I will send *Porchester* to help you.' And to the group, '*Porchester* assist *Launceston* as hunting ships. *Pevensey* and *Kenilworth* are to form square search round diving position. Legs of box – four miles.'

A dull underwater thud.

I called *Launceston Castle*, 'Was that you?'

Reply : 'Not made by me.'

'Consider it was torpedo exploding on the bottom. Target is a U-Boat all right.'

From *Launceston Castle* : 'Am attacking.' A long reverberation shakes the ocean. I went up to the bridge. I could hear the attacking ships chattering away to each other, 'Are you still in contact?' 'Yes, loud and clear.' 'Do you smell oil?' 'Lots of it, all round me.' 'Are you in contact too?' 'Yes – plain as a daisy.'

When we were out on the sides of the box search I called up the hunting ships, 'So long as you two can hold contact I do not propose to attack again until dawn. We might get survivors.' And to *Launceston Castle* alone, 'What is your assessment of attack?'

'Absolute copybook. Have wonderful trace, both range and depth. Target is on the bottom now.'

'Buoy the position as closely as you can. We've got to stay here for seventy-two hours.'

The following morning I took *Pevensey Castle* over the U-Boat, and obtained a lovely trace on the echo-sounder. The boat was lying on the bottom with a slight list to starboard. I then carried out a careful attack with our squid, and blew to the surface a tin of oil with a Hamburg address on it. There were a lot of big air bubbles and a smell of diesel oil; but no survivors. We stayed there for three days, and continued our patrol for another fourteen days.

We went back to Londonderry by the St. George's Channel at the end of the patrol. I had been suffering from a feeling of lassitude ever since the U-Boat episode. When we had rounded Rathlin Island and were approaching the entrance to the River Foyle about an hour after sunset, we found a full gale blowing from the north. The river mouth is on the west side of Lough Foyle, and the mouth of the lough is closed, except for the river, by a long sandy spit called Magilligan Point, which runs like a breakwater right across as far as the narrow river entrance. As we approached the mouth of the river we had the sea on our beam, and the sand spit for a lee shore less than a mile away. Suddenly the ship's head swung violently to port.

'What the hell are you doing with her, quartermaster?'

'Ship won't answer the wheel, Sir.'

I telephoned at once to the engine-room, 'Chief, there's something wrong with the steering engine. Better get there dam' quickly and let me know what's happening. Hurry or you'll be swimming. We've a lee shore under us.'

A few minutes later, but it seemed years, the Chief telephoned from the steering flat, 'Bad break. Will have to put her in hand steering.'

'Can I go astern?'

'No, Sir, the rudder is right over to port, and if there's pressure on it we'll never get the hand steering connected.'

'Be as quick as you can – you haven't much time.'

I had hoped to improve matters by going astern, because most single screw ships will then put their sterns up-wind. But with the rudder hard over to port it would have been useless to do so. There was nothing I could do but wait, and pray that the Chief would get the hand steering fixed in time.

I told the First Lieutenant to muster the men in the waist with their life jackets, and blew up my own. Unlike the time when I had tried to blow it up on *Warwick*'s bridge, it now held the air. I wedged myself in a corner. The motion was quite indescribable. I began to think, – 'An eye for an eye, a tooth for——' Better not start to think like that – better not to think at all.

Signal from *Porchester Castle*: 'Am preparing to take you in tow.'

Reply: 'Thank you, no. We are rolling too heavily to

222

handle towing gear. I am very near to touching. We must not lose two ships. If I go ashore please make signal to coastguard to meet swimming party.'

I looked over the side, and shone an Aldis lamp on to the waves. The water was brown with churned up sand. It could only be a question of minutes. The telephone from the steering flat buzzed.

'Hand steering connected, Sir.'

It could hardly have been a quarter of an hour since the steering engine had broken down.

'Starboard thirty, full ahead.'

Rolling horribly she brought her bow up into the wind. The group were scattered, steaming into the sea, holding their own with the waves, and waiting to see what would happen to us. As we limped slowly through the entrance they formed up astern. The Engineer Officer came on to the bridge, 'Serious defect, Sir. Only the dockyard can mend it.' I was shivering so much that I had to hold on to the rail to stand upright.

I told the group to anchor, and to follow me up-river the following morning. I went up that night and, as I was in hand steering, I made a signal for a tug to assist me to berth. We were alongside shortly after ten o'clock, and I went down to my cabin.

'Well,' I said to myself, 'this is it – you are round the bend.' It was true. I could no longer trust my own body to obey orders. Catching sight of myself in the glass made me pause. There had been a time when people ashore had said, 'You look very young to be a Commander,' but they hadn't been saying that recently. There wasn't now any reason why they should. The candle was burned out. I went on to the jetty to telephone to the Commodore. I knew he would be in even at that late hour, because it was Max Horton's habit to do his telephoning after his own dinner. I told the Commodore.

'I've expected this for months. When do you want to be relieved?'

'If it must be – the sooner the better, Sir.'

'I can do you a relief by noon the day after tomorrow.'

'Thank you, Sir.'

'Come and see me tomorrow morning – and congratulations on your U-Boat.'

I went back and lay long in a bath. Two days later I went ashore for the last time from my own ship. It was five years and two months since I had stepped on to *Loch Tulla*'s deck.

CHAPTER 10

SENIOR OFFICER OF ESCORTS (CHAIRBORNE)

In fact it was to take me much longer to leave Londonderry than I had at first thought. There were a great number of things which would be completed more quickly if I continued to handle them myself. Also there were certain formalities by way of visits to the doctors. Even though the executive side might know full well that an officer had become too tired for further service afloat, and should be given a spell ashore, they must obviously seek confirmation from the medical branch. It was greatly to the credit of the Navy that an officer who felt his efficiency to be sinking could always go to his seniors, and talk to them quite frankly without any fear that he would not receive a sympathetic hearing.

It was early December when I eventually arrived home. On the way through Liverpool I had called on Max Horton.

'I'm terribly sorry to let the side down like this, Sir.'

'What does the doctor say, Rayner?'

'Three weeks' sick leave, Sir.'

'Will you be fit for sea again then?'

'I very much doubt it, Sir. There is nothing physically wrong with me – I've just lost my nerve for the sea. Can you find me a job in the Command?'

'As a matter of fact I can. The U-Boats are coming right inshore now, and often my groups are working under the control of other commands, Portsmouth, Plymouth, Rosyth, and even the Nore. The two Channel Commands, Portsmouth and Plymouth, will I think be the scene of a last desperate attempt to cut the life line to the continent. The staff in those two commands don't understand the limitations of the groups, or their capabilities. Already some dam' fool has sent a signal to a group of Castle Class Corvettes ordering an impossible course and speed in bad weather. Result – six asdic domes punctured, and the whole group must be dry-docked. I've just had Admiralty approval to send a Senior Officer of Escorts to each Command to which the groups are attached. I am sending Pryse (Commander H. L. Pryse, R.N.R.) to Plymouth, and you could go to Portsmouth. Let me see – three weeks' leave. That will be just right. You'll report to Commander-in-Chief, Portsmouth on the 1st of January. You'll have to use a lot of tact I expect. Remember you are my ambassador. If you want any help get on to my Chief of Staff right away.'

The reader can imagine how grateful I was to be given such an appointment, for one of the most bitter pills that I had to swallow was that after five years of 'grooming' I had lasted only two months before I cracked. The chance to do something so obviously useful was the best medicine I could have been given.

I enjoyed a splendid three weeks, including Christmas, with my family. I had not been at home for more than ten days consecutively in five years. After Christmas and before the New Year I saw the Chief of Staff, Western Approaches, and then joined Commander-in-Chief, Portsmouth's staff at Fort Southwick on the 1st January 1945.

This was my first appointment to a staff. Until then I had always been on the other side of the great divide between those who sail in ships carrying out the orders of the various staffs, and the shore-based officers who plan the operations. How many times had I railed against the staff officer who, shut in the warm operations room where no winds blew, nor rain nor snow penetrated, had ordered me to take my ship down the River Foyle in a blinding snowstorm? Once I had even gone so far as to telephone to Jove in the fastness of his Olympus.

'Don't you ever open the scuttles in that fug-house of

yours and see what's going on outside? Do you really expect me to hazard my ship by taking her down the Foyle in a snowstorm when I can't even see my own bows?'

Jove was at least prepared to talk.

'I'm sorry, but I've got to have a ship at sea off Inistrahull tomorrow morning at six o'clock to take the Clyde portion of the convoy. All the convoy escorts have weather damage, and we've got to have them mended and back at sea in a week.'

'Well, let me wait for a couple of hours until I have the flood tide against me all the way. If I can't see then, I can at least anchor without the ship turning round on her cable. Agree to that and I'll promise to be there on time.'

And so we compromised on that occasion. But I also remembered incidents which, in my conceit, I felt that I would have handled quite differently if I had been in the operations room myself. I was now about to find out if I had been right. I felt very much of a new boy, and had only the vaguest idea of what would be expected of me. To make matters worse I was a representative of another Command, and a great deal would depend on the amount of co-operation I could extract from my new colleagues. At once I was made to realize that my personal position might be extremely difficult. All the Commanders on the staff were Royal Navy men, but only held the rank of 'Acting Commander'. They were fifteen to twenty years older than myself. Most, if not all of them, had left the Navy before the war with the rank of Lieutenant-Commander, and had been given Acting Commander's rank on their recall. They were a very high powered team, and had been at Fort Southwick for the assault on Normandy. There was some reason for them to think that they could well compete with the arrival of a few U-Boats in the Command, without any help from the Western Approaches. To my consternation I found that because of my 'qualified status' I was actually the senior Commander at Fort Southwick. I would have thrust on me such dignities as President of the Mess, and would have to sit at the head of the table; and my arrival meant that one of them would have to leave his cabin. These things may appear trivial and petty when a war is being fought, but when men are herded together they are not to be dismissed lightly. Friction anywhere can spoil the work of the whole machine.

The President of the Wardroom Mess invited me to his cabin after tea. On the way we passed my baggage in the hall. It was still waiting for a decision about my cabin.

'This is very awkward,' he said, waving me to a chair.

'Yes – I can see that. I would very much rather that it had not happened.'

We sat and thought for a bit and then I said, 'Look, you people all think that I'm on Commander-in-Chief, Portsmouth's staff. But in fact I'm not. The Admiralty has only appointed me to Portsmouth because I had to be borne on the books of the *Victory* for pay. I belong to Western Approaches. Obviously I can't belong to both. Let us look at it in this way – I don't belong to your household. I'm a guest, come to do some specialist work; and so long as I have a cabin to myself, *I* don't care whether it is in the Senior Officers' Tunnel or not.' Honour was satisfied, and neither the table nor cabin plan had to be changed.

The actual duties were something quite new to me. Radar had completely changed what little I had been taught about staff work before the war. At that time if ships were ordered to patrol certain waters the manner of doing this was left entirely to the initiative and skill of the Senior Officer. Now with radar covering almost the whole Channel, the staff could plot the minute-by-minute position of the ships, and could see how their orders were being carried out. What is more they could actually guide (or interfere with) the tactical conduct of operations at sea. Taking a leaf from the book of the Royal Air Force, they could control their ships in the same manner as the R.A.F. handled fighters – vectoring the groups on to the enemy. Once again, as when Commander Boyle and I had sailed together in *Havelock*, I discovered that he who controlled the plot controlled the battle.

I always had three or four groups from the Western Approaches, totalling fifteen to twenty frigates or corvettes, as well as the Portsmouth command's own anti-submarine force of twenty-five trawlers, and about a dozen asdic fitted Motor Torpedo-Boats. With these I had to provide close escorts for the outward- and homeward-bound convoys passing through the command, and also patrol the entire area. I must guide the hunt that followed an aircraft sighting report or an enemy attack; and I had to maintain very close relations with Coastal Command, to see that their patrols dovetailed in with those of the surface vessels.

The anti-submarine trawlers were operated by a W.R.N.S. officer, 1st Officer Audrey Parker. I think she was the only Wren officer to be given an operational job. She sat at the next table to mine in the office, and we worked together in perfect harmony. She really knew about ships, and had it not been for this partnership I could never have left the Fort, even for the hour's bicycling exercise which I forced myself to take every day. One never knew when the enemy would appear. The plot was many feet underground, and had no daylight whatsoever. This seemed to make one unconscious of the passing hours and if interesting operations were being carried out it was tempting to stay down in the tunnel for very long periods. Only the insistent clamour of one's stomach would drag one away, probably to find that breakfast, lunch or dinner in the wardroom was long since over; and coffee and buns in the canteen was then the only way to satisfy one's hunger.

As Fort Southwick was some way from the ships, I hardly ever saw my friends when they were in harbour. However, when a very particular friend did bring his 'Captain' Class Frigate in with a defect that would take some considerable time for the dockyard to repair, I strained every nerve to get aboard his ship. For this 'operation' I co-opted Audrey Parker, and we arranged a system of cars and motor boats in case I was needed back in the plot. When the day came for my expedition I sent a signal to the Captain telling him I was coming aboard, and asked if he could give me lunch. On telephoning to the signal tower to make certain that my signal had been sent, I was surprised to learn that they were having difficulty in passing it. It sounded so unlike that ship's usual efficiency that I began to wonder if her Captain had been changed. However, after some time it was reported that the signal had been passed, and I left the Fort.

When the motor boat arrived alongside there was no sign of life aboard. No quartermaster to take a line – nobody. I scrambled aboard, and in the silence of the deserted ship could hear the clatter of the signal lamp. It stopped, and the Captain's head appeared over the rail of the bridge high above me.

'Sorry not to be down to meet you. I was just taking a signal. Do come up.'

'What,' I shouted back, 'all that way? What's wrong with your cabin?'

'I'll tell you when you get here.' His head was withdrawn.

I clambered up three or four ladders until I reached the open bridge, rather breathless from lack of practice. I had met nobody on the way up.

'And what have you done with the ship's company?' I asked my host when at last I sat down on the compass platform.

'Well as a matter of fact they are all on leave.'

'Good God! Every one of them?' I exclaimed.

'Yes,' he nodded with great seriousness. 'You see I gave one watch leave until the 10th, and naturally gave the other watch leave from the 10th. What I overlooked was that those going on leave today would want to go in the morning, and of course those returning won't get back until the afternoon. So there isn't anybody aboard in the meanwhile.'

'Just like that?' I asked.

'Just like that,' he agreed.

'You're a ruddy marvel. That's what you are. And so we are to have our lunch up here in the March winds so that the Captain can keep signal watch?'

'That's right,' he said. 'You don't mind do you? I've got just one bottle left of that wine you like so much.'

'Of course not – but how I wish you were "operational"! I'd love to order you to sea, and find what you'd make of that one! Can you imagine the newspaper headings, "Captain goes to sea alone in 1,500 ton Frigate"!'

When the motor boat came back for me in two hours' time, he did come down from the bridge to see me 'over the side'.

'I'm going to send you one heck of a long signal' I shouted as the boat drew away from the ship's side.

'I shan't read it – only the time of origin. The signalmen can ask for a "repeat" when they get back from leave.'

In the Western Ocean I had always been able to get some sleep after lunch. Only once, in the case of the torpedoing of the *Salopian*, had I ever heard of the enemy starting an attack in the afternoon. Also the hours from 4 a.m. to 8 a.m. were nearly always clear for sleep, unless you were helping to clean up a mess made earlier in the night. It almost seemed as though the German captains played to a 'convention' as far as those times were concerned. I was soon to discover that the plot knew no such off-periods. For the first three weeks I slept only in snatches, because sighting reports followed each other almost continuously, and whether they were suspected to be true or false, they must all be investigated with equal care. Fortunately we had an excellent Chief of Staff in Commodore R. V. Symonds-Tayler, R.N. I had first met him when he was First Lieutenant of the *Hood* in 1932, and I was serving in the same ship. He gave me a remarkably free hand, and under him I really found myself enjoying life in a way which I would not have believed possible away from the sea.

The enemy always kept at least two U-Boats in the area. Sometimes, if my opposite number at Plymouth, Commander Pryse, made things too hot for one of his visitors, the U-Boat would slip over the frontier to see if things were quieter in my part of the Channel. Whereupon I would chase him back again. Similarly I would sometimes drive one over to Pryse's side of the net, but he would very soon return it to me. We kept about forty ships and four aircraft continuously searching for the U-Boats in the waters roughly bounded by a line due south from Dover to one due south from Portland Bill. But we only killed two in four months. One we killed outright after it had attacked and sunk a merchant vessel, and one we attacked after an aircraft sighting report, and drove it into a mine field.

Against these slight successes we only lost two merchant-men – the one already mentioned, and another which might possibly have been sunk by one of our own contact mines which had broken adrift. There was a conflict of opinion over the cause of this loss. I maintained that the weather had been far too bad for a submerged attack, and that although the attack could have been carried out by a surfaced U-Boat I was sure that it would not have dared to surface there, however bad the weather.

As we were the nearest naval plot to London we were always being surprised by special parties of notables who wanted to see what a plot was like, or to study some aspect of D Day. One such party was actually standing round the plot, having it all explained to them, when the merchant ship was torpedoed and we laid on the groups to kill the U-Boat. These particular officers came from the Polish Navy. They were being groomed to go back home to teach their re-formed Navy how to do things. From our point of view the actual sinking of a merchantman caused no more fuss than an aircraft sighting report, and we were all well drilled by this time in the routine to be carried out. Two Escort Groups were covering the convoy. One was sent to hunt the U-Boat, and the other was spread round the limits of the zone which the enemy could have reached. It was our lucky morning. The U-Boat was caught and despatched. The group that did the killing was left to watch the wreck. Survivors from the merchantman were picked up and brought in, and the second group was sent off on another patrol. To us it was a busy morning which, although it started badly, had a successful conclusion – no more. But our guests were amazed.

Afterwards in the Wardroom one told me, 'You English are a very *calm* race. I do not understand you at all. There is no excitement, no——,' he waved his arms, unable to find a word – 'It is not natural. A ship is torpedoed. A Wren is sitting beside the plot. She has such nice legs – she puts a red disc on the plot. She is so calm. No one shouts. You write out the signals. The ships are moved on the plot, and still there is no excitement. The Wren sits swinging her nice legs. When the U-Boat is sunk the Wren still goes on sitting there, and you say to me so quietly, "Come on, let's go and have a drink." I think you English are the most dangerous people to fight in the whole world.'

I was rather taken aback by this fulsomeness. 'You're going to Liverpool next, aren't you? You'll see the plot at Derby House. That really is a big one. It covers the whole North Atlantic, but it's not on a table like the one here. It's on a wall and the Wrens have to go up tall ladders to mark the positions.'

'The Wrens go up ladders?' he asked eagerly.

I saw the way his mind worked.

'But they wear trousers,' I told him.

When I had first joined a big staff which included both sexes in almost equal numbers, I had wondered just how they would work together. I wondered still more when, after my conversation with the Mess President, I found myself given a cabin on the other side of the Fort, where the ten rooms were occupied by five Wrens and five junior naval officers.

I wonder if there is another country in the world where such an arrangement could have been made without trouble developing. Beyond the fact that the ladies were inclined to occupy the one bathroom for rather longer than one would suppose necessary to clean the human body, they were excellent companions. Their feminine touch made their cabins into something nicer than a mere hole in the ground equipped with the usual naval chest of drawers, wardrobe and bed. Most of the girls had stoves of some sort, and it was no more than usual to find a cocoa party in progress. Just occasionally high spirits would break out, and for a short time chaos would reign while sponges, pillows and human bodies flew up and down the long corridor. But such outbreaks were few and far between. Nearly everybody in the tunnel, except Audrey Parker and I, was a watchkeeper; and we were practically in 'watch and watch'. If one of us was not down in the Plot the other was. The chance to sleep was too valuable to be thrown away. I mention this only because so many books written after the war have suggested the exact opposite. The women in our services not only released men to active duties, but contributed a very special sum of their own to final victory. While marriages certainly grew out of many war-time encounters, of what is sometimes mis-called romance there was very little at all.

But to return to the war, the truth of it was that we were using a relatively enormous force, and had achieved the destruction of two submarines; but the continuous threat of attack in our coastal waters had also achieved virtually nothing. I declare that the second round was a draw, with both sides impotent to damage the other. But the Walter-engined high-speed U-Boat was only just round the corner. What would have happened if that weapon had arrived? It was nearly always an aircraft which sighted the U-Boats' Schnorkels, and they would attack by dropping one or perhaps two depth-charges. Nearly all these reports were made at night, and the aircraft attack was little more than a warning to the U-Boat that he had been observed. We would throw round the position such a net of A/S vessels that he would know himself surrounded, and so would become ever more cautious. Given a clean bottom with no wrecks to mislead the hunting vessels, and no tide-rips to upset the asdics, he would have been 'dead mutton' very quickly. But with the wrecks of the first World War, the wrecks of D Day and those of the second World War to confuse us, and the water full of tide-rips, he escaped us time and time again. True we held him on the defensive. But the net we threw round him could not have enclosed the new U-Boat, which could travel faster under water than our hunting craft could travel on the surface.

We had taken our soldiers from Dunkirk, Norway and Crete. We had supplied them at Tobruk and Benghazi, and escorted their supplies over the long route round the Cape. We had landed a vast army in North Africa, and seen it ferried across to Sicily and Salerno. We had guarded the approaches to the D Day invasion, and now the soldiers repaid our efforts. They brought Germany to her knees, and the third round of the U-Boat battle was never fought. When Germany fell, the first Walter boat was nearly ready for sea. She was scuttled in harbour by the Germans, and raised by us so that her secrets were revealed.

The two U-Boats that surrendered in the Portsmouth command were in excellent condition, outside and within. Morale was good, and their crews waited only for the new boats. They may have hoped that if the war had gone another six months they would prove the saviours of their nation. Such hopes of course were nonsensical. Germany was utterly defeated.

EPILOGUE

So there you have it – the war as seen by an amateur sailor, who was fortunate enough to take advantage of the training the Navy offered, so that when war came he was capable of taking command of a ship. If there was one thing that the war taught me, it was to appreciate the innate decency of the many hundreds of men, from all walks of life and from all parts of the Commonwealth, who served in my ships. In the whole time I was at sea I only once had to deal with an offence which would have incurred a prison sentence if it had been committed ashore; and we never sailed short-handed because men did not return from their leave.

If few women figure in these pages it is because they were barely discernible against the background of the ships themselves, each of whom had – or so it appeared to me – a character as complex and as interesting as that of a woman. *Loch Tulla* was the diligent nursemaid, who would take me for a nice walk round the islands and bring me back for tea. *Verbena* the busy housewife. *Shikari* the rather raffish thoroughbred of whom my mother would have said 'A very nice girl, but (and you knew the sting was coming) just a little unreliable I always think.' *Warwick* the widowed lady who had once been a girl herself. *Highlander* the best-loved, in the prime of her life. Lastly *Pevensey Castle*. Poor little *Pevensey*! The girl who had been to the university; the blue stocking; the one who had everything – but had not yet learned how to live.

On the 14th May 1945 Admiral Sir Max Horton made the following signal. It was the last one to be put in my 'In' basket at Fort Southwick, for I was leaving that night for home, and my desk was empty. The groups had gone back to the ports on which they were based. The Command itself was closing down and, although one was glad that the long, weary war was over, one felt a sharp pang of regret that the life we had led was ending. It was more than the finish of a chapter. The book that held such tales of friendship, heroism, and endurance was being closed, and put away for ever. From henceforward it would only live in the memories of many men.

'To : F.O.I.C.'s and N.O.I.C.'s in W.A. From : C.-in-C. W.A. Pass to all ships and establishments.

'In saying goodbye to the Command it gives me great pleasure to communicate the following letter which I have received from the Admiralty.

' "Before the Western Approaches Command comes to an end Their Lordships wish to place on record their recognition of the large part which it has played in the war with Germany now successfully completed. The Command has participated in virtually every form of Naval activity and in most on a large scale.

' "In the campaign against the U-Boats and in trade protection it has been pre-eminent and its record in this vital sphere will form one of the enduring chapters of the Naval history of this Kingdom.

' "Never has the existence of the Nation encountered so grievous a maritime threat as the German attack on its shipping during the years 1939–45, and with the triumph over that threat the name of the Western Approaches Command will always be pre-eminently associated. All who have been members of the Command, whether afloat or ashore, are entitled to take pride in the contribution which it has

235

made to the long and bitter struggle which has so recently been brought to a victorious conclusion."

'I thank you all for your loyal help and support and send you my best wishes for the future.'

WHEN THE MOON RISES

TONY DAVIES

A trainload of British prisoners of war steams
slowly through the Italian mountains.
Suddenly there is a screeching of brakes and
the sound of shots from the guards. Two
British officers have made the leap for
freedom . . .

Tony Davies's first escape bid ends in
recapture and transfer to a new camp in the
north. When he escapes again he and his
companions are faced with a 700 mile walk
along the spine of the Appenines to the Allied
beach-head at Salerno. The journey begins as
a schoolboy adventure: it ends as a terrifying
and deadly game of hide-and-seek where
the Germans hunt down the fugitives like
animals and courageous Italian peasants risk
their own lives to save them.

SS

SS PANZER BATTALION
LEO KESSLER

JANUARY 1940 . . . the coldest winter within living memory and the phoney war still paralyses the Western front. But at the Adolf Hitler Kaserne, a new battalion of SS troops trains for a mission so secret that it is known only by its WEHRMACHT code name, ZERO.

THE VULTURE — Major Horst Geier — is the only man who knows that the objective is the key Belgian fortress guarding the junction of the River Meuse and the Albert Canal — the most impregnable fort in Europe, which must be taken regardless of the cost in human lives if Hitler's hand-picked SS Panzer troops are to turn the flank of the Maginot Line.

SS PANZER BATTALION is the first novel in a new series about ASSAULT REGIMENT WOTAN, a crack unit in the Waffen SS.

ESCAPE FROM THE RISING SUN
IAN SKIDMORE

'The oily dust fell everywhere, on hungry stragglers searching for their units, on armed deserters who roamed the streets searching for loot, on . . . fear-crazed men fighting their way at the point of a gun or bayonet, pushing women and children aside . . . The dead lay in the streets . . . but no one collected the corpses now.'

Singapore had fallen. The British Army, retreating in disorder before the onslaught of the Japanese shock-troops, had been told to surrender. One man was convinced he could escape.

Geoffrey Rowley-Conwy seized a junk and sailed for Padang. There he joined a group of fellow officers for a desperate escape-bid in a dilapidated sailing boat across the Indian Ocean to Ceylon. 1,500 miles of open sea swept by the fury of the monsoon and patrolled by Japanese fighter planes on the lookout for British survivors.

'One of the best and liveliest escape stories of the Second World War . . . enthralling.'
Times Literary Supplement

——————CHARLES DENNIS——————

STONED COLD SOLDIER
CHARLES DENNIS

**The most savage and scurrilous satire
on war since CATCH 22 and M*A*S*H.
'Beautifully managed. A very funny book
made funnier by a passionate indignation'.**
——————THE TIMES——————

When the men of 'B' Company's Wichita
platoon simply vanished into thin air, a lot of
people started asking awkward questions.
David Maxwell, ace reporter and darling of the
T.V. networks, a man terrified that it was his
destiny to get crabs and die, was sent to find
the answers.

What was the purpose of the outsize quonset
hut that appeared overnight at the edge of the
jungle ? Why did the army deny that the camp's
medic, Dr. Markson, ever existed ? Why did
Father Doolan carry a revolver ? What was the
role of Cashbox, the exquisite $100 whore ?
Why was 'the Murder Man' sent out to Saigon ?
Who was Chy Ming ?

It began as a mystery : it ended as a scandal
that could rock the Pentagon.

**'Carries all along in a torrent of scurrilous
abuse. He loves words and uses them like
bullets from a machine-gun.'**
THE SPECTATOR

'Ingenious . . . a really good tale'.
SUNDAY TIMES